Ladies of Lucknow

Ladies of Lucknow

The experiences of two British Women
during the Indian Mutiny 1857

A Lady's Diary of the Siege of Lucknow
G. Harris

Day by Day at Lucknow
Adelaide Case

LEONAUR

Ladies of Lucknow
The experiences of two British Women during the Indian Mutiny 1857
A Lady's Diary of the Siege of Lucknow by G. Harris
Day by Day at Lucknow by Adelaide Case

First published under the titles
A Lady's Diary of the Siege of Lucknow
and
Day by Day at Lucknow

Leonaur is an imprint of Oakpast Ltd

ISBN: 978-1-84677-954-1 (hardcover)
ISBN: 978-1-84677-953-4 (softcover)

http://www.leonaur.com

Publisher's Notes

In the interests of authenticity, the spellings, grammar and place names used have been retained from the original editions.

The opinions of the authors represent a view of events in which she was a participant related from her own perspective, as such the text is relevant as an historical document.

The views expressed in this book are not necessarily those of the publisher.

Contents

A Lady's Diary of the Siege of Lucknow

Contents

WRITTEN
FOR THE PERUSAL
OF FRIENDS
AT HOME

Preface

The writer of the following *Journal* arrived at Lucknow with her husband in March, 1857—only a few weeks before the *Sepoy* outbreak. The annexed extracts from a subsequent letter point out the precise circumstances under which this record, of events so painfully interesting, was kept. As no lady's diary has hitherto been given to the public, the friends of the writer have thought that it might interest others, beyond the family circle, to communicate additional information on a subject in which the British nation feels so deep an interest.

> "I have kept a rough sort of journal during the whole siege, often written under the greatest difficulties—part of the time with a child in my arms, or asleep on my lap; but I persevered, because I knew if we survived you would like to live our siege life over in imagination, and the little details would interest you; besides the comfort of talking to you. For the first month (July) we had so little hope of escape, that I did not feel as if you would ever receive it; so you will find the records rather bare; but such as it is, I shall send it, if possible, by post, for I know you will like to have it. I have found in my desk two June letters also, which I will send you."—Allahabad, December 14, 1857.

NOTICE TO SECOND EDITION.

Here and there a verbal alteration has been made, and an inaccuracy corrected. One or two short passages from the manuscript journal, omitted in the First Edition, have been inserted; and an extract from a recent letter of the Authoress, which it is thought may be both of interest and service to truth, has been added at the end of the book. Otherwise this is simply a reprint.

Journal and Letters

La Martinière, *May 15*

4 p.m.—Since writing to you this morning such awful news has come, that I still feel paralysed with horror. There has been an insurrection in Delhi, and the Chief Commissioner (Mr. Fraser), Captain Douglas, Mr. and Miss Jennings, have all been murdered in cold blood. The news came by electric telegraph. No particulars are known, nor even the extent of the insurrection; or who have risen, whether people or *sepoys*. They have cut the telegraph wires between Delhi and Meerut, and destroyed a bridge to prevent the passage of troops.

At Meerut there was a rising among the native troops, on Sunday evening, when several Europeans were killed and wounded: the rebels showed fight till they had received a volley from the Rifles, and then they all ran away; but there are no particulars, so we know not how many English have lost their lives. There has been no post for four days from up country, and we are in complete ignorance of what horrors may be going on. Poor! poor Captain Douglas!—or rather, one's heart should bleed for his miserable wife, who little knows now that she will never look upon his face again in this world.

May 16. I was interrupted yesterday; but you may well fancy we can think of nothing but the dreadful tidings. No post in from Delhi, nor any further news by telegraph. I cannot describe our horrible state of anxiety, alarm, and gloom. These are fearful times, and it seems as if our tenure of India hung by a thread; for if the native army turns against us, nothing humanly speaking can save us. We must trust to God, and hope for the best We are fortunate in having such a man as Sir H. Lawrence at the head of affairs here; and European artillery as well as a Queen's regiment. The stoppage of post is most alarming; no one knows what to think. Poor Miss Jennings! she was by all accounts such a very nice dear girl, the comfort and delight of her father's life. I have heard it was beautiful to see the two together.

Mrs. Jennings is in England, educating her younger children, and this poor girl came out to be her father's companion about a year and a half ago I do so wish we could know about Mrs. Douglas: such a sweet creature, and so fondly devoted to her husband: how I do grieve for her! he was such a noble-hearted Christian gentleman, respected and liked by all; his valuable, useful life to be sacrificed to those bloodthirsty villains, it seems too dreadful. You must not feel over anxious I don't think I should have told you all this, only you will see it in the papers. Every precaution is taken for our safety here, but at present all is quiet; and we trust such a due degree of severity will be used, in time, as shall prevent further mischief: the great mistake has been not overawing the *sepoys* at first. There have been three regiments disbanded, and the men turned loose on the country to foment ill-feeling; whereas, if the first which mutinied had been annihilated with grape-shot, there would have been an end of tumult, and many lives saved. You can only rule these Asiatics by fear: if they are not afraid, they snap their fingers at you.

From the Writer's Husband.

Lucknow, May 18, 1857.

G. has I know written to you very fully as usual, but I wish to send a few lines also, particularly as I feel that the news probably taken home must make you all anxious. I really have hope we may ride over the crisis yet; there does not seem to be perfect combination amongst the alien troops, and hence the chance for us. It is certainly fearful to know that this, humanly speaking, is our only hope.

The number of European troops in this country would, in case of a general insurrection, only go to swell the death list; yet, as I said before, it is hoped that this may be averted; our great trust is in prayer to the Almighty, who can help in time of peril, and save by few as well as by many. Every human precaution has been taken here, and the troops are as yet firm; we cannot say what these horrible reports may do towards rousing their enmity.

I imagine a few days must, at all events, put us out of this horrible suspense. We are concentrated as much as possible, and, being warned, shall, at any rate, not be surprised. As communication with other stations is cut off, we have no certain news of what is occurring elsewhere. I fear everybody at Delhi is murdered. Poor Mrs. Douglas! her being away has saved her child which else would not have been—for children, women, and even half-castes were sacrificed. The insurgents were repulsed at Meerut, but in the first surprise many were cut off.

You must all try and be trustful, as we do; God has given us a good chief in Sir H. Lawrence, and I believe everything is being done to avert peril. I shall try and get the people to come to morning-prayer at church. I went down to city church last night (Sunday), leaving G. much against her will with C, but am sorry to say the people congregated at the Residency did not come. I believe the Meerut massacre began as people left church, so, perhaps, this had some effect in keeping them away, but there really was no danger to them, as the church is within the Residency compound, and there are one hundred and fifty Europeans on guard.

I had to go through the crowded streets alone after dark, and met with no molestation, but I thought it best to refuse a guard which was pressed on me (and in whom, by-the-bye, I had no confidence), and to sneak back to cantonments. You may be sure I will not expose myself to unnecessary danger, if only for dear G.'s sake. She is, thank God! well, and more resigned about her great sorrow.[1]

Today ought to bring us our letters from home, but this awful state of things scarcely allows us to hope it. If the Europeans in this country now survive the insurrection, I should suppose the Government will at last see the necessity of sending, at least, twenty thousand troops to keep the alien army in check—these have now felt their power, and can never be trusted again. God bless you all, and may He mercifully preserve us through this emergency, to meet you again in England!

Cantonments, Lucknow, May 18, 1857.

How I grieve for the heartsickening anxiety I know you will

1. Her Father's death.

all suffer on our account when the terrible news this mail will take home reaches you! It seems so cruel to add to your great sorrow by telling you of our dangers; but as you are sure to see all that has happened and is dreaded in the papers, we think you will like best to hear from us the worst as far as we know.

At Delhi the people rose in the city, and it seems were joined by the *sepoys*; so have murdered every European there, Captain Douglas, Mr. and Miss Jennings, Mr. Fraser (Chief Commissioner), the Judge, the bankers, post-office and newspaper people, shopkeepers, clerks, writers, even women and children, and half-castes—all who had European blood in their veins.

Among the slain is a Mr. Mocatta, a very great friend of F. F.'s, who we met at Lahore, and who was staying with Mr. Jennings on his way to England, to join his wife and six children, whom he had sent home before him. Poor Mrs. Jennings and Mrs. Douglas are both in England, and we fear there will be nothing to soften the shock to them. Delhi is in the hands of the insurgents, and no post could go out from there, even if there were a survivor to write: all we know is from electric telegraph by way of Agra, so that if I were to write to Mrs. Douglas I could tell her but the bare horrible facts; and there is every aggravation to the horror of the awful affliction, for the dead bodies of our countrymen at Delhi are being exposed to insult in the streets, and there is no one to give them Christian burial.

At Meerut last Sunday night the 3rd Cavalry and three Native Infantry regiments rose, set fire to the officers' bungalows, and murdered them with their wives and children as they tried to escape: so utterly unprepared were they for such a catastrophe, that all the Native Infantry and cavalry lines were in a blaze before the Rifles, 6th Dragoons, and English artillery could be brought to the rescue. At the first volley from the Rifles the insurgents ran away to add to the horrors perpetrated at Delhi only thirty miles off.

There are rumours of risings all over the country, at Benares, Allahabad, Ferozepore, Moultan, &c.; but these are only reports, and almost every hour we hear rumours of fresh horrors to add to our terror. God only knows what the end will be, or if the lives of any English in the country will be spared.

All this discontent and mutinous spirit among the *sepoys* has been going on some time, but Government has shut its eyes to and laughed at it, till now it may be too late. As yet everything here is perfectly quiet, and every precaution, as far as human means, has been taken for our safety. The 32nd has been brought up to garrison cantonments, and all the ladies and children are come up here from the city; we came yesterday morning and are with C.[2] The *Sepoy* regiments here are supposed to be faithful, and everything is being done to secure their allegiance.

Sir H. Lawrence is a most able man—we could not have a better head, and everyone is on the *qui vive*, but our best security is to pray that the danger may pass, and that the troops marched to the rescue of Delhi may take such signal vengeance as shall overawe any attempt at further outbreak; but there is no doubt that this is a most fearful crisis, and that the life of every European here is in great jeopardy: the city is quiet at present, but fears of a rising are great. The natives have all such a defiant, impertinent manner, as if they knew their power, and turn round and scowl at us as they pass.

Oh! mother, mother darling! these are fearful times. Pray for us, dearest. God only can help us. It is very awful to feel this terrible danger hanging over us; it may come at any moment. It would be impossible to describe the state of apprehension we are in and the gloom that hangs over us. Do not be frightened for us, you dear ones, but, oh, pray for us, that we be accepted for our blessed Saviour's sake, when he sees fit.

It is a great mercy that we have warning. Darling mother, pray that we may be spared to come back and see you; but in any case, and above all, commend us to God. If it be His will, He can confound the devices of our enemies, and we shall weather the storm. I am so grieved for your anxiety—but you cannot be saved from hearing about . . .

I am so loath to leave off writing and say goodbye; but what more can I say? We are all well, and in as good and brave spirits as we can be.

Do not be very much alarmed if you do not hear from us next mail, for communication is so uncertain, I cannot feel sure that even these letters will reach you. The insurrection has been put down at Allahabad, and we have just heard the Calcutta mail is in. [*Then follow greetings to many loved ones, both friends, relations, and servants, evidently thinking it might be the last letter.*]

2. Her cousin, Lieutenant Barwell, 71st N.I.

Lucknow, May 20, 1857.

How anxiously will you all be looking out for the next mail! Thank God, all is still quiet, and the *sepoys* seem to be faithful and well behaved at present, though, of course, no one can feel confidence in them, the disaffection seems so general; and their plots have been carried on so secretly, that till they broke out into open mutiny they were not suspected. It is a great blessing that we have such a firm, well-judging chief in Sir H. Lawrence, who is vigilance itself, and is doing all that man can do to ensure our safety: hitherto, by God's help, he has succeeded in preserving calm here in the midst of great danger.

We are earnestly hoping now that the crisis may pass and leave us unhurt. An army of eight European regiments and a large force of artillery, with the commander-in-chief at their head, was to assemble on the 18th at Kurnaul, and will arrive at Delhi tomorrow to take summary vengeance on the miscreants who are now triumphant masters of the city.

It is impossible to describe the horror of the last few days, every hour bringing dreadful intelligence. Poor young Campbell MacNabb was one of those murdered at Meerut, on Sunday, 10th, in the 3rd Cavalry; poor fellow! that was the first regiment that mutinied. Captain and Mrs. Macdonald and their children, 20th Native Infantry (we knew them at Peshawur), were murdered; the poor babies snatched out of their parents' arms, and cut to pieces before their eyes.

This morning tidings came of the revolt of the Sappers and Miners at Roorkee, near Meerut, and of one of the officers, Captain Fraser (husband to her of the Blenheim), being shot through the head. Some of the officers and their wives in the cantonments at Delhi, it is hoped, have escaped; but no hope of those in the city. We saw a letter from an officer at Meerut, giving an account of the insurrection. General Hewett, who commanded the division, is under arrest; he seems to have done nothing to stop it; and with 2500 European soldiers in the place, atrocities were allowed to go on from four o'clock Sunday afternoon till Tuesday morning, without any effectual opposition; and the insurgents actually permitted to march off with flying colours to Delhi on the 12th, where they went to the heir apparent, proclaimed him king, and being joined by the city people, and three regiments of Native Infantry, proceeded with their massacre.

Yesterday there was a false report that the 71st had risen: the 32nd and Artillery were all under arms immediately; the Brigadier and Sir H. Lawrence went down to the lines in the heat of the day, but found all quiet. Overtures have been made from this place to the King of Oude, offering to restore him to the throne, but he very sensibly laid the whole before Government, for which he deserves to be well rewarded.

If we can only hear in a few days that the wretches in Delhi have been punished, we may hope that, for the present, our fearful danger is over: but all say that our Indian empire trembles in the balance, and very, very nearly had we lost it: such a combination against us has never been known in the annals of its history, and never again can a native army be trusted. The native corps will have to be reduced to a small number, and European regiments raised to take their place, as the only chance of retaining the country. Yesterday we had the great happiness of receiving our home letters.

May 21st, Ascension Day. There is terrible fear now that something is wrong at Cawnpore. The 2nd Cavalry have been some time suspected of disaffection; and last night Sir H. L. received despatches, which are kept a profound secret. No one knows what has happened, which makes us all the more anxious and nervous. Every time we hear the slightest noise—loud voices, a horse galloping by, a gun fired, or any calls to see C, and they speak in an undertone—one's heart is in one's mouth. The excitement will be terrible if bad news from Cawnpore should be confirmed. The depot of the 32nd is there, and most of the women and children; and the poor soldiers would be frantic if they suspected their families were in danger.

There would be no holding them. Their indignation already is intense at the murders of helpless women and children that have occurred at Meerut and Delhi. They are frantic to avenge them; so Sir H. L. is quite right to be close; but it greatly increases our suspense being thus kept in the dark. No news has come for eight days from Delhi; but it is known that several officers and ladies have escaped from cantonments; two arrived at Meerut disguised as natives.

We saw a gentleman yesterday, Mr. Martin, who knew Campbell MacNabb, and told us everyone liked him very much, and that at the outbreak he did his duty nobly—he went down at once to the lines to try and bring the men to order, and was immediately shot.

This morning I went with J. to the Residency church in the city. The congregation consisted of two people besides myself, which just enabled J. to administer the communion. Is it not dreadful that in these times of terror and danger people will not come for help where only it can surely be found?

The church is inside the Residency compound, in which all the Europeans of the city have taken refuge, with a battery of artillery and 150 of the 32nd to defend them, so that they could run no more risk in church than inside the houses, and yet none come. It was just the same last Sunday. At this church there were not above a dozen people. It does seem so very strange, and frightens one more than anything; for it seems almost daring the Almighty to show us how utterly useless all our human means of defence are, by thus trusting to them, and neglecting to seek Him who alone can succour us.

The prayer in times of War and Tumult is now always used in church, as well as in our private devotions, and is most applicable to our present condition. It seems to come so much more home now than at the time of the Russian war, when I used to think it did not seem quite suitably expressed. Last Sunday James gave the Holy Communion in the barracks, Colonel Inglis having made an urgent request it might be administered there once a month. The regimental school is much reduced, owing to the absence of the greater portion of the 32nd regiment. Mrs. Inglis took great pains with it, and had the children at her own house on Sundays. It is such a rare thing in this country to find ladies interesting themselves about the poor women and children; but the Inglises, from what I hear of them, must be excellent people.

This is frightful weather for Europeans to be marching on service. How I pity the poor fellows! but they say excitement will keep them up, and prevent them suffering much. All the regiments from the hills are sent for, 75th from Kassowlie amongst others. They had just settled themselves, as they thought, for a three years' sojourn in the Himmalayas, and now most likely will never go back, as no regiments will be spared to recruit themselves in the mountains, at all events till very strong reinforcements come from England to keep the peace in the plains.

So perhaps there will be no Dagshaie for us after all (supposing we are spared); but, indeed, one does not look forward for ever so short a time, much less months. Hour by hour none can tell what may happen. Sir H. Lawrence has been made Brigadier-General, so that in this emergency he may possess full military as well as civil authority. His post is a fearfully responsible one; he must be nearly worn out, taking no rest, and his mind constantly on the stretch.

Those who understand them say that his conduct and all his arrangements have up to the present time been perfect, and as yet not a sound of disturbance has been raised in these parts. C. is nearly worked to death now as acting brigadier-major.

May 22. We were very much frightened last night by a fire, so very close to this house, that it seemed as if nothing could save it. The stables and outhouses of Captain Green, of the 48th, were burnt down; but, providentially, the wind, which has been blowing a gale this way all day, had subsided, and the flames were prevented extending. The blaze was awful, and it is supposed to have been done on purpose. Several bungalows were in great danger. The thatch is so combustible, the least spark sets it in a blaze.

At Umbala incendiarism has been going on at a furious rate, and numbers of houses destroyed. J. went to the Residency this morning in the city: all the sick soldiers, the women and children are there, in a state of great alarm, poor things! So many false reports get about and frighten people more than there is cause for. There was a placard stuck on to the Residency gates last night in Hindostanee, calling upon all true people to rise and exterminate the *Feringhees*, and invoking curses on those who should help us. A pleasant sort of publication!

Everything, however, in city and cantonments continues outwardly quiet. The troops are expected to be at Delhi today. Queen's 84th have been sent up to Cawnpore from Calcutta in post-carriages, and will arrive tomorrow. There is no news today from any place. A company of the 32nd, some guns, and an Irregular cavalry regiment, were sent off to Cawnpore in the middle of the night before last; so there must be mischief there, but we know no particulars.

We are hoping in a few days order may be restored, and we able to return in peace to our quarters in the Martinière, and resume our quiet life. But can you conceive the folly of having no European troops at Cawnpore, and only one regiment in Oude—a country of which we have so lately taken unjust possession, and where a rebellion might have been expected any day? Again, at Delhi, not a single European soldier within thirty miles. However, I should think the lesson now given won't be forgot in a hurry, and that the defences of India will not again be confided to native troops.

Tuesday, May 26. Yesterday, at 3 o'clock a.m., we were roused by C. telling us to get up and dress ready for flight at the shortest notice. He had been sent for to the brigadier's, and great alarm prevailed, as the different guards were going to be changed, and then a rising was feared. Of course, we got up and dressed as expeditiously as possible, waiting C.'s return in fear and trembling. He came back at five with the longest and gravest face, announcing that it was Sir H. L.'s most peremptory order that every woman and child should leave cantonments immediately, and take refuge in the city Residency-house, which is fortified, barricaded, and provisioned for a regular siege.

C. said the precaution was most necessary, as we were in frightful danger, and the horrors of Meerut and Delhi might at any moment overtake us, so we were not to delay. Poor Emmie was, as you may imagine, dreadfully upset at the idea of being sent away, and leaving Charlie to encounter such peril. The officers of the native regiments are to remain in the lines, and do all they can to keep their men quiet; but, if the outbreak takes place, they are to retreat with the 32nd on the Residency; and here we are to try and hold out as long as possible, till European troops come to our rescue.

I do feel so sorry for E. and C, and so thankful that my dear husband's duty does not separate him from me. We put together all the things we had with us, and Emmie all her valuables, as quickly as we could, and came down here at once. On arriving we found all in such confusion at the Residency, all the unfortunate ladies and children hunting for quarters, that we were most thankful to accept an invitation from kind Dr. Fayrer to come to his house in the Residency compound; and here we are an immense party of unprotected females, Mrs. Fayrer and I being the only ladies who have the comfort of our husbands. Besides E. and myself, there are here Mrs. Dashwood and her two children, Mrs. and Miss Halford, Mrs. Germon, Miss Schilling, Mrs. Thomas and child, Mrs. Anderson, and Mrs. Stanley Clarke.

There are two civilians, Mr. Gubbins and Mr. Ommanney, whose houses attached to the Residency are also full to overflowing, and all the other ladies, about thirty in number, with children innumerable, are in the Residency, which also contains the sick and women and children of the 32nd. We have two companies of the 32nd and a battery of artillery to defend us, besides barricades erected at all the entrances and guns mounted all round the walls. E. and I have a small room together, and think ourselves most lucky in being so comfortable.

In the Residency there are as many as eight and nine ladies with a dozen children in one room, and the heat is awful. J. sleeps in Dr. Fayrer's study. The reason of our all being packed off here in such a tremendous hurry was that the news from Cawnpore and other stations round was so alarming. An outbreak was expected every moment, and the effect of revolt at Cawnpore would be instantaneous mutiny at Lucknow. Sir H. L. did not impart all he knew, and we are kept in utter ignorance of what is going on in other parts of the country, but I believe our condition is frightful, and God only knows what the end of it will be.

The panic in Calcutta they say is terrible. Native regiments there and at Barrackpore are mutinous to the heart's core; and if European troops do not soon come to our relief, there will be none perhaps left alive to tell the tale. Every station in the country is in equal danger. At Allyghur the 9th Native Infantry had the consideration to spare their officers' lives. They were permitted to escape, leaving all their property behind them. Lady Outram (the wife of Sir James, who is in Persia) was staying with her son at Allyghur, and obliged to run several miles, fleeing for her life.

We are all most anxiously looking for news from Delhi: the army must have arrived yesterday, and we trust such a signal vengeance will be taken on the desperate wretches who have shut themselves up there as shall intimidate any from attempting to follow their example. This seems to be our only hope; and if General Anson does not act with vigour, we shall be at the mercy of our enemies. Oh, my darling sister! you can little imagine what an awful position we are in, but God can help us. He only can. Since we left cantonments there has been no disturbance. C. came over this morning to see E., and reported all quiet and news good from Cawnpore.

They were in hope the rising there would not take place; the troops had not actually mutinied, though in a very excited state. Part of the 84th (Queen's) will arrive this evening, and that gives us fresh hope and courage. The ladies at Cawnpore have taken refuge in the church, which is the only stone building, consequently not so easily set on fire.

Oh! the accounts of the massacre and burnings at Meerut are something too horrible and make one's blood run cold. The murder of the unfortunate women was not enough; they were made to suffer worse than death, and numbers of little children were brutally killed. The Punjab seems quiet, and no alarm felt there,—at least so the papers say; but we have not had a line from any of our friends, and feel really anxious about F. F. at Lahore, for I think he would have written; but then the posts are so uncertain, his letter may be lost.

I am in an agony of fright that our last letters home may have been lost. I shall send this by Calcutta. Nothing has been heard of the harmoniums, which are very likely lost, as neither property nor persons are safe travelling. If they don't arrive we shall be out of pocket 100*l.*, but one really cannot think of pecuniary losses now, when if we only save our lives we must be thankful. Yesterday we were all a very sad, panic-stricken party, besides being completely overcome with the heat; but as no bad news came today, all are better, and the sound of the piano has been heard in the drawing-room.

It is thundering, and if only rain would fall it would be a blessing, as if the thatched roofs of the bungalows were well soaked it might save the cantonment from fire. I shall never forget the alarm we had on Sunday night in church. Several shots were fired, and all felt sure the outbreak had come. Several officers left the church. J. went on with the prayers in a firm voice, though he thought, as we all did, that our last hour might be near. Soon all was quiet, and the fright we had was caused by the Mussulmans having seen the new moon, which terminates their long fast the Ramazan and commences a great festival. At the first glimpse caught of the moon they fire off a *feu de joie.* I hear such a storm now, the rain pouring; never was it more welcome.

May 27. Yesterday afternoon a telegraphic message from Cawnpore. Still quiet there, and some of the 84th expected that evening at Ferozepore. Two Native Infantry regiments had mutinied, but were instantly surrounded and overpowered by our old friends the 10th cavalry (Captain Harvey's regiment), who behaved right loyally. At Lahore a regiment mutinied and were marching off to join those at Ferozepore, but were fired into and disarmed by the other troops of the station, and no officers lost their lives.

This news is cheering, as it shows the disaffection is not universal. Yesterday Dr. F. and J. rode to cantonments, and brought back news that three wretches had been captured in the 13th Native Infantry lines trying to incite the men to revolt. One of the native officers invited them into his house and kept them in talk while he gave warning to the European officer on duty, who immediately came and had them secured. They are emissaries from Delhi.

I think they are all to be hung today, but there is some hesitation about it, for our position is so weak that they hardly dare do anything which might provoke a rising, and at Cawnpore, where a villain was caught doing the same thing, they have not ventured to put him to death, for they knew his execution would have been the signal for an immediate outbreak, and the life of every European there would have been the forfeit. I think nothing speaks so much for our defenceless state as this.

No news today—we are so anxious to hear of the fate of Delhi. This morning Miss Schilling, J., and I went to the top of the Residency to see the view, which is wonderful. I never saw a more beautiful panorama,—the whole of Lucknow spread out below us, with its innumerable fine buildings, gardens, gilded domes, and tall minarets—it was an enchanting sight, and the air so fresh and lovely. Dr. and Mrs. Fayrer, our host and hostess, are very kind people; they are quite a young couple and have one cherub of a baby boy eleven months old, who is the plaything of us all—he is the image of Murillo's St. John the Baptist in the National Gallery.

The heat is so dreadful I cannot write more. The piano has been going today a good deal; several of those here sing and play well; I think I shall go and listen. I forgot to tell you the harmoniums arrived this morning from Calcutta and are stowed away in the church; I am so glad they came safe. We are awfully punished here by late dinners and noise; but the poor things in the Residency are miserably uncomfortable compared to us. We are close prisoners, cannot go beyond the walls, but as all continues quiet still we are hoping to be allowed this evening a drive to cantonments. It must be a tremendous expense to those kind Fayrers entertaining so many people.

May 28. I must close this today, as I intend sending by Calcutta, not being sure of the upcountry post. I heard from —— this morning: she says the panic in Calcutta is frightful: what would we not all give to be safe in England! We drove to cantonments this morning, and took E. to pay C. a visit, but were not allowed to stay long. Our danger is still most imminent; the city is in an awfully excited state, and *sepoys ditto*; but at present no open outbreak.

All the officers and European soldiers are getting worn out with the harassing duty, and as for Sir H. L. it is little short of a miracle how he keeps up, for he gives himself scarcely a moment's rest night or day.

His measures are all to gain time for European troops to come up to our relief before anything occurs. Messages were received last night containing good news from Cawnpore and other doubtful places, which remain peaceful by the good providence of God, for no one can understand how it is that the threatened rising at Cawnpore did not take place.

I grieve for your state of suspense and anxiety, but we are all hoping now that the fearful crisis is nearly over, and that He who has hitherto so mercifully preserved us will yet bring us safely through the danger. No English letters; we are beginning to get anxious for their safety; but there has been no post from Lahore for twenty days. No news yet from Delhi. The natives have a report in the city that we have been beaten; but this I doubt not originates in their own hopeful imaginations: most anxiously do we long for the real news. It is so painful to see that poor dog Bustle panting—he suffers dreadfully in this weather: poor old dog! I should be grieved to lose him; he has shared all our joys, sorrows, travels, perils, and adventures the last three years.

Whit Sunday, Lucknow, May 31.

I hardly know how to begin to tell you of the horrors of the past night, knowing how anxious and unhappy it will make you, but it is kinder, I think, to conceal nothing. The insurrection, so long dreaded, has taken place. Last night, at nine o'clock, the three *sepoy* regiments stationed in the cantonment, the 71st (C.'s), 48th (Dashwood's), and the 13th, flew to their arms, and attempted to take the big guns, in which, however, they did not succeed.

Poor Brigadier Hanscombe was killed, and Mr. Grant of the 71st, son of Sir Patrick, quite a young man, who was on station duty at the centre picket, was murdered—two bullets sent through him, and his head cut off, by his own men; and Mr. Raleigh of the 7th Cavalry, a poor boy who only joined two or three days ago—just out from England—was cut to pieces. These are all the deaths, but several officers are wounded: poor Mr. Langmore, a great friend of Charlie's, is dangerously wounded; they say he will die.

The whole of the cantonment has been burnt to the ground; some few houses have escaped burning, but everyone ransacked and pillaged. The B.s have lost every single thing they possessed in the world, and our three large boxes containing all our worldly goods, with the exception of my mourning, and a dozen of linen we had with us, are all gone too; also 350 *rupees*, deposited by C.'s advice in the regimental treasury for safety; however, we cannot think of our pecuniary loss—ours is less than so many others.

Poor C. is quite ruined, for they had furnished their house so nicely, and had so many beautiful things they brought out with them: but we can think of nothing but his merciful preservation. You know he's been Acting Brigade Major for some time, and his duty therefore was close attendance on the poor Brigadier. Volley after volley was fired at him, and he was close to the Brigadier when he fell, but, by God's great mercy, escaped without hurt.

If Sir H. Lawrence had not sent all the women and children out of cantonments, we should inevitably, every one of us, have shared the fate of our countrywomen at Delhi and Meerut; and it would have been scarcely possible for any of the married officers to escape, hampered as they would have been with the care of their families; as it was, a poor sergeant's wife, and her two children, who happened to be in cantonments, were cut up on the road.

Oh, mother! mother! how dreadful it is! We have just heard there is a rising in the city. God help us! Last night we were at dinner when the servants came running in to say there was firing heard in the cantonments: we heard it distinctly, and from the top of the Residency the whole place was seen in a blaze. We were all told to be ready to take flight if necessary to the Muchee Bhowan, a strong place which has been fortified, and in which we are to take refuge as our last resource, and try to hold out till European relief can arrive; but, oh, when can that be?

There is scarcely an available regiment in the country. The Governor-General has sent to stop the troops, on their way to China, at Ceylon, and bring them to India. There certainly is a disturbance in the city; they have proclaimed the King's brother King. We sat up in our clothes all last night; E. in a dreadful state of anxiety about C.; messengers kept arriving from cantonments with reports of what was occurring; firing has been going on all the morning.

The insurgents have all decamped and spread themselves over the country; the troops have been pursuing them, but, having no cavalry, it was useless; only a few stragglers were caught. A poor half-caste has just been brought into the Residency, cut to pieces; he went down to his house in the city, and was murdered. Two companies of the 84th have arrived at Cawnpore, and they sent back the company of the 32nd which was sent over there last week. Cawnpore is almost sure to rise now. (Residency.)—I was interrupted in this by the alarm of the rising in the city, and we had all to leave Dr. F.'s house, and take refuge in the main building of the Residency.

Here we all are—God only knows how it will end! Do not grieve very much, mother; we are in His hands, and He can take care of us, and preserve our lives if He will. I do try and pray to feel resigned whatever may happen. I know not if this will ever reach you, very likely not. There is such noise and confusion, and my hand trembles so I can hardly hold the pen. A gentleman is going to send all our letters to the post at once, so I can add no more. . . .

Lucknow, *St. Barnabas' Day*, 1857.

I sent off three letters to you and darling mother on the 9th,[3] and have now little more to add, though I could not bear not to write, this day of all others, when we have so many thoughts and recollections in common. Some news came in from Cawnpore this morning, brought by two spies; they said 500 European soldiers arrived there the day before yesterday, and that the insurgents had been driven back. They had been pounding into the unfortunate Europeans inside their intrenchments for three days with artillery and a twenty-four pounder: every house in the cantonment has been burnt; the blaze has been going on for days. No official news has come yet: the enemy has still possession of the road and river, so we can't tell when we shall hear anything positive. A letter came last night from General Wheeler, but it was dated the 8th: he described their position as nearly hopeless, but we hope he has had reinforcements.

They had under two hundred European soldiers, and only a few nine-pounders, which were of no use, as they could not touch the enemy with them, whereas the insurgents were

3. They never were received.

pounding into them with a twenty-four pounder: the casualties are not known, but are probably considerable, and what the poor women and children must have gone through is horrible to think of; still, if they are saved from falling into the hands of those wretches, any amount of alarm and suffering will be nothing.

The bare idea of the fate of the unhappy ladies at Seetapore is too horrible; there was no indignity that was not inflicted on all the women the wretches got hold of. The children were murdered, and thrown in a heap; one pretty little woman, Mrs. S., whom we knew at Peshawur, was shot down as she tried to wade through the river. Yesterday about six people, sergeants and their wives, who had made their escape, arrived: they contrived to creep into the jungle, where they wandered about for two days, when a native *rajah* had compassion on them, and sent them in here.

One poor woman is badly wounded in the hip, and they are all in a dreadful state of illness and exhaustion. J. went to see them all, and he says the accounts they give of the dreadful scenes they witnessed, and what they went through themselves, are too horrible to be conceived. Many ladies and children have fortunately made their escape from different small stations in the district, just in time to save their lives, leaving all their worldly goods to be burnt and plundered.

I am sure we should not think of our losses when there are such numbers here with families of children who have not so much as a change of clothes. A Mrs. Boileau, and her four children, are in this house:[4] she came in yesterday from Secrora on an elephant, and was from 4 p.m. till 10 a.m. on the road; half of their escort wanted to murder them, but the other half was steady, and persuaded the rest not to molest them, so they came in safe. As the mutiny at Secrora had not taken place when the ladies were sent away, the officers were obliged to stay with their men, but on the 10th (yesterday) the outbreak came. They have got away in different directions: three officers came in here yesterday, but Captain Boileau is supposed to have taken refuge with a friendly (?) *rajah*, and his poor wife is terribly anxious, as they can have no communication, and she cannot even hear of his safety.

4. Fayrer's.

The fortifications here are now nearly complete, and the engineers say that, if the insurgents keep off only two days longer, they will not care how many come against us, as we shall be impregnable so long as provisions last, and we hope for relief long before they are expended. I have just heard of a lady, Mrs. Benson, who escaped with her husband (a civilian) from Harriabad: they were disguised in native clothes. She dressed as an *ayah*, and had to walk seven miles, when they found some ponies, which they mounted. Her feet, poor things are in the most dreadful state.

They met some *sepoys*, who looked very suspiciously at them, and followed them some way, but at last thought better of it and turned back. We hear that most of the insurgents here are making off for Delhi: it is to be hoped they will meet with a warmer reception there than they will like, but it is strange that nothing has been known, or is known, of what our troops are about up there; we ought to have heard something long ago: now all communication between us and the rest of the world is cut off, and we know not what may be going on at other stations. At Benares, at Allahabad, and indeed every station in India, there seem to have been mutinies: we are so afraid the Government at home will be difficult to rouse from their usual state of indifference about this country, and if there be delay in sending out an army to our rescue, the native prophecy that this year the English will be driven out of India is pretty sure to come true.

If they will only let us depart with our lives, I am sure I shall be thankful to quit. I have such a dreadful cold I can hardly hold up my head, and feel as stupid as an owl; it is so odd to have colds with the thermometer at 93°, but they are going through the house. The *sepoys* in cantonments are not disarmed yet; they tried to get rid of them by offering them furlough, which they all refused. I will leave this open to finish tomorrow. Oh! how I do hope you will receive it, and the others sent on the 9th!

Sir Henry Lawrence has been very ill: he was completely worn out in mind and body, and in danger of breaking down; but Dr. Fayrer insisted on his keeping quiet, and having forty-eight hours' entire rest, not even receiving a note, or being told a single thing. He is now much better. J. has been taking a census of all the people, European and native, inside the walls of this house, and including servants, *punkah coolies*, *ayahs*, &c., they amount to 110.

There are eleven ladies and six children staying here. J., Dr. Fayrer, and a great friend of his, Dr. Partridge, are the male portion of the community. Dr. P. belongs to one of the Oude Irregular Cavalry regiments, and very narrowly escaped with his life when out in the district on detachment duty the other day; the men showed such a mutinous spirit, that the officers expected every moment to be murdered, but they succeeded in getting back and bringing them in here; and after this you will hardly believe Sir H. Lawrence ordered them out again last night, and was going to send them to Seetapore, but, happily, changed his mind, though they are still under orders to be in readiness.

To her Sister.

Lucknow, June 13, 1857.

I sent a scrap of similar dimensions to this yesterday in the hope of its going by the Calcutta mail, but, as I hear of another messenger starting for Agra this morning, I will not lose the opportunity of writing you a few lines on this your wedding-day, wishing you both many happy returns of it. You little dream the state we are in here, and our prospects seem to grow darker instead of brighter. I hope you will receive this note; I sent to dearest mother yesterday, to assure you of our present welfare and safety, for I fear you will all be very anxious about us. I pity poor Aunt Ellen with her three sons in this horrible country.

We are very anxious about W. B.; his regiment is at Bareilly, and there is a horrible rumour that every officer there has been murdered, as well as those at Shahjehanpore. Of course C. can get no news of him, as all communication is cut off between ourselves and the rest of the world: it is more than a week since any certain intelligence has been received from Cawnpore, only 48 miles off. The insurgents are besieging the Europeans there, who have less than two hundred English soldiers to protect them, but they are supposed to be still holding out bravely.

Yesterday there was a small disturbance here. The military police mutinied and went off with their arms; they were pursued by a couple of our guns and two hundred of the 32nd; and I fear there never was a more mismanaged affair: the poor soldiers nearly died from exposure to the sun, and lost two men from apoplexy, without ever getting the chance of a shot at the enemy. Some *Seikh* cavalry went in at them, and behaved splendidly, killing between thirty and forty.

One gentleman, a Mr. Thornhill (who says he has often danced with us at Kew, but I don't remember him), was wounded. I walked round our fortifications yesterday evening with James; they are wonderfully strong, and the engineers say we can hold out against any number as long as provisions last, and long before they are expended we hope for relief. As yet none of the insurgents have appeared in the neighbourhood, and I expect they are much too cowardly to make any attempt on a place so well prepared: it is only when they can take you by surprise and murder defenceless women and children that they dare attack Europeans.

When you hear of all the atrocities which have been committed, and the wholesale murderings and plunderings which have been and still are going on all over India, your blood will run cold. How it is all to end, God only knows; we do not dare look forward; but humanly speaking, all depends on an army being sent to our assistance from home without delay. We are quite well and keep up our spirits, trusting that our prayers will be heard, and that we shall be delivered from our dangerous position. I have very long letters written to you, but there is no chance of sending them at present. These notes have to be concealed about the person of the man who is to try and take them to Agra for the Bombay mail: it is very doubtful if he will accomplish his errand. Goodbye.

June 13. I have just got off a very wee note, darling, though doubtful if you will ever receive it. I wrote one to darling mother yesterday. They did not go by post; a messenger starts for Agra tonight with small documents concealed about his person, which he will try to convey to their destination in safety. This is your wedding-day, dearest, and many happy returns of it do I pray that you and dear Willie may enjoy.

Yesterday we had a great alarm: the military police mutinied and made off with their arms. The guns and 200 of the 32nd went in pursuit, but never came near enough to get a shot. Some *Seikh* cavalry behaved well, and did a good deal of damage to the wretches, who fought well and executed a most masterly retreat. The poor European soldiers suffered dreadfully from their bootless exposure to the sun, and two of them dropped down dead. We have a most imposing show of guns, and I cannot help thinking the villainous wretches will be afraid to attack us, for they are arrant cowards.

There is no news again today from Cawnpore or any place. They say it is not true about the 500 European soldiers having arrived there; no firing has been heard in that direction for twenty-four hours. There is dreadful news, which is thought to be true, that all the English at Shahjehanpore have been murdered, without the escape of one, and that the mutineers proceeded to Bareilly, the next station. I went yesterday over to the Residency to see Mrs. Polehampton, who is getting much better. Oh! I do feel so glad now I have no children. Fancy the babies at Seetapore being dashed to the ground and bayoneted—one has no words to express one's horror and indignation. This house now swarms with children.

J. had no less than five funerals this morning. I am happy to say the church has not yet been blown up, and we hope it will not be necessary. Mr. Polehampton has lent us 12 volumes, of *Sharpe's Magazine*, which is quite an acquisition in our dearth of books, and it is delightful to me to meet such a dear old friend. Our life, as you imagine, is extremely monotonous. We get up at four and sit in front of the house, where we have tea and biscuits; at eight we go to our rooms. When Emily and I are dressed, we send for J., and read the Psalms and Lessons together, and he says prayers.

At ten we have breakfast. We sit in the drawing-room working or playing with the children as the case may be. We dine at four, and if it be cool enough when the sun sets we go out again and sit in front of the house, where we have tea and ices; at half-past nine we come in to prayers and go to bed. The only change or excitement of any kind we have is in the shape of bad news or horrible alarms. The heat is greater than I ever felt it for so long together; in the drawing-room the thermometer is at 93, in our bedroom 97.

When we are sitting outside the house we have many gentlemen visitors over from the 82nd. It is reported that one of those poor Miss Jacksons at Seetapore has been carried off prisoner by the *sepoys*. This, if true, is a worse fate than her sister's, who fainted and was lifted up and thrown by the wretches into the middle of the burning bungalow. The poor girls were so much liked and admired, I am quite glad I never knew them. Their brother, Sir Mountstuart Jackson, is supposed the first killed.

June 16. Day after day has brought only bad news. I have really felt too downcast to write, having only horrors to record. The Shahjehanpore massacre seems worse than any one we have ever heard of yet. A survivor, Captain Orr, has written to his brother here. It seems the outbreak commenced on Sunday, and a few people were murdered in church; the rest of the officers were told they might go away with their families where they pleased, they did not want their lives. They all started immediately in every available conveyance, and had proceeded about six miles when they were overtaken and surrounded.

The gentlemen were first bayoneted on the spot, wives and children looking on; resistance was useless, so they made none, and died praying with their hands crossed over their breast, like noble English martyrs. The ladies were equally calm and heroic; they knelt down with their little ones under a tree praying, and as soon as their husbands were slaughtered their turn came.

Captain Orr is half a native, was spared, and invited by the mutineers to take the command; but he put them off, and finally escaped into the jungle, where, after wandering four days, he met or heard of (I don't know which) Sir Mountstuart Jackson and one of his sisters, with a little child of Mr. Christian's. They were all in the jungle, dependent for food on the *rajah,* who says he cannot protect them, but daily sends them food.

The sufferings of poor Miss Jackson and the little child must be extreme. Sir H. L. has written to offer the *rajah* a handsome reward if he will protect and send the poor creatures safely into Lucknow, but one cannot tell if he will or can do it. The idea that our rule in India is come to an end seems firmly to have possessed all the natives. The day before yesterday our bearer, who has been with us almost ever since we came to India, and to whom J. has been most kind, walked off, taking with him all his goods and chattels, and one of our *punkah coolies* to carry his bundle. We did not find out he was gone till some hours after his departure. A *khitmutgar* of Mrs. Boileau's, who had been sixteen years in her husband's service, walked off today in the same manner.

People's servants seem deserting daily. We expect soon to be without attendants, and a good riddance it would be if this were a climate which admitted of one's doing without them; but if they all leave us, it will be difficult to know how we shall manage. Their impudence is beyond bounds: they are losing even the semblance of respect. I packed off my tailor yesterday: he came very late, and, on my remarking it, he gave me such an insolent answer and look, that I discharged him then and there; and he actually went off without waiting, or asking for his wages.

On Sunday we were able, thank God, to go twice to church, which was a blessing we had scarcely dared to hope. The artillery horses are picketed in the churchyard, and stores stowed away in part of the church. Vestries and outhouses are given up to refugee families, so it looks terribly warlike, but we hope to avoid the necessity of blowing up the sacred building: it would only be done in case of the enemy's getting possession of our outer defences—which God forbid!

For some days it has been reported by scouts that a large force of insurgents are within twelve miles of us, but they have not yet appeared, and we hope they will not dare come. A letter was received by Sir H. L. this morning, from Sir Hugh Wheeler, brought in by a trusty native: it was dated 14th. No reinforcements had come, and they were sore pressed, but still holding out: many lives lost; and the top of their barracks blown off: the enemy had possession of the magazine and one of our 18-pounders.

It is most despairing; no troops having yet been sent up, we cannot but fear that all the country below must be in the same predicament; and if they have to fight every inch of their ground on the way up, one does not see how we can escape, as it will be months before any help can arrive. There are great fears about Patna. Benares and Allahabad are known to have risen.

On Sunday came the certain intelligence of the fate of those officers who were supposed to have been carried off to Delhi by their mutinous men: they were every one of them murdered—Captain Burmester and Mr. Farquharson of the 48th; Captain Staples, Mr. Boulton, and Mr. Martin of the 7th Cavalry. The latter, such a gentlemanly nice handsome fellow, who dined with us at the B.s' a few days before our flight from cantonments. His brother is a civilian here, and has a pretty little wife: they are the sons of Dr. Martin, the celebrated Indian physician. Mr. Boulton was wounded, and rode for his life seven miles, when he was met by another party, who surrounded and cut him down.

This morning brought news to another poor lady, living over at the Residency, of the murder of her husband, poor Major Galle: he started from here on the 12th, disguised as a native, to try and carry information to Calcutta; it was such a perilous attempt, we all felt that it would be miraculous if he succeeded: he was accompanied by ten men from his own regiment (which since his departure has mutinied and made off for Cawnpore); he selected them himself, as those he felt confident he could depend upon; but, alas! people are being now taught by sad experience that no trust can be placed in one of the race.

He was about eighty miles from this, on the road to Allahabad, when his faithful (?) followers betrayed him to some of the enemy they met: he was murdered at once. Five out of the ten men were *Seikhs*, and they came back here and told of the fate of their master, pretending they stood by him and were true; but at all events they did not shed any of their blood for him, as they were perfectly unhurt It is beginning to be suspected that the *Seikhs* are playing a double game, and, if so, it is a great pity Sir H. L. trusts them as he does, and has brought so many inside this place.

The remaining *sepoys* of the three regiments in cantonments have been disarmed and sent away on leave; they did not at all approve of going, but made no resistance: all the officers, except the colonels and staff, are come down here, and the rest are expected to follow in a few days; there are one hundred and fifty of the 32nd, and some artillery in cantonments, as it is necessary to keep possession as long as possible, for the sake of getting in supplies. Charlie, being quartermaster and acting brigade major, is obliged still to remain up there.

At Sultanpore, another of the Oude outlying stations, the officers have been massacred, but the ladies are safe in some fort. Colonel Fisher, one of the most splendid old soldiers in the world, whom one has always heard spoken of in India as quite a hero, was savagely murdered by his men, whom he trusted and loved like his own children. He was wounded first by the *sepoys* of another corps, upon which he rushed into the midst of his own lines, telling his men he had come to them for protection, as he knew they would stand by him to the last. The words were scarcely out of his mouth when three of his regiment rushed upon him with their spears and killed him.

Such an awful thing happened here yesterday! Because there are not murders enough done by the heathen, two Christian Englishmen quarrelled, and, in the heat of passion, one of them seized a pistol and shot the other through the body. James buried the murdered man this morning. He was the riding-master of the 7th Cavalry; so respectable a man that he was to have had a commission given him. His murderer, the sergeant-major of the same regiment, also bore the highest character, and was liked and respected by everyone who knew him, and the two were bosom friends. It seems the quarrel began with the wives disputing about the drawing up of a curtain; this trivial matter led to words between the two husbands, and in an instant the dreadful deed was done.

The poor women are perfectly distracted. The poor wretch who killed his friend is a Roman Catholic, James was going to see him this evening, but found the Roman Catholic priest with him. He was told that the poor fellow had lain all day hiding his face, and would not speak a word. The officers of the 7th Cavalry all went to the funeral this morning; they are dreadfully grieved about it—both men were such favourites, and thought so very highly of by all—it is very shocking. I earnestly hope when next I use my pen I may have something more cheering to relate; today has been nothing but horrors. The native report is that Delhi is again in the hands of the English. If we could only hear that this was true, it would indeed be good news. Charlie has heard that nearly all the officers effected their escape from Bareilly to the nearest hill station, so we hope poor Willie is safe.

June 18, Waterloo Day. Emmie is in bed today, feeling poorly. No enemy has appeared to attack us yet, though we have daily rumours of their near approach, and that a powerful *rajah* has joined them, and is leading them on. From Cawnpore no good news. It was reported European troops had got in there, but this was never confirmed. The last terrible piece of news was that all the English at Futtyghur had tried to make their escape, and that when they arrived as far as Cawnpore they found the insurgents lining the banks of the river. They were fired into, compelled to land, tied together, and marched up to the parade-ground in front of the barracks, where our poor people are intrenched, and grape-shot fired into them before the very eyes of their countrymen, who could not move a finger to save them.

I think Mr. Thornhill lost an aunt, uncle, and two cousins, but I think it must be a mistake that they were killed in front of the European camp, for nature could never have stood it. There must have been a rush to their rescue at any sacrifice; but such is the story that came here. Yesterday brought the sad tidings of the murder of Mr. Longueville Clarke and Mr. Cunliffe as they were endeavouring to escape from Burrnitch; the latter was engaged to Miss ——, and the 6th of this month was to have been their wedding-day; the other sister was to have been married on the same day: poor girls! now all their happiness has been turned into mourning; their engagements were announced about six weeks ago, when we none of us suspected what a frightful time was coming upon us.

Mr. Schilling and the Martinière School were all ordered inside the fortifications this morning, so the Martinière is abandoned, and I suppose we shall lose all our remaining property, which we have been obliged to leave there to its fate, as nothing more can be brought in here; we got our small remnant of clothes, but furniture, harp, books, carriage, horses, &c, are left at the Martinière. The poor boys are all stowed away in a hot close native building, and it will be a wonder if they don't get ill. I am grieved to say there have been a great many deaths, and some of them from cholera, among the 32nd, but I trust it is not increasing; it is a great mercy the garrison is as healthy as it is, considering the immense crowd of human beings that are congregated in this small space.

In the Residency alone there are upwards of one hundred ladies and children; there are, I think, sixteen hundred Europeans here altogether, and, amongst these, nearly one thousand fighting men. They have taken the church for stores, and nearly filled it with grain. The top of the church is barricaded, and will be used to shoot from in case we are besieged; we shall have no more service in it, I grieve to say—is not this a horrible, terrible state of things? We are a very melancholy party here, as you may well imagine, and today that sweet little Bobbie Fayrer is ill, which makes us worse. There are many sad and anxious hearts here; now scarcely a day passes without bringing bad news to someone or other.

There is a poor lady at the Residency, a Mrs. ——, whose brother, mother, and sister were all murdered at Shahjehanpore. Oh, how my heart aches to think of my darling mother's and all your anxiety! when you get no tidings of us, what will you think? If I could but let you know we are safe now,—but even if we are spared, it will be so long before you hear it; and as to getting your letters, we dare not hope for them for ages to come. There, it does not do to think of these things, it makes one too miserable. Goodbye, my dear sister, &c. &c.

June 19. I went yesterday evening with James to the *Begum's* house to see the poor women who came in from Seetapore, and gave them a few old dressing-gowns and things of mine which I thought would be useful, as they had lost all their own clothes. One of them is expecting to be confined immediately. They were very cheerful, and seemed quite to have got over their troubles. It is wonderful how little that class of people seem to feel things that would almost kill a lady.

After our visit to them, James took me with him to see poor Mrs. Eldridge, the widow of the riding-master who was murdered three days ago by his comrade. I don't know when I have seen such a nice well-spoken respectable woman; she spoke most kindly and charitably of the wretched murderer, and seemed to pity him very much. I hear that the poor wretch has never spoken a word since he committed the deed, and will have nothing to say to the Roman Catholic priest who visits him. His wife, a most violent woman, who excited him to the fatal pitch of fury, is perfectly distracted and wild.

Mrs. Eldridge has two children, a poor girl of thirteen who is half-witted, and a fine little boy of six years old. She told me she had two daughters comfortably married at Jellunder, and that if she could get to them she should never want a home. All her things were burnt in cantonments the night of the outbreak. Dr. Fayrer has ordered us today not to go to the Residency any more, as smallpox has broken out there. Cholera, too, is raging in the city, and there have been several deaths from it among the 32nd. Intelligence reached this today that all the poor ladies and children from Sultanpore, who were thought to be safe in some fort under the protection of a *rajah*, have been turned adrift and fallen into the hands of a party of the insurgents, and all been massacred.

James went this morning to see the soldiers in the Muchee Bhowan Fort: it is a very unhealthy place, and all tumbling to pieces, so they would never be able to hold it against an attack. They are moving all the guns, stores, and ammunition down here, and when that is done they will blow it up, and the garrison, 150 strong, will come in here: they have sent the baggage from cantonments down here, and the force is held in readiness to come away at the first notice of the enemy's approach, but it is determined to hold the position there as long as possible; and also it is not advisable, till absolutely necessary, to bring any more human beings into this already crowded space.

Charlie came down to see Emmie this morning, and is looking quite well. The nearest force of insurgents to us is said to be forty miles off: it is the general opinion that we are too strong for them to venture an attack; of course the longer they delay the stronger our defences will be. It is those unfortunate women at Cawnpore one trembles for, if aid does not speedily arrive.

The troops are to abandon cantonments at last, and all come in here this evening. Two children died of cholera at the Residency this morning, and a lady who came in from Secrora, Mrs. Hale, is dying of it tonight: James has been sent for to see her at the *Begum's* house.

June 20. I am extremely unhappy today at having been obliged to send away our dear old Bustle. Poor dear dog! I expect he will break his heart, for never did I see such an attached creature; he is always miserable when James is out of his sight. An order has been issued that all dogs seen outside the compound are to be hung, and, as it would fret poor Bustle's heart to be tied up, we have sent him down to the Martinière to be with the horses, and I trust the *syces* will take care of him till we are able to have the fond old pet back again.

Every child in the house is at this moment screeching, and we are all distracted: both the poor little D.s are ill and wearing their mother out; they will go to no one else, so one cannot help her with them. I never heard such a chorus of squalling in my life. The heat seems to increase every day, and no signs of the rains yet. Dr. Partridge read out loud to us in the drawing-room this morning *Guy Mannering*.

A letter came today from General Wheeler to Sir H. Lawrence; no reinforcements arrived at Cawnpore up to the 18th, but the brave people still holding out gloriously, and say they have provisions and ammunition enough for another fortnight; their sufferings are extreme. General Wheeler says, "It is useless to state the extent of our losses;" by which one fears they must be terrible. He says the sun is their worst enemy. Their consolation in their distress is that their devotion may be our salvation. Dear, brave, generous creatures! how heart-rending it is that no aid can be sent them from here! if it were not for the river between us, it might be done.

—— was speaking at dinner today of the iniquity of the annexation of Oude, and thinks the tribulation we are now in is a just punishment to our nation for the grasping spirit in which we have governed India; the unjust appropriation of Oude being a finishing stroke to a long course of selfish seeking our own benefit and aggrandisement. No doubt it is a judgment of God, and that we have greatly abused our power; and, as a Government, opposed the spread of Christianity; while individually, by evil example and practices, we have made our religion a reproach in the eyes of the natives. God grant that this heavy chastisement may bring all to a better mind!

June 21. The poor church is converted into a storehouse, so we had service in the drawing-room this morning at 11 o'clock. James had a service at 9 in the hospital. Mr. Polehampton went to cantonments and gave the troops there an early service, and had one in the Residency at 11. There is to be a general one out of doors this evening at 7 in Mr. Gubbins's garden, where everyone who likes may go. How little they are thinking at home how intensely applicable to us are those petitions in the Litany, From plague, pestilence, and famine, from battle, murder, and from sudden death, good Lord deliver us! It seems as if they never came home to one's heart before; indeed the whole of the Liturgy and the Psalms appear so wonderfully suited to our present condition, as if composed expressly for the occasion, taking in all our necessities and all our feelings. They are most comforting.

June 21, Sunday. Charlie came down to see Emmie this morning, and told us they had had an alarm in camp last night; some of the scouts came running in to say that a body of cavalry were seen, so they all got under arms, but no one appeared. Fifty of Captain Weston's men (the City Police) deserted last night, with their arms. I wish every armed native would go; we should all feel much safer, for not one can be trusted. It is three weeks today since the memorable Whit-Sunday when we fled in such alarm to the Residency, expecting to be attacked immediately.

Captain Weston was saying yesterday it was perfectly unaccountable why they did not molest us that day, when our defences could not possibly have stood an assault, but now we are so well prepared we could hold our own against any number of the enemy. What a merciful Providence it was that withheld them! Our great fear now is of traitors in the garrison. Sir Henry L. will go on trusting the *Seikhs* and a few others who have un- fortunately not yet joined the rebels, and no one but himself has the smallest confidence in them. At Benares, Cawnpore, and other places, the *Seikhs* have turned against us, and it is not likely these will be better than the rest. At Cawnpore, where the garrison was entirely composed of *Seikhs*, they rose and murdered all the Europeans; amongst the rest Mr. Fane, a cousin of the D.s.[5]

The native artillerymen have been true, or rather stuck to us as yet, and half the guns are manned by them; but one feels very uncomfortable at the idea they are pretty sure not to fire on their countrymen if they appear; and it is impossible not to be afraid of the mischief they may do us. But we have been so mercifully preserved hitherto we ought not to despond, especially when we remember those poor distressed people at Cawnpore.

June 22, Monday. Dear F. and G.'s wedding-day. Five years ago now,

5. This report was untrue at the time.

and how fresh every incident is in my memory! I have been recalling every little circumstance, and living it over again in my mind. What a sad anniversary for poor F.!—the first he has passed alone since his darling was taken away. Their dog Toph died on their wedding-day last year, and they wrote to tell us how grieved they were about it, little dreaming of the great grief which was so soon coming. What would I not give to hear of the safety of F. and the children! One trembles at the idea of what may be going on in the Punjaub if the *Seikhs* should have revolted. This uncertainty about the fate of one's friends in other parts of India, and the impossibility of hearing of them, are very hard to bear. Charlie is very anxious about Teddie and Maggie;[6] they are at Hansi, far from any European troops or place of refuge.

There has been no news from any quarter today, except that twenty gentlemen-volunteers with thirty *Seikhs* rode out on the Secrora road last night to try and gain some intelligence of the insurgents. They came back about one today, having seen and heard nothing at all, but there is a strong force at Secrora. We had a very heavy shower of rain early this morning, and were in hopes it was going to continue, but all signs of it very quickly departed, and the heat is greater than ever. James took Mrs. Boileau and me this evening to walk round the fortifications of the P. O., which are very strong. Mr. Brice, an old Peshawur friend, has the command there. He told us half his native gunners deserted last night. I wish they would all go, we should be much safer.

June 23, Tuesday. James had fever on him all last night, and is very poorly today, but I hope will be better soon. A great many people are suffering from boils. Mrs. Dashwood's little boy and Mrs. Boileau's children are covered with them. I hear they are very common at Lucknow. I am thankful to say there have been no fresh cases either of small-pox or cholera the last few days. Charlie came down this morning. I have got dear old Bustle back. Mr. Schilling, who went down to the Martinière yesterday, told us such a touching account of the poor dog's misery and pining that J.'s heart relented, and he consented to his return. The order about the destruction of dogs has never been attended to, and while I see so many *pariahs* allowed to run about with impunity there is no reason for Bustle's exile.

Dr. Partridge has been reading *Guy Mannering* aloud to us the last three mornings, which passes them pleasantly, and causes Chip's frock

6. Edward Barwell and wife, murdered at Hansi.

to proceed apace. I wonder if the darling boy will ever have it when finished. All the officers have had their white jackets, trousers, and cap-covers dyed slate or mud-colour, partly to save the washing and partly because that colour is so much less prominent a mark for the enemy. They look such queer figures.

June 24, St. John the Baptist's Day. Such terrible news from Cawnpore yesterday. It has made us all miserable again. General Wheeler writes to say the insurgents have got mortars, and are shelling the besieged in their intrenchments. They had thirty shells sent amongst them in three hours, and have lost a third of their number. They have retired underground, and do not suffer so much from the sun therefore, but unless relief comes now in a few days they are lost. Oh God, help them! It is too agonizing to think of their perishing after all their bravery and devotion. And the poor women and children; how heart-sick it makes one to think of them!

It is certain that an enormous force is gathering with the intent of coming down upon Lucknow. There are 15,000 troops they say now in Oude, independent of the Cawnpore force, which numbers about 5000, and which will join the rest if Cawnpore falls. They have eighteen guns, but the shells are worse than anything. It was supposed, till General Wheeler's note came yesterday, that the rebels had none, and, if they had, did not understand how to use them. But, alas! they have proved they know too well. They can shell from a distance of two miles, where our guns cannot touch them, which just suits the cowards.

Poor Sir H. Wheeler is much to blame for not having removed all the guns and ammunition into the intrenched camp when there was time. They had a good three weeks after the first outbreak at Meerut before the troops mutinied at Cawnpore, and ample time for every precaution. We are indeed in an awful strait. It may be God's will that we should all perish, and that I should never see my darling mother and sisters again in this world. . . .

Meanwhile I will strive to bear all we may have to endure with patience and fortitude, and, as much as I can, help and comfort my companions and husband: he is still very poorly with a bad sore throat, and extremely weak and pulled down; but I am thankful to say the fever has gone, so that I hope tomorrow he will be much better.

There is a report among the natives that Delhi has fallen; if this be true, it will perhaps awe the insurgents, and prevent their venturing to attack us here. It is surmised the cause of the delay at Delhi was waiting for poor old General Reid to come down from Peshawur and take the command, as he is the senior general in the Queen's service out here. We imagine something terrible must be happening in Bengal which prevents European troops from coming up.

We expected four regiments long ere this; they will now be obliged to wait for the China force, and send up a large army, for there are thousands in arms between Cawnpore and Benares, and two or three regiments would hardly make their way through them. It is all very, very dreadful, and one does not see a glimmer of sunshine in the dark clouds. The rain too is keeping off most unusually late: if that came down in torrents it would very much discompose the enemy, as niggers abominate wet weather. Today is very blowing and dusty: I hope it is a sign that rain is not far off.

June 26. Good news has cheered us up today, for we have heard really and truly of the fall of Delhi from Sir H. L., who received a letter this morning with the joyful tidings. Our army was in possession of the city on the 13th—dear G.'s wedding-day. The insurgents were still in the fort, so that had to be taken, but no doubt they have driven them out long ere this. A royal salute was fired from this place, the cantonments, and the Muchee Bhowan, with a view of impressing our triumph on the natives, and causing their hearts to melt into water.

Positive news came yesterday too, that the 84th Queen's and Madras Fusiliers had driven away the rebels at Allahabad and got possession of fort and cantonments; they were to proceed towards Cawnpore as soon as arrangements for carriage could be made. God grant they may be in time to save the unfortunates there. No news from Sir H. Wheeler for two days past. There are 10,000 of the rebels with ten guns camped at Nawab Gunge, twenty miles from this; but it is hoped that the news from Delhi will deter their coming to attack us, and dishearten those at Cawnpore.

We hear the post goes regularly between Allahabad and Calcutta, and that the telegraph is at work again and communication opened from up country till within twenty miles of Cawnpore, and telegraphs working between Agra and Delhi; all this cheers us, and gives us great cause for thankfulness. Mrs. Boileau has heard of the safe arrival of her husband at Goruckpore, where he has fallen in with some European troops. The officers of those regiments that have made themselves scarce are all learning gun drill, that they may serve as artillerymen in time of need; there is also a volunteer cavalry corps formed of a select few; numbers had to be rejected, from being such abominable riders.

Captain Weston told us this morning, to our extreme dismay, that the little notes we sent on the 12th and 13th did not get far; those going up country were destroyed, and those going down buried, and the man cannot recollect where their grave is; so all the dear ones at home will be terribly anxious, not even getting a line to say we are alive: I hope though now we shall soon be able to write by post. Mr. Schilling's bearer followed the example of ours the other day, and decamped, robbing his master to the tune of 150 *rupees*; ours took nothing with him; fortunately the rest of our people are all behaving very well, and have not even plagued us for money, as some of them are doing. Our *Syces* come from the Martinière every morning and report the horses quite well.

All the clouds are gone, and the weather as hot as ever. I am making a flannel coat for little Bobbie Fayrer. Dr. Partridge has done *Guy Mannering*, and begun *Quentin Durward* to us. Dear James is much better, though his throat and chest are still bad.

June 27. It is dear old Ben B.'s birthday:—many happy returns of it do I wish her. Little Bobbie Fayrer is a year old today. Sweet little fellow, I never saw a more lovely boy than he is. A letter from Sir H. Wheeler last night; they are still holding out bravely; but he says their sufferings have exceeded anything recorded in history. Nearly all the children and most of the women have died from the effects of the sun; and there is a fearful list of killed and wounded.

The general's son, Mr. Wheeler, of the 1st N. I., who was our landlord, and lived next door to us the first six months we were at Peshawur, was killed by a round shot at his father's side as the poor old man was finishing his letter. The enemy have two 24-pounders, three mortars, and eight other guns, which they fire on the besieged night and day. Ten days after the barracks were knocked down, the unhappy people had no shelter whatever from the sun. Ladies and children sat under tables and chairs out in the open. The general says they can hold out till the 2nd, by which time they hope to obtain relief from Allahabad.

Two regiments of infantry and two guns, and 200 *Seikhs*, were starting from there on the 24th: Oh, I trust they will be in time. They say our salutes yesterday put the insurgents at Nawab Gunge in a great state of excitement. News has been received that eleven persons, ladies and gentlemen, escaped from Seetapore, and are hiding in the jungles, protected by a *rajah*, who is very civil to them, and that the two Miss Jacksons and their brother are among them; it was positively asserted that they had been killed at Seetapore, the natives declaring they had seen their bodies, which leads one to hope that others reported dead may be found alive some day.

There are 800 soldiers arrived at Allahabad, and two of the Persian Gulf regiments have returned and are started from Calcutta, so we may hope soon to have a sufficient number for our protection up here.

June 29, St. Peter's Day. I think it must be ten years since uncle Augustus was consecrated Bishop of ——, and M. first dined at our house. They will be remembering this anniversary at home. How sad all anniversaries seem now! But, alas! how little they are thinking at home that, perhaps, this is the last that we shall ever see. I have no heart to write, for it appears next to impossible that letters or journal will ever reach the dear ones for whom they are written. There are such terrible reports from Cawnpore, I can hardly bear to put them down.

Lucknow, *June 30,* 1857, Tuesday. A most disastrous day. Early this morning we were awoke by the sound of guns passing the house, and found that a small force of 300, with seven guns, were going out to meet the advanced guard of the enemy, which was reported to be at a place called Nawab Gunge, in hopes, by driving them back, of preventing the rest from coming on. When they reached the village of Chinhut, about five miles from Lucknow, instead of a small force they found the whole rebel army, amounting to between 12,000 and 15,000.

Our unfortunate troops were taken at a disadvantage, completely surrounded, and obliged to fly back in terrible disorder, leaving nearly 200 killed and wounded, and five of our guns, one of them a howitzer, in the hands of the enemy. It was little less than miraculous that any of them came back alive. Poor Colonel Case, Captain Stevens, Mr. Thompson, and Mr. Brackenbury, and Captain M'Clean, of the 71st N. I., were killed. Sir Henry Lawrence and Colonel Inglis returned all safe.

At nine o'clock we were in a state of siege, completely invested by the enemy, and tremendous firing commenced. A very fierce attack was made on the Bailee Guard Gate at the back of this house. The enemy's guns opened upon our intrenchments while we were dressing for breakfast; and we were shouted at to rush down to the underground room before we were half ready: so I seized my hair out of the hands of the frightened *ayah*, and cut it off just at the plaits. She instantly burst forth into piteous lamentations and decamped this evening, thinking the loss of my hair was a sign that all was up with us.

And now the ladies and children were all huddled together in the underground room, called the Tye Khana, damp, dark, and gloomy as a vault, and excessively dirty. Here we sat all day, feeling too miserable, anxious, and terrified to speak, the gentlemen occasionally coming down to reassure us and tell us how things were going on. James was nearly all the day in the hospital, where the scene was terrible: the place so crowded with wounded and dying men that they had no room to pass between them, and everything in a state of indescribable misery, discomfort, and confusion.

The Polehamptons have left the Residency, and got a little room in the hospital to live in. Mrs. Polehampton will make herself useful there in nursing. I wish I could go too, but there is no room for us, and James says it is too great a risk for me going backwards and forwards under fire each time, so I must try to be of use here instead.

July 1, Wednesday. Poor Miss Palmer's leg was shot off this afternoon at the Residency. Sir Henry L. too had a very narrow escape; a round shot passed just above his head through the room in which he was sitting. The firing has been incessant the whole day, and we have been close prisoners to the Tye Khana.

July 2, Thursday. Sir Henry Lawrence was mortally wounded about half-past eight this morning, from the bursting of a shell in the Residency. He was on his bed, and Captain Wilson was reading some papers to him, when he was hit by an enormous piece of shell, and his left leg nearly taken off just below the thigh. He was brought over to this house immediately. James prayed with him, and administered the Holy Communion to him. He was quite sensible, though his agony was extreme. He spoke for nearly an hour, quite calmly, expressing all his last wishes with regard to his children. He sent affectionate messages to them and to each of his brothers and sisters; he particularly mentioned the Lawrence Asylum, and entreated that Government might be urged to give it support; he bid farewell to all the gentlemen who were standing round his bed, and said a few words of advice and kindness to each.

His nephew, Mr. George Lawrence, he blessed most affectionately, and told him he regarded him as a son. He spoke of his wife, who died about four years ago, most affectingly, and expressed the deepest penitence and remorse for his own sins, and most perfect trust and faith in his Saviour. James says he never met with such a humble-minded Christian, or attended a more truly beautiful and edifying death-bed. There was not a dry eye there; everyone was so deeply affected and grieved at the loss of such a man, and we all felt as if our best friend and support was taken from us. I shall never forget the miserable feeling of despair which seemed to take possession of us, as if our last hope were gone.

Poor Sir Henry's screams and groans of agony all day have been fearful to hear. He has named Major Banks as his successor in the chief authority. This has been a wretched day. Lieutenant Dashwood was severely contused by the falling of bricks from the striking of a round shot at the Post-office battery. He was brought here soon after Sir Henry L.; and Captain Power, an officer of the 32nd, was shot in the front verandah. The fire all day has been more tremendous than ever. The enemy seem to have found out that Sir Henry is still alive and where he is, for they direct their fire especially on this house.

Last night we were very much startled by the blowing up of the Muchee Bhowan Fort; the shock was terrific, and at first we did not recollect what it was, though we had been told what was to happen. The garrison arrived here quite safely, not a shot having been fired at them.

July 3, Friday, I was upstairs all day, nursing Sir Henry, who still lingers in extreme suffering; his screams are so terrible, I think the sound will never leave my ears; when not under the influence of chloroform, he is quite conscious, and J. has been reading to him all day psalms and prayers as he was able to bear them. He several times repeated them after him in quite a strong voice. Once we thought he was going, but he rallied, and has taken an immense quantity of arrowroot and champagne during the day. Once when I was feeding him he looked at me so hard, as if he was trying to remember who I was. The firing has never ceased for a second the whole day.

July 4, Saturday. Sir Henry L. died at a quarter past eight this morning. His end was very peaceful, and without suffering. J. was with him. I came into the room a minute after he had breathed his last: his expression was so happy one could not but rejoice that his pain was over. Half an hour before he died, his nephew, Mr. George Lawrence, was shot through the shoulder in the verandah. I have been nursing him today, poor fellow; it was so sad to see him lying there in the room with his uncle's body, looking so sad and suffering.

About twelve I was obliged to ask J. to have the body carried outside, so he called some soldiers to help carry the bed into the verandah. When they came in, one of the men lifted the sheet off poor Sir Henry's face, and kissed him. Last night nearly all the servants ran away: two *khitmutgars*, five *punkah coolies*, three sweepers, four *ayahs*, and Mrs. D.'s baby's wet-nurse, only remained behind. We are all obliged to put our shoulders to the wheel and divide the work between us. Mr. Schilling has sent us three little Martinière boys to help.

A soldier of the 32nd, called Metcalfe, has taken charge of dear old Bustle for us. He was so much in the way down in the Tye Khana, and received such black looks from —— and ——, we were afraid we should have been obliged to condemn him to death as the most merciful way of getting rid of him, when this delightful man, who is on guard at this house, offered to take charge of him for us till better days should come. Mr. Ommaney, the Judicial Commissioner, was shot through the head yesterday, and is not expected to live. He came here to see poor Sir Henry, and was wounded on his way home.

July 5, Sunday. We had service, and all received comfort in the Holy Communion downstairs in the Tye Khana. Work was portioned out, to each of us who are strong enough to do any, by James this morning. My share is to act housemaid, and keep the rooms we inhabit tidy and clean: I am also to nurse Mr. Lawrence, and any sick or wounded who may be brought to this house. We all sleep (that is, eleven ladies and seven children) on the floor of the Tye Khana, where we spread mattresses and fit into each other like bits in a puzzle, so as best to feel the *punkah.* The gentlemen sleep upstairs in a long verandah sort of room on the side of the house least exposed to fire. My bed consists of a *purdah* and a pillow. In the morning we all roll up our bedding, and pile it in heaps against the wall.

We have only room for very few chairs down there, which are assigned to invalids, and most of us take our meals seated on the floor, with our plates on our knees. We are always obliged to light a candle for breakfast and dinner, as the room is perfectly dark. Our usual fare consists of stew, as being easiest to cook: it is brought up in a large *deckger,* so as not to dirty a dish, and a portion ladled out to each person Of course we can get no bread or butter, so *chapatties* are the disagreeable substitute. We have large stores of beer, wine, tea, arrowroot, sago, &c, which will last a long time.

Our rations of meat, rice, wheat, *dhol*, &c. , we draw from the commissariat. We are all kept close prisoners to the dismal Tye Khana, only Mrs. D. and I go upstairs at all during the day—she to see her husband and I to look after Mr. Lawrence. For about half an hour in the evening we are permitted to sit in the portico and breathe a little fresh air. After sunset the firing generally slackens considerably for a time, and it is supposed the *sepoys* are engaged just then in cooking their dinner. Mr. Ommaney died this evening: what a dreadful blow it must be to his poor wife and daughters!

July 7, Tuesday. Mr. Polehampton was shot through the body this morning. He was in his own room, shaving, and a musket-ball came through the window. I am delighted to say the wound is not mortal. The bullet entered his side and came out at his back, but no vital part was touched, and he is going on well. Captain Francis of the 13th N. I. had his leg taken off by a round shot today.

July 8. Captain Francis died. A little girl at the Begum Kotee was killed today by a round shot. James has five or six funerals every night. He has very hard work of it now Mr. Polehampton is laid up; and going down to the churchyard to bury, he is exposed to a hot fire the whole time. I feel so terribly heartsick and anxious till I see him come back again safe; but God will, I trust, protect him in his perilous duties.

July 9, Thursday. This has been a dreadful day. Poor Lieutenant D. died of cholera: he was taken ill about four o'clock this morning, and before two he was dead. His poor wife never left him from the time she was first called, which was about five. At first Dr. Fayrer was not alarmed, thought it a very slight case, and that he would recover; but he never rallied at all. James said prayers with him and gave him the Holy Communion. His brother was with him when he died. My patient, Mr. Lawrence, went back to his own quarters this morning, convalescent.

July 10, Friday. Young Mr. Dashwood wounded himself in the leg while cleaning his own pistol this morning. He is likely to be laid up some time, as they cannot find the ball.

July 12, Sunday. We had service upstairs in the hall. Tremendous fire kept up all last night.

July 13, Monday. Mr. Charlton of the 32nd shot through the head.

July 14. Very heavy firing all day: ten Europeans wounded: five buried this evening.

July 16, Thursday. Poor Mrs. Thomas died of smallpox. She was staying here before the siege began, and has since been living at the Begum Kotee. Mr. Lester, who was shot yesterday, died today. There were six funerals this evening.

I finished a flannel "jumper" for Captain Weston, and began a flannel shirt for Mr. Polehampton; his wife is so much engaged nursing him and other sick in hospital, she has no time to work. James had a most providential escape *today*. As he was going down to the graveyard a round shot fell between him and the *dhoolie* next to which he was walking, and threw up the earth all over him. Mr. Brice of the artillery, an old Peshawur friend, was wounded today. Little Mary Strongways died of cholera.

July 17, Friday. Four round shot came through the house today mercifully none of us were touched.

July 19, Sunday. Mr. Arthur of the 7th Cavalry was killed this morning, and two officers wounded in the Residency. Poor Mr. Polehampton was seized with cholera: James went over to see him, and found him as ill as he could be, and frightfully altered; he would hardly have known him. There is no hope of his recovery.

July 20, Monday. Mr. Polehampton died at half-past eight this morning. J. sat up all last night with him, and was with him when he died. His poor wife is stricken to the earth by this terrible blow. God help her! J. says she is wonderfully calm. This evening he read the funeral service alone with her over her husband's body, before taking it away with the others for burial. She was extremely anxious he should have a coffin, a wish it seemed impossible to gratify; but J. instituted a search, and found one stowed away with some old boxes under the staircase in the hospital; and he also had a separate grave dug for him. Since the siege the bodies have always been buried several in the same grave, and sewn up in their bedding, as there are no people and there is no time to make coffins.

The enemy made a very strong attack today; it began at 10 o'clock and lasted three hours, when they gave it up. Two 18-pounders came through the room Em. B. and I used to sleep in, and where we have since always gone to perform an alarmed and hurried toilet; it was impossible to wash and dress down in the Tye Khana, so we have hitherto braved the danger. J. was in the room this morning at his ablutions when the round-shots came through; he was quite smothered with dust, as a great piece of wall and ceiling came down, but was most mercifully saved from hurt.

I was dreadfully frightened when I heard the noise, for I knew he was in the room. I really felt paralyzed with terror, till I heard him call out he was "all right!" He was obliged to creep out of the rubbish almost in a state of nature, as he was just in the act of bathing when the shot struck the room.

We have by degrees crept upstairs during the day and sat in the little entrance-hall, which is considered tolerably safe; but this morning we were all hurried down to the lower regions in double-quick time. We dress now in a tiny barricaded closet out of the dining-room, where no balls have come yet.

We had two killed and nine wounded this morning during the attack. There were nine funerals tonight—the largest number since the battle of Chinhut. Mrs. Polehampton has left the hospital and gone to a room at the Begum Kotee, which she shares with Mrs. Barbor and Mrs. Galle, both widows, whose husbands were murdered by the mutineers.

We have had no less than eight round-shot through this house today.

July 21, Tuesday. Three weeks since the siege began. Poor Major Banks was shot this morning on the top of the Gubbins's house. There was a fierce attack made on that side today. Dr. Bryden of the 71st was wounded, but not mortally; he was shot whilst at dinner.

July 22, Wednesday. Mrs. Dorin, one of the fugitives from Seetapore, was killed in the Gubbins's house today, shot through the head in her room. Two shells burst in the churchyard last night not forty yards from the grave where J. was standing.

Now that Major Banks is dead, there is no chief commissioner. Colonel Inglis of the 32nd is brigadier, and commands the garrison, which is entirely under military authority.

July 24, Friday. No casualties today, and only one funeral.

Mrs. D. is very poorly, and quite unequal to the charge of her children; so I am now head nurse as well as housemaid, and find plenty to do, which keeps my thoughts from dwelling too much on the misery and horror that surround us. Ally D. is a dear little boy of two, and Herbert, the baby, is ten months old; their poor mother is expecting her confinement again before long.

I am making her a black dress.

July 25, Saturday, St. James's Day. Poor Mr. Polehampton's effects were sold today, and realised 700 *rupees* (70*l.*)

Both the little D.s are ill with diarrhoea, and I am up half the night with them. The Boileau children and Bobbie Fayrer have it too; our rest is much disturbed; what with the frequent night attacks of the enemy, the crying and illness of the poor children, the rats and mice which run over us, the heat, and the sleepiness of the *punkah coolie*, unbroken sleep is a luxury we have long been strangers to.

We take it in turns to watch during the night for an hour each; mine is the second watch, from 10 to 11. Mrs. Boileau takes from 9 to 10, and wakes me just as I am in my first slumber. I don't exactly know what is gained by these night watchings, except that we are all very nervous, and are expecting some dreadful catastrophe to happen, so that the rest go to sleep more easily, if one of the party is known to be awake. The ladies who are delicate, as Mrs. D., Mrs. Fayrer, Mrs. Anderson, and Emily B., are exempted from keeping watch.

July 26, Sunday. The first news that greeted us this morning was, that a pensioner, Unget by name, who had been sent to Cawnpore with a letter, had returned with a despatch from Colonel Fraser Tytler, the quarter-master-general of the troops under General Havelock, who is advancing to our relief with a large force, and hopes to be here in four days. These joyful tidings put us all in the highest spirits. It seems as if one could never be thankful enough for the deliverance which is at hand.

Smith, one of our little Martinière servants, was shot through the leg this morning, running with a note from Miss Schilling to her brother.

J. was sent for to see a lady at the Gubbins's house, dying of cholera (Mrs. Grant); her husband was on another bed in the same room, and one of their children died yesterday. The husband and wife partook of the Holy Communion together for the last time on earth. Mr. Lewin of the artillery was killed at the Cawnpore gate; his wife is expecting her confinement; she has one little girl, the age of Herbert D.

July 27, Monday. There was an attack in the night which alarmed us, but the enemy as usual were soon driven back. Captain Shepherd was killed. Mrs. Grant died this morning.

July 29, Tuesday. Colonel Halford died this morning; he has been ill with a carbuncle ever since the siege began, but we had no idea his end was so near.

J. said prayers with him this evening. . . .

The poor daughter is much to be pitied. . . .

There was great excitement in the garrison this afternoon; firing was distinctly heard, and we all came to the conclusion our much longed for relief was near; some of the soldiers began to cheer, and sentinels on the top of the house declared they could distinguish the advance of European troops in the direction of the Martinière park; time passed, nothing came of it, a reaction took place, our spirits fell to the lowest ebb, and at length we were told the guns which had so rejoiced our hearts were fired in honour of a puppet King of Oude, aged 11, who was proclaimed today.

I have finished Mrs. D.'s black dress, and feel rather proud of it, as I have done every stitch myself. Captain Grant died of his wounds today: he has been unconscious the last two days, and never knew that his wife was dead; the last time he spoke of her, he thought she was better, and was too ill to be told she had preceded him. The doctors forbade it; but I should think it would have comforted him.

August 2, Sunday. This is the *Buckraeede*, a great Mahomedan feast, and a grand attack was consequently expected from the rebel forces, but it has been instead an unusually quiet day, and we imagine therefore that many of them have gone off to oppose the relieving army. Poor little Bobbie Fayrer is very ill; I never saw such a sad change as there is in him from the lovely cherub of a child he was some time since; he is now quite a skeleton, and looks like a little old man. All the children are very bad; the want of fresh air and exercise, and the loss of their accustomed food, have made them all ill.

Little Herbert D.'s wet-nurse is in such a bad humour, and always threatening to run away, and declaring her milk is gone, so we have been trying to wean the poor child, and I feed him with thin arrowroot and sago mixed with a little milk, but he dislikes the change very much, and I fear it does not agree with him, for he has had diarrhoea, and now it has turned to dysentery.

James has had some correspondence with Brigadier Inglis about the state of the churchyard; the smell there became so horrible, owing to the shallowness of the graves and the want of workpeople to make proper arrangements, that the medical men pronounced it positively dangerous for the living to go there, and J. for two nights read the funeral service over the dead in the hospital porch, and did not accompany them to the graveyard: having reported the state of it to the proper authority, it ended by the brigadier giving orders that the graves should be dug the necessary depth, and a plentiful supply of charcoal spread over them. James considered that as he is the only chaplain here, he must think of his duties to the living before the dead; if he were made ill by the noxious vapours rising from the graves, the former would be the sufferers.

One of the most serious inconveniences we endure in consequence of the desertion of the servants is the loss of a *dhobee*; there is only one left, and he has neither soap nor starch. James made an arrangement with him to wash a few things occasionally, but he merely dips them in water, and brings them back no cleaner than he received them. I have washed some myself, but it is such dreadful hot work it half kills one.

Since Smith was wounded I have undertaken, in addition to my other work, to wash up the cups and saucers for the early tea; and I find every hour of the day fully occupied. It is a great comfort to have so much to do, and to feel oneself of some little use, and helps to keep up one's spirits much better than would otherwise be possible under the circumstances. Dear James is very hard worked, and does not spare himself the least, so we don't see much of each other.

August 4. One of the gunners was shot dead in the verandah this morning. When I came up stairs to dress, I saw the poor fellow lying there in a pool of blood.

August 5. A soldier of the 32nd was shot in hospital this morning, while sitting on a comrade's bed.

August 6. Mr. Studdy, a 32nd officer, had his arm shot off by an 18-pounder.

August 7. Unget returned last night with another letter. General Havelock's force was obliged to return to Cawnpore to oppose the rebels, who were gathering in their rear, and will not be able to come to the relief of Lucknow till they get more reinforcements. Dear James is very poorly today, and indeed we are none of us feeling well. Hard work and want of fresh air, together with hope deferred, are beginning to tell upon most people.

August 8, Saturday. Poor Mr. Bryce died of cholera today, and also Dr. M'Donald. Mr. Bryce had nearly recovered from his wound. He was ill a very few hours. James was with him; but the poor fellow was in such extreme agony until the collapse came on, he could not speak or attend to anything.

Aug. 9, Sunday. Dear J.'s 35th birthday; and a little siege baby cousin came into this stormy world. E. presented Charlie with a small son and heir at eight o'clock this morning. She felt very unwell all yesterday, but until the evening we never suspected the cause, as she did not expect herself to be confined for another fortnight. I sat up with her all night, and was with her till master baby made his appearance. Dr. Partridge attended her, and was very kind. She suffered very much, poor thing! but bore it most bravely. Charlie went off at dawn of day, and got a very nice 32nd woman (Mrs. Roberts), who only just arrived in time.

Poor Mr. Studdy died today of his wound. Mrs. Hersham's and Mrs. Kendal's babies died. It is sad the number of children who are dying: they get diarrhoea, for which there seems no cure. We have by mutual consent given up the night watchings. I suppose we are grown braver, so we voted there was no necessity for anyone to keep awake, and composedly resign ourselves to the arms of Morpheus.

August 10, Monday. I was called up in the night to attend to my wee siege cousin. Charlie took Mrs. Roberts's place for some time, but could not manage to pacify his infant son, who was crying lustily, so at last came down to call me. I went up and found the poor little thing required dressing and feeding, both of which operations I successfully performed, and then put him to sleep. Charlie went off at daylight to find another nurse, and brought back a copper-coloured individual of the name of Scott, who seems a good sort of woman; and Emmie and baby are both flourishing today. Captain Power has died of his wounds. He was shot here the same day as Sir H. Lawrence. The enemy made two heavy attacks on our intrenchments—one in the middle of the day, and the second this evening: it began just as we were kneeling down to prayers.

August 11, Tuesday. Part of the roof of the Residency fell in this morning, and buried six men of the 32nd: only two were dug out alive.

August 12, Wednesday. Major Anderson, our chief engineer, died: he will be a great loss to the garrison.

August 14, Friday. The smell in the churchyard is again so offensive that it has made J. quite ill; and when he came back he vomited about two hours incessantly, and frightened me very much.

Mrs. Fayrer is very ill. She had alarming choleratic symptoms today. They have barricaded the windows in Mrs. D.'s old room, and put her to bed.

August 15, Saturday. Dear J. all right again today. Mrs. Fayrer very ill, and little Bobbie too. I fear little Herbert cannot recover: he seems to be sinking. It makes one's heart ache to look at his little suffering face. He is so weak he scarcely ever cries, and when he does, it is such a little feeble wail it is pitiable to hear. We are all coming to sleep upstairs in the dining-room tonight. The Tye Khana is so damp, everyone is ill, and the dining-room is tolerably safe. Mrs. Clarke and I have been busy arranging beds under the *punkah*, and sewing on a good deep frill to whisk away the mosquitoes. This is the first night there has been no funeral.

August 16, Sunday. Emily's baby a week old. A shell burst in the verandah outside Mrs. Fayrer's room. She was very much alarmed, and it is wonderful how she escaped being hurt. Dr. Fayrer carried her bed into Emmie's room, which, being quite in the centre of the house, is comparatively safe. Now the two invalids are together in a sort of hospital. A letter was brought in from Cawnpore last night. General Havelock still waiting for reinforcements, and no hope of relief for us at present.

August 19. Dear little Herbert D. died at half-past three this morning. Yesterday he seemed so much better that Mrs. D. was quite happy about him; but fever came on in the night, and we were alarmed at the way he gasped for breath. Mrs. Boileau happened to wake, and heard him first. Directly she looked at him she saw he was dying, and woke his mother and me. I called up Dr. Partridge, who ordered a warm bath; and we sent the *dye* down to prepare some water, but before she came up with it the little spirit had fled.

One could not grieve; he looked so sweet and happy; the painful look of suffering quite gone, and a lovely smile on his dear little baby face. We closed his pretty blue eyes, and crossed his little hands over his breast, and there he lay by his mother's side till daylight; then she washed the little body herself, and put him on a white nightgown, and I tied a lace handkerchief round his face, as she had no caps.

Charlie D. came over to see her, and we left her quiet with him and the dead baby till eleven, when I was obliged to go in and ask her to part with it. She let me take it away, and I sewed the little sweet one up myself in a clean white cloth, and James carried it over to the hospital to wait there for the evening burials.

Poor little Ally is so ill, it prevents Mrs. D. thinking so much of the loss of Herbert as she else would. She is so anxious, poor thing, about her last remaining treasure. He has fever and dysentery, and his life seems hanging on a thread. Bobby Fayrer is just as ill, and his mother also, but the poor little fellow has found a most devoted nurse in Miss Schilling; and if he lives, humanly speaking, the Fayrers will owe their child's life to her unremitting care and attention. She watches him night and day, and never leaves his crib for a minute.

The poor child is not allowed to be moved or lifted up. The only fear is Miss Schilling getting ill herself from over-fatigue and anxiety, and I wish much I could help her; but what with looking after Emmie's wants, and nursing both Mrs. D. and Ally, besides my housemaid's work and washing up cups and saucers, &c, I have as much on my hands as I can manage.

August 23, Sunday. We had service, with the comfort of the Holy Communion, at half-past three. Emily and Mrs. Fayrer came out to church, and lay on two sofas, looking very interesting invalids. Mrs. Polehampton, Mrs, Barber, and Mrs. Lewin came to the service. It was very affecting to see so many newly-made widows assembled together; with Mrs. D. and Mrs. Halford there were five in the same room.

August 26, Wednesday. Mr. Webb, an officer of the 32nd, was killed in Mr. Gubbins's compound by an 18-pounder. We are reduced from this date to half rations.

August 27, Thursday. A 32nd man badly wounded in the verandah this morning. There was an auction held today of some stores which belonged to poor Sir Henry Lawrence. The price things were sold for was quite laughable. A dozen of brandy fetched 170 *rupees*; two small tins of soup 55 *rupees*; a ham 75; a quart bottle of honey 45; beer 75 a dozen, &c.

August 29, Saturday. The pensioner Unget returned again from Cawnpore last night, bringing a letter from General Havelock, still waiting for reinforcements. Oh! when will they come? Sir Colin Campbell is arrived in Calcutta. Delhi is not yet taken, but expected to fall in twenty days. The Rajah Pattiala has declared himself on our side, and sent a large force to Delhi. The Punjaub is all quiet; the *Seikhs* prove faithful.

August 30, Sunday. This is the last day of the Mohurrum, and there was a report that the enemy intended attacking us in force, but they must have changed their minds, for the firing has been less than usual. Our only two *kitmughars* ran away last night, and great was the dismay in the household this morning when their desertion was discovered. No one to light the kitchen fire or boil the kettle for tea; we began to think some of us should be obliged to turn cooks, not at all a desirable office in such melting weather; but happily a friend indeed turned up in Mrs. Need, a woman Mrs. Boileau engaged some time ago to take care of her children, who volunteered her services in the kitchen. The new *chef de cuisine* served us up such a capital breakfast and dinner, we began to think the departure of the kits rather a good thing than otherwise, especially as we shall be saved paying them a large amount of wages due for the last two months.

August 31, Monday. Mrs. D. was taken ill this morning and confined in less than half-an-hour. I had just time to rush into the gentlemen's room and wake up Dr. Partridge, fly into Emmie's room and get a *purdah,* which we rolled her on to carry her into her old room where the shell had burst, before her third little son made his appearance. I was never more astonished in my life. When we had set down the bed I ran to ask Emmie for some baby clothes, as there were none ready; before I got back again I heard a cry, and the first thing I saw was the little new-born; the very image of his poor father; everyone who saw it remarked it instantly.

Emmie's nurse came in to wash and dress the poor little thing, and James has been all day trying to find a nurse, but has not yet succeeded, so I have been in attendance when necessary; but poor little Ally is too ill to be left, so I hope we shall find someone to come soon.

After breakfast Emmie vacated the hospital-room, as she is now quite well enough to come out, and we have moved Mrs. D. into her place opposite Mrs. Fayrer's bed. I have not sat down today a minute; what with nursing and cooking for invalids, I never was so busy in my life.

September 1, Tuesday. I sat up with Mrs. D. and baby last night; both were very restless. The baby would not be quiet, except in his mother's bed or my arms; the nurse came this morning, whom J. succeeded in getting yesterday. Her arrival was a great relief to me, little Ally requiring such constant nursing I could not attend to his mother and him at the same time. Two Martinière boys have been taken away to grind grain by order of the Brigadier; so we are again distressed for servants and obliged to work harder than ever.

September 2, Wednesday. J. engaged Mrs. Weston, the sexton's wife, a half-caste, to come and help in the kitchen, and wash up plates and dishes. A very sad thing occurred this evening: Mr. Birch was shot through the body by some fatal mistake through one of our own loopholes. His wife was the daughter of Colonel Brown, who commanded the artillery at Peshawur, and whose death-bed James attended a year and a half ago. She was only married last January, and escaped with her husband in here from the massacre at Seetapore a short time before the siege began. Her poor husband lived a few hours after he was wounded, and James was with him when he died. Mrs. Birch is expecting her confinement; her father-in-law, Colonel Birch, was murdered at Seetapore; it is altogether a sad story.

September 4. Major Bruère, 13th N. I., was killed this afternoon on the top of the brigade mess; he has left a wife and four children.

September 5. Mr. Graham, one of the officers who escaped in here from Secrora, committed suicide this morning; he was quite out of his mind. His poor wife was only confined a few days ago, and has just lost one of her children. The enemy gave us an attack today about breakfast time, but it did not last long; they blew up three mines, none of which did us any damage.

September 6, Sunday. It is four years today since we sailed from Portsmouth, and I looked my last on my own dearest father's loved face; shall I ever see Mamma and the other precious ones again? God only knows, and I pray that His will may be done. Baby B. was christened this afternoon; his name is Percy Arthur. I stood proxy for his godmother, who is Emmie's sister, Mrs. Fulcher; Henry O'Dowda stood for his godfathers, Uncle Will and a brother of Emmie's. The dear little babe looked lovely; he is so fair and white, and has such pretty blue eyes; he should have been a girl.

September 8, Tuesday. Captain Simonds, of the artillery, died today; he was wounded at Chinhut, and has been suffering ever since; his wife and children went to the hills just before the disturbances began. Mr. Schilling is staying here for a little change; he is very unwell.

September 10, Thursday. Darling little Mary Farrer's fourth birthday; God bless and keep the dear child! I long to hear she is safe and well. The enemy have been comparatively quiet the last day or two. The report is that many of them are departing towards Fyzabad, which makes us hope that Delhi has fallen. Mrs. Boileau's youngest child is very ill indeed; the others are all better—the two siege babies flourishing. The weather is much cooler, for which one can't be too thankful. I have the sole charge of little Ally D., and now he is getting better, but is not well enough to play about, nor ill enough to lie down as he used to do; I seldom have him out of my arms, and feel rather as if he must be my own child; he is getting such a darling.

September 13, Sunday. Poor little Ina Boileau died in the night; she was so very ill all yesterday, we knew she could not live; her poor mother, who had been watching her all night, had fallen asleep quite exhausted, and when she awoke she found the poor child quite cold in her arms; her cry of anguish awoke us all; poor creature! she is distracted, and reproaches herself with having gone to sleep; but of course she could not help it, and she would not allow anyone else to watch with her. Captain Mansfield of the 32nd was seized with cholera during the night and died this morning.

This day year we started for Cashmere from Murrie: what a contrast to our present captive condition, and how little we then dreamt of what was coming to pass! The service here was at half-past two, and we had the comfort of Holy Communion. Mrs. Polehampton, Mrs. Barbor, and a few outsiders came. James generally holds four or five services on Sunday in different parts of the garrison—this house, the brigade mess, the Tye Khana of the Residency, the hospitals, &c. Besides visiting the sick and burying, he administers the Holy Communion at one place or another every Sunday, taking the different houses in turn.

A prisoner was taken last night; he was a grass-cutter of the 7th Cavalry, found straying inside our intrenchments; he gave information that news had been received in the city of General Havelock's advanced guard having crossed the Ganges; that many of the *sepoys* had gone off to their villages with plunder, and that the enemy now surrounding us consisted of the city people and *zemindars* of the country; that the whole of Oude to a man was hostile to us, but they were very much disheartened at not yet having been able to take us, and were of opinion now that if they besieged us for twelve years they should never succeed, which is satisfactory for us to hear at all events.

September 14, Monday. This evening, when James went over to the hospital, he was dreadfully shocked to find poor Captain Fulton had just been brought there killed by a round shot at Mr. Gubbins's bastion; his head was completely smashed, and nothing but the mask of the face left; he was the chief engineer after Major Anderson's death, and his loss to the garrison is irreparable; he has a widow and six children at Simla—poor things! Mrs. D. came out of her room this evening for the first time; she has got on famously.

September 15. Captain Fullerton died last night; he walked out of the hospital window in the upper story, whether in sleep or delirium is not known; he was taken up insensible, and never spoke again. A round shot came through the hospital whilst James was there this evening and passed from one end to the other two feet above the men's beds, alarming the poor invalids most terribly.

September 17, Thursday. The eightieth day of the siege. We were all sitting out in the verandah this evening when an 8-inch shell fell and exploded in a lane opposite, not twenty yards off. No one was touched, but we all flew into the house like frightened sheep. Mrs. D. came back to the common sleeping-room today, and Miss Schilling and Bobbie turned into the hospital-room with Mrs. Fayrer. This entailed a fresh arrangement of beds, which took up some of my time this afternoon.

September 18. There was a partial eclipse of the sun between nine and ten this morning. The natives look upon it as a bad omen, and predict a famine, which, as the successor of war, is not unlikely to happen.

September 19. James was sent for last night to see a poor woman, the wife of a writer, who was shot through the lungs as she was sitting at work in her room with her children round her, when a musket ball came through the window. With this exception yesterday was a white day in the siege—no funerals, and no admissions into hospital. The season is extraordinarily healthy for the time of year; there seems to be a special Providence guarding us from the usual sickness prevailing this month.

Dr. Fayrer says, in his seven years' experience of India, he has never known so healthy a September. We have also been mercifully spared epidemics, which would inevitably have destroyed us, and at one time both cholera and smallpox seemed impending. There were several fatal cases both in July and the beginning of August, but they have since totally disappeared. An auction took place this morning on the property of a 32nd officer who had died. The value of things has undergone a curious metamorphosis; three very old flannel shirts sold for 105 *rupees*, while a handsome new uniform went for twelve. A pair of old boots sold for twelve *rupees*, and a bottle of brandy for twenty.

September 20, Sunday. I was made quite miserable this morning by the loss of my dear little old Christian Year given me by darling mother on my seventeenth birthday, and which has been my constant companion ever since; I left it on the hall table for a minute, and when I came back it had disappeared, and, upon inquiry, I got out of Anna Boileau that Master Georgie had walked off with it: the little wretch, however, denied all knowledge of it, and after vainly endeavouring, by scolding and coaxing, to make him tell where it was, and searching every hole and corner of the house I could think of, I gave it up as hopeless, and felt quite unhappy all day.

In the evening, just after dinner, up comes Captain Weston with my lost treasure in his hand. Something of his had fallen out of window, and in picking it up he discovered my dear little book among a heap of empty bottles, where the magpie boy must have hidden and forgotten it. We had service here with the Holy Communion at half-past two today. It is little Georgie F.'s first birthday—a sad anniversary for dear Fred. James and I did not forget the precious little one. What would we not give to know that both children and Fred are safe and well!

September 21, Monday. It began raining in the middle of the night, and we have had quite an English wet day, delightfully cool.

September 22, Tuesday. Rain all day. Poor Mr. Cunliffe died.

September 23, Wednesday. We were all awoke between one and two last night by the arrival of Colonel Palmer with joyful tidings that delightful old pensioner Unget, who has always brought us in the only letters we received from outside, has come back with one from Sir J. Outram, dated the 20th, in which he states that he crossed the Ganges on the 19th with a complete army, and, by the blessing of God, will relieve us in a few days. Mrs. Boileau and Mrs. Anderson happened to be awake, and heard Colonel Palmer telling the gentlemen in the next room; they listened anxiously to every word, and then woke all the rest of us to impart the happy news.

Oh, it seems really as if one never could be thankful enough! the looked-for relief will come just as all hearts are beginning to fail. There will doubtless be very hard fighting before our brave friends are able to raise the siege for us. The enemy seem as determined and active against us as ever, and not one whit daunted by the news they must have had that help for us was at hand.

May God in his great mercy grant us the victory! Heavy distant firing was distinctly heard this afternoon. A round shot, 24-pounder, came through the window of Mrs. D.'s room today and filled our little dressing-room with dust, but did no other mischief, though the poor *bheestie* who was filling the water-jugs rushed out in a most awful fright, and could scarcely believe he wasn't killed.

September 24, Thursday. Distant firing heard all the morning, and numbers of *sepoys* seen flying in disorder from the direction of Cawnpore. The enemy round us have been remarkably silent. The excitement in garrison is intense. Dr. Partridge and Captain Weston went to the top of the Residency and distinguished plainly the smoke of the guns, which they fancied were about four miles distant. Unget, the bearer of good news, who has brought in all the letters, is to receive 500 *rupees* for each; he will get 1500 for the three.

Well does he deserve it. We are indebted to him for every scrap of news we have been able to procure from the outer world during three weary months, so closely have we been invested. He stated in his last deposition that the number of the besieging army was 15,000, and the force with Sir J. Outram 6000, of whom 5000 were Europeans, and the rest *Seikhs*. Among the former are 200 gentlemen volunteers, who form a body of cavalry. Delhi has not yet fallen.

September 25, Friday. The enemy made two attacks during the night. Captain Ratcliffe of the 7th Cavalry was mortally wounded at the Cawnpore battery by a round shot. He will be a terrible loss to his wife and a very large family.

Continued firing in the city all day.

September 26, Saturday. Yesterday evening, on the eighty-eighth day of the siege, our long-looked for and so often despaired-of "relief" arrived. Never shall I forget the moment to the latest day I live. It was most overpowering. We had no idea they were so near, and were breathing air in the *portico* as usual at that hour, speculating when they might be in, not expecting they could reach us for several days longer, when suddenly, just at dark, we heard a very sharp fire of musketry quite close by, and then a tremendous cheering; an instant after, the sound of bagpipes, then soldiers running up the road, our compound and verandah filled with, our deliverers, and all of us shaking hands frantically, and exchanging fervent "God bless yous" with the gallant men and officers of the 78th Highlanders.

Sir James Outram and staff were the next to come in, and the state of joyful confusion and excitement is beyond all description. The big, rough-bearded soldiers were seizing the little children out of our arms, kissing them with tears rolling down their cheeks, and thanking God they had come in time to save them from the fate of those at Cawnpore. We were all rushing about to give the poor fellows drinks of water, for they were perfectly exhausted; and tea was made down in the Tye Khana, of which a large party of tired thirsty officers partook, without milk or sugar, and we had nothing to give them to eat.

Everyone's tongue seemed going at once with so much to ask and to tell, and the faces of utter strangers beamed upon each other like those of dearest friends and brothers. In the crowd I suddenly found myself caught hold of by both hands and warmly greeted by my old friend Walter Birch. Two old Peshawur friends also turned up, Captain Commeline and Mr. Battine. From the latter we heard the terrible fate of poor Edward and Maggie B. at Hansi. They were both murdered in May, soon after the disturbances first began at Delhi. Edward was shot on the parade-ground, and Maggie cut to pieces in the house.

Willie B. has escaped to the hills from Bareilly—he and a Mr. Hunter of his regiment (18th N. I.). The Punjaub has remained quiet—thanks, humanly speaking, to the vigorous and stern policy of Sir John Lawrence. Poor Mrs. Fayrer's brother was killed at Saugor. Dr. F. has not told her the sad news, as he does not think her strong enough to bear it. Mrs. Boileau has letters from her husband, who is safe at Benares.

The enemy's fire was very heavy all yesterday, as if in defiance, and just before dinner an 8-inch shell fell and burst in this house; the pieces were picked up in all directions, several in Mrs. Fayrer's room, yet wonderful to relate no one was struck. The "reinforcement"—for alas! "relief" is the wrong word—turns out to be very much smaller than we were led by Unget's statement to expect. They only started 3000 strong from Cawnpore. The force consists of parts of the 78th and 90th Highlanders, Her Majesty's 84th, 64th, 5th Fusiliers, and the 1st Madras Fusiliers, the Ferozepore regiment of *Seikhs*, 200 volunteer cavalry, and some artillery.

They had a tremendous day's fight to get in here; every inch of the ground through the city was contended for, and the loss of life has been terrible, some 30 officers and 500 rank and file killed and wounded. The heavy baggage with about 500 men and a couple of guns were left outside the city at a garden called the Alumbagh, so that the force which reached us brought with them no stores or provisions of any kind. Sir James Outram has made this house his head-quarters; he and his staff occupy the long room, in which the gentlemen sleep, and the drawing-room.

This morning a force was sent out to bring in the guns which were left outside the intrenchments last night, and Mr. Thornhill, who acted as guide through the streets, was dangerously wounded. Colonel Cooper, of the artillery, one of the gentlemen who was drinking tea here last night, was killed. The guns, however, were safely brought in. The enemy's fire still continues very annoying, though it is now from a greater distance, as our troops occupy the ground immediately round us, and have taken possession of the Tera Kotee, and one of the palaces at the back of this house, about a quarter of a mile off, called Ferreed Bux.

Our prospects today look gloomy enough. The disappointment is severe at finding the force which has arrived, instead of being strong enough to relieve, will in a manner increase our difficulties, by giving us treble more mouths to feed out of the scanty provisions left us. All at present is dire confusion and dismay, and faces in garrison longer even than before. Councils of war are sitting; as yet no line of action is decided on.

Whether we are to evacuate Oude, and attempt a retreat on Cawnpore, or remain at Lucknow, and endeavour to obtain provisions by force, has yet not been determined—a retreat through the streets with so many women, children, sick and wounded, would be a terrible alternative, and I fancy would only be adopted as a very desperate measure. There was a little gleam, however, of sunshine in the shape of good news of success at Delhi. An extraordinary event happened today.

Three prisoners were brought in, and undergoing a summary trial by drum-head court-martial, when a round shot struck and killed the trio. We heard that fifty people, among whom were several ladies and gentlemen and native Christians, were murdered in the city at the approach of General Outranks force; also that a party of nine, four gentlemen and five ladies, tried to join the force on the road coming in, but were followed by some *sepoys*, and all cut up almost within reach of our troops. J. had nineteen funerals this evening.

The hospital is so densely crowded that many have to lie outside in the open air, without bed or shelter. J. says he never saw such a heart-sickening scene. It is far worse than after Chinhut—amputated arms and legs lying about in heaps all over the hospital, and the crowd and confusion such that little can be done to alleviate the intense discomfort and pain of the poor sufferers.

I heard last night for the first time the particulars of the horrible tragedy at Cawnpore. (Then follows an account, which is here omitted, being already so well known in England.)

At Jhansi, where Louisa R. had been stationed, not a soul escaped.[7] The account of that tragedy is still more dreadful—children were burnt before their parents; wives insulted, mutilated, and murdered before their husbands, who were kept to the last and then bayoneted. The Futtyghur people were blown from guns, and those who escaped butchered at Cawnpore. How shall we be thankful enough for the mercy which has hitherto so miraculously been shown to us? I am very happy to hear that Simla has been quiet; so I hope the dear little ones up there are safe. At Murrie there has been disturbance, but it was soon put down.

September 27, Sunday. A sortie was made to take some guns on the Cawnpore side. The expedition was a failure—only 150 went out, not enough to do any good: lost many lives, and only spiked three guns, which will be unspiked as soon as their backs are turned. Our position seems more precarious than ever, as there is more danger now of starvation. The enemy surrounds us again on all sides, so that retreat from this dreadful place is next to impossible.

One great danger the arrival of the reinforcement, however, saved us from, for which we cannot be too thankful. Three mines were discovered, which had not even been suspected by the old garrison, and which, if completed, must inevitably have destroyed us: one was under the Redan battery, and two under the Treasury and Bailie Guard, close to the back of this house.

Mrs. D.'s baby was christened this afternoon Arthur Frederick;

7. Yes, a few did, and Mr. Ryves was one.

Charlie D. was one godfather; I stood proxy. There were twenty-five funerals this evening.

September 28. Our siege is as close as ever. The enemy have returned in great numbers and broken down all the bridges leading from the city, so that retreat for us is out of the question. A *kossid* arrived this afternoon with a despatch from Delhi. We have been victorious there, and taken every part of the city but the palace, which was expected to fall in a couple of days. The loss of life has been terrible. Colonel Nicholson, who commanded a brigade, is mortally wounded.

It was only this time last year we were dining with him, and feasting on the delicious grapes he used to send us in Cashmere. He was such a splendid soldier I am sure his loss will be severely felt; and how the death of such a very dear friend will grieve Colonel Edwardes! The troops have been resting today; they much needed. The enemy has been tolerably silent.

Michaelmas Day, Tuesday. Dear old B.'s wedding-day. God bless the dear old thing! I daresay she is anxious enough about our fate. A sortie was made this morning by a thousand of our men. They blew up four of the enemy's guns, brought two inside, and spiked others, besides blowing up about a dozen houses and killing many of the enemy. The loss on our side was thirty killed and wounded, among whom I hear five officers.

We had the *Home News* of the 30th August lent us today. We were all ready to devour it, so I read aloud all the morning to a most attentive audience of ladies. It is a comfort to know that there are 20,000 troops on their way out from England. I was so delighted to see in a bit of newspaper which came here, that both Mr. Ryves and Mr. Tyrwhitt had escaped the Jhansi massacre!

September 30. Three months today since the battle of Chinhut and commencement of our siege. I finished my darling little nephew's frock today—oh, I wonder if he will ever have it! I have done a great deal of work during the siege; besides dear Chip's frock I made a flannel-shirt for poor Mr. Polehampton, two for Henry O'Dowde, a jumper for Captain Weston, a dress for Mrs. D., *ditto* for myself, besides baby-things for the siege babies born in this house.

We bought some very pretty cups and saucers today from a soldier of the 90th. The Ferreed Bux was full of china and all sorts of valuable things, and the soldiers are constantly offering articles for sale. I got a prize in the shape of seven pairs of thread stockings, which I much needed.

October 1. The volunteer cavalry went out last night, with orders if possible to cut their way back to the Alumbagh, and on to Cawnpore; but they were compelled to return before they had gone a quarter of a mile. The fire which was opened upon them made it impossible to proceed. The enemy are all round us again in great force; they attacked our outposts in the middle of the night, and there was tremendous firing for about an hour. There are several officers here who were at Jellalabad, and they all say that siege was mere child's play to this. The investment of this place has been so complete, that with the exception of the three letters brought in by "Unget," we have had no communication whatever with the outer world.

Maun Singh, one of the most powerful of the Oude *rajahs,* with whom Sir James Outram has been trying to negotiate, has declared against us, and is heading the rebels; so no hope of aid from that quarter. We have heard that all the servants who ran away from the garrison and went into the city were shot, because they had served Europeans, and they offered a reward of five *rupees* for every servant's head: so the poor creatures gained nothing by their desertion.

Some troops made a sortie this afternoon to take the guns on the Cawnpore side. They went very cautiously to work, first taking possession of the houses which command the battery, and were very successful: we only lost two men killed and two wounded. A soldier of the Madras Fusiliers was discovered in a well, where the poor fellow had been hiding several days; he had fortunately some tea-leaves and biscuits in his pockets, on which he had managed to support life; he had heard the enemy all round him, and had not dared utter a sound; but his joy was great when he heard European voices, and he shouted loudly for help in spite of his exhausted state.

Both poor Mrs. Ouseley's children died today, within ten minutes of each other; the baby was born the same day as little Percy B.; the other was two years: they are first cousins of Sir Frederic's.

We made another sortie, took three more guns, and blew up several houses. J. took me a little walk this evening, and I saw for the first time what terrible destruction has been wrought by shot and shell on all the buildings round. The Residency I should never have recognised: it is quite a ruin. This house is so riddled with balls at the back and one side, you could scarcely put a pin's head between them.

I had a visit this evening from a Captain Scott, 12th N. I., a great friend of Louisa Ryves; he came to make acquaintance, having heard her speak of me. I heard from him of her safe arrival with her children in England, and her husband's escape from Jhansi: he fortunately happened to be out of the station, and made his way across country to Agra.

October 4, Sunday. A year today since dear G. F. died. I was glad the anniversary fell on a Sunday; and I had an opportunity of attending service and receiving the Holy Communion, and giving thanks for those dear ones who we trust are gone to their rest. There was a very large congregation at the brigade mess, and they nearly all communicated. It is a great blessing that now we can have a public service every Sunday. They arrange the mess-room very well, and it holds a good number of people. Walter Birch came to speak to us after church, and told us he was going out with a force this afternoon to try and reach the Alumbagh; and if he reached it in safety he would be able to send a letter home, and would let dearest mother know we were alive and well. The expedition however was countermanded. A horrible report was published in Calcutta, that Lucknow had fallen and we were all massacred: if this goes to England it will be dreadful. I am so anxious they should hear the truth as soon as possible.

Afternoon service was held at this house at three, and a great many came. In the evening I walked with C. and E. to call on their regimental doctor's wife, Mrs. Brydon, at the Ommaney's house, where they have a snug little room to themselves, instead of living in public as we do here; they looked so cosy we came home quite envious.

October 6, Tuesday. The enemy attacked our outpost at the Ferreed Bux this morning, but were repulsed with great loss; we lost ten, killed and wounded. The troops have been withdrawn from the extended position they occupied down the Cawnpore road—we were not strong enough to maintain it. The loss in killed and wounded since the reinforcement left Cawnpore was four days ago computed at 800 rank and file and 50 officers—nearly a third of the force.

At the commencement of the siege there were 150 officers in garrison, out of which number there are 90 killed or wounded. The casualties at this post, from the 30th of June to 25th of September, were thirteen killed and thirty wounded. Weston's (our clerk) child, Adolphus by name, was shot through the head in the verandah of the church this afternoon.

October 7. A 24-pounder came through the window of Mrs. D.'s room this morning. It was a spent ball thrown from a great distance, and did not penetrate the opposite wall. Sir James Outram received a letter from the Alumbagh this evening, with news of the safe arrival there of 60 carts of commissariat stores, escorted by 250 men with two guns. They had found the road perfectly clear from Cawnpore. The enemy have received reinforcements from Delhi.

It is now generally acknowledged, that but for our reinforcement on the 25th of September, we could never have held out against this tremendous increase in the number of besiegers: and it is very doubtful whether any natives would have remained with us after the 1st if no troops had arrived. In spite of excessively short commons, there is cause for great thankfulness for their timely help. Our rations are considerably reduced, and we often leave off dinner as hungry as when we began. The General has put out "an order," most lavish in praise of the Lucknow garrison, which he terms "more than illustrious."

October 8. A house blown up today, and a large number of the enemy destroyed.

October 9. James engaged a Madras servant, a smart-looking man in a very elaborate turban and yellow "*choga*," and speaks English: his name is Choonia.

October 10. News come of the complete fall of Delhi. King and queen in our hands, and complete possession of the place. It has been a dearly-bought victory—62 officers and 1300 men fallen; and when the news left Delhi there were 3000 wounded in hospital. A rebel force of 6000, with 18 guns, had escaped downwards, and are on their way to Lucknow; but Colonel Greathed with 3000 men was in pursuit on the left bank of the Jumna, and hoped speedily to overtake them.

October 11, Sunday. Service and Holy Communion at the brigade mess this morning. Afternoon here at three. J. also had service and Holy Communion at the Begum Kotee, for the wounded officers: this, with two services in hospital, besides visiting the sick and funerals, is hard work for one day, and he is quite tired out this evening. A letter came from Cawnpore this evening. Colonel Greathed's force had encountered the rebels at Allyghur, and given them a thorough beating. We may look for his arrival at Cawnpore in a few days, and other troops from Calcutta are on their way; so our hopes are once more raised. The weather is getting quite pleasantly cool, and it is wonderful how all the children have improved the last few days; dear little Ally looks quite a different child, and is getting fat and rosy again.

October 12, Monday. Poor Mr. Thornhill died; he was wounded the day after the reinforcements arrived, and lost his arm and his right eye; his poor little wife only lost her first baby about a week before: they were married last January. Dr. Fayrer is ill with fever.

October 13, Tuesday. The enemy made an attack on the 78th piquet this afternoon, but were soon driven back.

October 14, Wednesday. Emily and I took possession once more of the room we occupied before the siege. J. and Charlie have been hard at work getting, the rubbish cleared out and setting it all in order for us; it has had four round shot through it, and was so knocked about I did not think it could ever have been habitable again; we only use it as a dressing-room, but it is a great comfort, having a private retreat we can be quiet in sometimes; the windows are barricaded with boxes filled with earth, to protect us from musketry, and all the guns on that side are gone; so we are supposed to be safe from round shot at that end of the house.

A *Seikh sowar*, who deserted from the garrison some time ago, returned this morning: he reported that many deserters in the enemy's camp wished to return to their allegiance, but I hope we shall have nothing to do with such double-distilled traitors. We had nothing for breakfast this morning but *choppaties* and boiled peas—very scanty fare.

This evening dear James was coming out of the churchyard, when he saw a man in front of him tumble over, he ran to him and found that a round shot had taken off the poor fellow's leg; if it had come a yard or two farther, it would have struck James instead. There was an auction held today: cigars sold for two *rupees* a-piece, and a very old flannel-shirt of poor Captain Fulton's, which had seen service in all the mines about the place, and was covered with mud and dirt, sold for forty-five *rupees*.

October 15. James was told today the sad details of the fate of the poor Moncrieffs at Cawnpore. They were murdered down the river. Mr. Moncrieff begged for a few minutes, and began offering up a prayer, but before he had said many words the butchery commenced. His wife, who had been dragged off with the other ladies, rushed across to him and clung to him so closely that the wretches could not separate them, so they were both killed together. Their little child had died before. We have provisions enough, according to the present rate of rations, to last till the 25th of November. Our store of wine and beer is come to an end, and I have finished my last piece of soap, and am obliged to use some stuff called *basin*, which is a sort of oatmeal, as a substitute.

October 16. We had a visit this morning from Mr. Delafosse, one of the two officers who escaped the massacre at Cawnpore. He gave us a long account of the horrible tragedy. . . . Out of 900 English at Cawnpore, 400 of whom were women and 200 children, only four people survived;—Mr. Delafosse, Mr. Thompson, and two soldiers, one of whom has since died of cholera. Three boats succeeded in getting away down the stream, but the enemy pursued them with two 9-pounders, and they were all sunk before they had gone a mile.

Fourteen men saved themselves by swimming. They effected a landing, and took refuge in a tower, but were soon surrounded, and the enemy set fire to it and smoked them out. They then made a rush, and charged through them, but only four out of the fourteen reached the river. They swam six miles, and at last landed on the other side, in the territory of a friendly *rajah*, who treated them very kindly, and under whose protection they remained till they heard of General Havelock's advance, and joined his force.

October 17, Saturday. Mrs. D. and her baby removed to the Ommaneys'. Mrs. Ouseley persuaded her to come and occupy a little room which was vacant just above hers, which she will have to herself. Ally is left in my charge, as she is anything but strong, and one child is quite enough for her to take care of at present. A letter was received this evening from Cawnpore, giving little information though about movement of the troops this way, and we are still ignorant when we may expect relief.

October 18, St. Luke's Day. We went to church at the brigade-mess this morning and had service here at three. Since the arrival of the reinforcements we have been able to get a few more servants. James has got me a bearer, who relieves me of the dusting, and now we have our Madras man and the B.s have got a kit there is no need for ladies to wash up cups and saucers, so I only superintend the general work and see that it is properly done. Ally takes up a great deal of time and attention. Now he is kept away from natives he begins to talk English and understand anything I say to him in his mother-tongue.

He is a dear little fellow, and wonderfully improved. After he has gone to bed I go down and make tea in the Tye Khana. Mrs. Clarke makes it in the early morning, and Miss Halford for breakfast; so we divide the labour between us. It is a long time since we tasted milk or sugar in our tea; the goats have been dry for months, but Mrs. Ouseley sends Ally a little every day. I am quite used now to no sugar, and don't mean ever to take to it again.

October 19, Monday. The enemy gave us an attack last night, and kept up a tremendous fire for some time. I went to see Mrs. D. early this morning. She is very comfortable in her little room, and looks better for the change. An officer's servant found his way in from Alumbagh last night with the *Home News* of the 25th of August. We had only a glimpse of it here, and Captain Weston read out loud just the heads of news—Interest about the state of India in England intense—Troops started overland—A meeting in London and subscriptions made for the sufferers by the rebellion—The news of Sir H. L.'s death and investment of Lucknow had been received.

The crisis of our fate is now approaching awfully near. We have only provisions till the 25th of next month, and no certainty yet of relief. The good health prevailing in the garrison now is quite extraordinary. This is generally the most sickly time of year, yet there are no cases of fever, and the wounded are the only invalids. Soldiers are all the better for having no grog, and there is no grumbling about the privation. They are all in excellent spirits, and the poor 32nd improving every day.

October 20. General Outram received letters from Cawnpore last night. A large force is assembling there fast. Sir Colin Campbell arrived as far as Allahabad. The Delhi column was thirty-six miles from Cawnpore on the 17th. Maun Singh has been making offers of submission. There was a report in garrison today that the enemy intended making a desperate attack at 3 p.m. The troops were all under arms, but nothing came of it.

October 21. Maun Singh sent a letter to Sir James last night putting himself under his orders. He has been desired to send in a *vakeel*, or accredited ambassador, tonight. Heavy firing heard out at the Alumbagh while we were at breakfast. A boy of the 32nd was killed by a round-shot at the hospital today, and a man of the 78th Highlanders at the Residency lookout-tower. Three natives were shot in Mr. Gubbins's compound. The enemy sprung two of their mines, but did no mischief.

October 22, Thursday. No *vakeel* from Maun Singh appeared last night. Very heavy distant firing heard; today some say at Alumbagh, others pronounce it to be much farther off.

October 23, Friday. No news in, and no explanation of the distant firing. I had an escape this evening: a bullet went through the leg of the chair I was sitting on; it just glanced upwards and struck me on the side, but having expended its force on the chair, I was not hurt

October 24, Saturday. A rumour is rife in the garrison that the English troops at Cawnpore have given the rebels another beating at Bithoor, the *Nana's* place, and also that two regiments have arrived at Alumbagh,

October 25, Sunday. A month today since the force which was sent to relieve us arrived, and here we are as closely besieged as ever. The distant firing we heard the other day was an attack on the Alumbagh, but the enemy were easily repulsed. Maun Singh sent a letter to the general today; the purport of it has not transpired. We went to church at the Brigade mess, where we received the Holy Communion. Service here at 3 p.m.

October 26, Monday. Two letters were received from Cawnpore last night, and news good. The rebels had been defeated at Agra, all their guns and ammunition taken, and 1000 of them killed, with only the loss of six on our side. The Delhi column, under the command of Colonel Hope Grant of the 9th Lancers, was to arrive at Cawnpore on the 1st. An army of 6000 will be collected there on the 10th, and on the 15th we may expect relief here. A large quantity of supplies have safely reached the Alumbagh.

October 27, Tuesday. Another letter from Cawnpore during the night. Two officers wounded today—Captain Graydon shot through the lungs, and Dr. Darby hit on the head by a piece of shell. Maun Singh's *vakeel* really appeared this afternoon, and was closeted for a long time with Sir James Outram's secretary, Mr. Money, but the nature of their conference is the profoundest of secrets. Captain Orr has had news of his brother and wife, Sir Mount Stewart Jackson and sister, and some other persons, fugitives from Seetapore, seven altogether, have been brought into the city loaded with irons, and are now prisoners at the Kaiser Bagh.

October 28, Wednesday. A letter from Cawnpore was received last night. The Delhi column arrived on the 26th. After Agra they had two fights with the rebels—Mynpoorie and a place near Cawnpore; at Mynpoorie we captured two *lacs* and a half of treasure. Charley Dashwood managed to get a small letter sent out last night concealed in a quill. He mentioned both of us in it, so if it ever reaches England the D.'s will be sure to let darling mother know that we were alive at this date. I hope in less than a month we shall be able to write ourselves. Captain Graydon died today.

October 30. We have been besieged four months today. This morning an 18-pounder came through our unfortunate room again, which we flattered ourselves was so safe, and which we had made so comfortable. It broke the panel of the door, and knocked the whole of the barricade down, upsetting everything. My dressing-table was sent flying through the door, and if the shot had come a little earlier, my head would have gone with it. The box where Emily usually sits to nurse baby was smashed flat: fortunately she was spending the day with Mrs. Bryden, or she would probably have been in the room. There was a sale today of Colonel Halford's property, and James bought some plated dishes a great bargain: they will be very useful to us if we ever set up house again in India.

Sunday, All Saints' Day. Thought much of my dearest father and also G. F. Church services as usual. Little Ally has a slight fever. I went to see poor little Mrs. Banks at the Brigade mess this morning; she looks very sad. Her baby is immensely grown, and the picture of health.

November 2, Monday. The enemy's fire was very severe all day. An officer was mortally wounded at the Ferreed Bux. A letter was received this evening from Cawnpore. The commander-in-chief was to be there today.

November 3, Tuesday. Little Ally D. has a rash which is said to be chickenpox. Dr. Partridge and Dr. Fayrer both say there is no use in sending Ally out of the house; by this time the other children most likely have taken the infection if they are to have it, and the complaint is so trifling that it is of no consequence if they do get it. I have therefore not urged Mrs. D. to take Ally away, and she thinks he had better stay here. As there are so many children in the Ommaneys' house, it would not be fair to take him there with the complaint on him, so the poor little man stays here.

November 4. The anniversary of my own dearest father's birthday.

This day year we crossed the Cashmere territory in our way back to Peshawur, and I wrote to wish him many happy returns of the day, little thinking he would never see another in this world, and now it is nearly ten months since he was taken from us. He has been spared all the grief and anxiety I fear my darling mother must have suffered all these weary months.

We have been more shocked and grieved today than I can express. Poor Charlie Dashwood has had both legs taken off by a round shot. He was sketching in the Residency compound when the fatal ball struck him. James has been with him several times during the day. Mrs. D. went to him as soon as the sun was down. He knew her, but spoke little, and was so low. I fear he will not live through the night. He will be a sad loss to her. Ever since his brother's death he has been so good and kind to her; he was such a very nice boy, a favourite with every one, and such a tall handsome fellow. He was in high spirits this morning because he had heard of the safe arrival of his home letter at Alumbagh. What a dreadful shock it will be to his dear ones when they hear what has happened since he wrote it!

November 5, Thursday. The enemy attacked last night, and kept up a very fierce fire between nine and ten. Poor Charlie D, is better today, and there is just a little ray of hope that he may yet live to go home.

November 6, Friday. I went over to the hospital this morning with Mrs. D. to see her poor brother, but he was having his wounds dressed, and we could not see him, poor fellow Mrs. D. is looking quite ill again; she is so knocked up with going to the hospital before breakfast, that J. has asked Dr. Scott to lend his *palanquin*, which is to take her over there in the middle of the day, which will be a much better arrangement for her.

Capital news has come at last. A letter arrived from Cawnpore this evening, and "by the 10th, at latest" a force of 6000 men is to arrive at the Alumbagh.

November 7, Saturday. The weather has suddenly become quite cold. A 24-pounder came through the house again this morning, but did no damage, though Mr. Chamier, the *aide-de-camp*, had a narrow escape. I have got a little dressing-room to myself now; it is a passage-room, leading into Mrs. Fayrer's bedroom, but Ally and I are very snug in it. Emmie is gone back into our old room, which Charlie has doubly barricaded. They say that ball was a chance shot; but I did not like the idea of risking such a visitor again.

I went this evening to see poor Charlie D. Oh, it was so sad to see him lying there with his two poor legs gone. They were taken off just below the knee. He spoke quite cheerfully, and is hopeful about himself. The doctors say he has done better than they could possibly have expected.

November 8, Sunday. Service and Holy Communion at the Brigade Mess; 55 communicants. After church we walked home with Mrs. Polehampton; she showed me the little sketch Mrs. Barbor has done for her of the church and churchyard, with her husband's grave. She is having a marble slab put over it. There is a stonecutter in the 90th, and he has got a bit of marble from the palace, and is doing it for her. She is so pleased about it, poor thing. Captain Maclean has taken some first-rate sketches of different places in the garrison; they are to be in the *Illustrated News.*

November 9, Monday. Poor C. D. took a bad turn in the night, and was quite delirious when J. went to him this morning. He has been wandering all day, but Dr. Boyd does not yet consider his case quite hopeless. It will indeed be wonderful if he lives, for not a single case of amputation during the siege has recovered.

The enemy have been annoying us all day with a 9-pounder. Two Europeans were mortally wounded close to our gate, and the compound and verandah are thought so unsafe we are not allowed outside the hall-door this evening.

Mr. Kavanagh, the head clerk in Mr. Cooper's office, disguised himself as a native, and went out tonight to attempt reaching the Alumbagh. It is a fearful risk, for the poor man is almost sure to be taken; but he volunteered, and would not be dissuaded. Should he get there safe, he will be able to give an exact account of our state, and show them the best way in.

November 10, Tuesday. Great excitement. Distant guns heard for several hours this morning. At half-past two every ear was listening for a salvo of artillery which was to be fired from the Alumbagh as a signal that the relieving army had arrived. There was some mistake however about it; and though guns were fired, we remained in a state of uncertainty as to their meaning till eight o'clock in the evening, when a bonfire lighted on the top of the Residency was immediately replied to by a blue light from the Alumbagh; and the general announced that his doubts were satisfied, and our friends really there.

A flag hoisted at the Alumbagh this morning, which was the signal that Mr. Kavanagh had safely arrived there.

November 11. A very quiet day. No news from the Alumbagh, but the arrival of the commander-in-chief seems generally believed, so I hope it will be made certain tomorrow.

November 12, Thursday. There was a good deal of firing. A telegraphic communication has been established with the Alumbagh by means of semaphores, and conversations have been going on continually all day. We have ascertained that Sir Colin C. arrived this morning, and intends advancing with the force on Saturday; that Mr. Kavanagh reached Alumbagh in safety; and that the enemy were so bold as to make an attack there this morning, and were repulsed, with the capture of two guns.

Our meat out of the kitchen was stolen while we were at breakfast today, so we had none for dinner; but fared very well on an extra quantity of rice and peas, flavoured with a tin of salmon and a *bonne bouche* afterwards in the shape of a bottle of honey presented by Captain Weston. Mr. Gubbins wrote to ask James for a description of the Highlanders rushing in here on the 25th September. I believe he is writing a book, and an account of the gallant fellows' emotions at the sight of the ladies and children will form an interesting page of his volume, for it was indeed a most striking and affecting scene.

They telegraphed from the Alumbagh just now that the force would advance tomorrow "without fail" On tomorrow's success, therefore, hangs our fate! After the most merciful—miraculous way we have hitherto been preserved, it would be wicked to doubt for a moment that our relief will be accomplished; and yet one cannot think of the crisis, now it is so near, without trembling; and it is awful to remember, too, how many precious lives must be sacrificed in order to ensure our safety.

Colonel Campbell of the 90th died today. He was wounded very slightly the day the reinforcements came in with Havelock and Sir James Outram, but yesterday his leg was obliged to be amputated. I fear poor Charlie D. is sinking. Mrs. Ouseley is dangerously ill. The enemy has been wonderfully quiet today. They blew up a mine, and blazed away furiously for about ten minutes this afternoon, but very soon subsided into silence again. My dear husband had a merciful escape this morning. As he was going into hospital a round shot passed close over his head, and entered the wall just above him.

November 14, Saturday. A very anxious day. The commander-in-chief advanced on the Martinière, which he now holds. There was no firing heard till about eleven o'clock, when it continued very heavy for about three hours, and totally ceased in the afternoon. A great many of the enemy have been seen from the "lookouts" making off in various directions. This evening a blue light was seen on the top of the Martinière. It is supposed that our force met with little opposition; but no messenger or news of any sort has come in.

Mrs. Ouseley died this morning: she has been ill only a few days, but she had no strength left; her two children died on the same day, 1st October; and her poor sister, Miss Palmer, was killed by a round-shot at the beginning of the siege. Mr. Ouseley is first cousin of Sir Frederick; poor man! I pity him very much: his whole family has been swept away in this cruel siege. Captain Weston was telling me this evening, that of the garrison of this house, maintained at 45, there had been killed or wounded 47, that is the whole strength of the garrison and two over.

James, in reading over my journal, is quite affronted because I have omitted to record that since the 30th of May, the night of the meeting in cantonments, he has gone to bed in his clothes, or rather has not gone to bed at all. Ready for any emergency, until a few nights ago he slept on the floor, with a wadded curtain or *purdah* to lie on.

The gentlemen have lately moved their beds into the front verandah, and found *charpoys*, or native bedsteads, to sleep on, which is much more comfortable. When we slept down in the Tye Khana the first two months of the siege, we all used to lie down ready dressed, in case of any alarm; and it is only lately that we have regularly undressed and equipped ourselves for the night, as in ordinary times.

November 15, Sunday. We expected great things to have been done today; but the commander-in-chief seems to have stayed quietly at the Martinière, and very little firing at all has been heard. There are various conjectures as to the cause of his delay. One idea, which seems probable, is that they have been throwing a bridge over the river close to the Martinière; and a village on the opposite side was seen to be in a blaze, so that it is not unlikely that part of the force may have crossed this evening—but it is very tantalising knowing nothing positive. The enemy continues pertinaciously popping into us. An *ayah* was shot in the eye this afternoon in this compound, and a shell burst on the roof of the Residency. This evening there is a great deal of firing going on all round. Oh! when will it all cease?

November 16, Monday. Our troops have had success today; but as I cannot remember the names of the places they have taken, and am quite ignorant of the localities, I cannot attempt to describe the movements which have taken place. A force went out from this garrison and stormed some of the enemy's positions, and I hear our loss was as small as could possibly have been anticipated. The commander-in-chief's army is now within a thousand yards of our force; so tomorrow there will be a combination.

It was very exciting listening to the sound of the battle going on so near us. The gentlemen spent most of the day on the top of the house looking out; but could not distinguish anything clearly on account of the smoke. They saw our horse artillery and some of the lancers galloping about, which must have been a truly delightful sight. Our artillery must have made tremendous havoc today among the enemy. The big guns have been at work incessantly.

November 17, Tuesday. Communication established today between the two forces. Sir Colin C.'s head-quarters are in the old 32nd mess-house, which was taken this morning.

We were astounded this morning after prayers by the news that tomorrow night this place is to be evacuated. We are all to leave it, with only as much of our worldly goods as we can carry in our hands. I feel utterly bewildered, and yet so relieved to think we shall both be together, and the dreaded separations between husbands and wives averted, that I cannot realise the utter ruin it will be to us all in the loss of property and money we must leave behind.

It is such a dreadful thing too for the sick and wounded ladies, close to their confinement, like poor Mrs. Anderson, and little children. It seems such an extraordinary step, after holding the garrison so long; no one ever dreamed for a moment of such a measure as evacuating Oude now. I trust it is all for the best. If we live to reach Calcutta, we shall be in a state of destitution. I think the best thing will be to return to our respective parishes.

November 19, Thursday. Left the intrenchments.

Yesterday the sick and wounded were all moved out to Dilkoosha, and today the women and children departed from the scene of our long imprisonment. J. and I started in a carriage of Dr. Fayrer's in company with Mrs. Anderson and Miss Schilling. We had a pair of starved horses of Mr. Gubbins's to drag us, but the wretched animals had been on siege fare so long that they had forgotten the use of their legs, and had no strength, so came to a standstill every five minutes, invariably choosing the most dangerous parts of the road for their halt.

At one place we were under so hot a fire that we got out and ran for our lives, leaving the vehicle to its fate, and two poor natives, who were helping to shove it on behind, were shot At the Ferreed Bux we had to wait a long time, as the carriage could not be got through a gateway till some stores were cleared away. Some of the officers of the 90th invited us inside, and gave us wine and water, which was very refreshing.

We walked after that every step of the way to Secunderabad, where we all had to wait several hours till *doolies* arrived to take on all the women, and we proceeded under a strong escort to Dilkoosha. The road to Secunderabad was frightfully dangerous in places. In one place we were passing a 24-pounder manned by some sailors of the naval brigade; they all called out to us to bend low and run as fast as we could; we had hardly done so when a volley of grape whizzed over our heads and struck a wall beyond.

At Secunderabad we found the place overflowing with women and children of the Lucknow garrison. We met several gentlemen, friends, belonging to Sir Colin's force—Captain Norman, assistant adjutant-general, and Mr. Roberts (two Peshawur friends), and Mr. Ryves. They were all very kind to us. Captain Norman gave me gingerbread nuts; Captain Ryves, biscuits; and Mr. Roberts, a delicious cup of tea, with milk and sugar, bread and butter, and beef, all such long untasted luxuries. We made a regular feast, especially as we had not tasted anything since a scanty very early breakfast, and were nearly exhausted.

About 9 o'clock p.m. we started again in *doolies*. Mr. Roberts lent me one, and J. walked by my side the whole way. The crowd and confusion were excessive, the enemy hovering round and firing occasional shots, and we were borne along in the most solemn silence; the only sounds were the tramp, tramp, tramp, of the *dooly*-bearers and the screaming of the jackals. It was an awful time; one felt as if one's life hung in a balance with the fate we had so long dreaded; but our merciful Father, who has protected us through so many and great dangers, brought us in safety to Dilkoosha, where we arrived about 2 o'clock in the morning.

November 20, Friday. There were tents pitched into which we all crowded, and found quilts spread on the ground, into which we rolled ourselves for the remainder of the night. The officers of the 9th Lancers very hospitably had a supper prepared for our refreshment, and we very much enjoyed some tea and bread and butter before going to sleep. We had none of us tasted bread and butter since the 30th of June till today, so it was indeed a treat.

This morning we went into a small tent with Captain and Mrs. Edgell and their child, and Mrs. Anderson, which is much pleasanter than being crowded with such numbers of others in a large, public, open tent, as we were last night. We drew very liberal commissariat rations today, and Walter Birch lent us his *khitmutgar* to cook our breakfast and dinner, as Chunia did not arrive till late. Mrs. D. and her children have been left behind in the intrenchments, having no *doolies* to bring them on. Poor Charlie D., I grieve to say, is very much worse.

We had the inexpressible delight of receiving our home letters this afternoon. It seemed almost too much happiness. How can we ever be thankful enough for all the mercies so lovingly vouchsafed to us? Dearest mother and all of them were quite well to the 8th of September, the latest date. Of course their anxiety for us has been terrible, but they have been, like us, mercifully supported through their trials. We had a perfect feast of letters, and felt regularly intoxicated before we had got half through them.

I have found out that John Coles is with the 9th Lancers, and have sent him word to come and see me. Emily B. has got a nice little tent of her own, into which she has taken Mrs. Germon. The air out here is so deliciously fresh after the close unwholesome atmosphere inside the intrenchments, one feels like another creature.

November 21, Saturday. Mrs. D. and the children arrived in the middle of the night. Dr. Fayrer found her wandering about the camp not knowing where to go to, and dreadfully frightened by a drunken soldier, who would accost her. He brought her to our tent, and James got up and took her to another one, where she got shelter, as we are unfortunately quite full in this one and could not possibly make room for her with us, which I was very sorry for, as we might help her so much if we were together. I wrote a short note home yesterday, as a post went out in the night.

We received another budget of letters this morning, and besides English ones there was one from dear old Fred, who is at Simla safe and well, with both his darlings. Also letters from Captain Harvey and Mr. Wale. They had just seen the list of the survivors of the Lucknow garrison published in the papers. John Coles came to see us today. He looks just the same as ever. He intends to be useful in letting us have things from the mess. There are two clergymen here with the troops. J. found them out today. One a naval chaplain, and the other belongs to the Additional Clergy Society.

The sick and wounded were all so delighted to see James when he went among them today. Poor Charlie Dashwood is as bad as can be. Major Stevenson, a Madras Fusilier, has died today. We have no news about moving from here, but all the treasure from Lucknow was brought in, and they have been blowing up guns in the intrenchments all day, which looks very much as if evacuation was decided upon.

There are terrible reports that those unfortunate prisoners in the Kaiserbagh have been murdered, and that Sir M. Jackson was hung. It is too horrible to think of their having been so near, and yet the utter impossibility of saving them. Mrs. Inglis came to tell me this morning Lady Thesiger had mentioned mamma in her letter, and desired her to let me know all my loved ones at home were well.

Poor dear Bustle was lost on the road, and I sadly fear we shall never see him again; it is heartbreaking after saving his life all through the siege.

November 22, Sunday. Bustle made his appearance this morning; we were so glad to see the dear old dog again!

We had prayers in our tent with just our own party, as there was no possibility in the utter confusion to manage a public service.

Dr. Darby died today. General Havelock is very ill, and they fear Mr. Delafosse, who escaped from Cawnpore, will not live.

There was a sharp engagement with the enemy this morning not far off. The lancers and horse artillery galloped off, and we heard a tremendous fire, but it did not last long. Ally D. came to spend the day with me; poor little man, he has got diarrhoea again, and looks sadly ill. Poor Charlie Dashwood died this evening. I went into the tent with Mrs. D. to see him about two hours before the end; he was quite unconscious, and did not recognise her; only when James was reading the commendatory prayer he opened his eyes, and for a moment seemed struggling to speak. I think he knew him, but it was only for an instant.

J. went again before bedtime and found him just dead; he had his poor body prepared for burial, and went to tell poor Mrs. D. It was a mercy the poor dear boy was taken before the march to Cawnpore begins, for he could not have lived through the hardships he would have had to endure, and his sufferings would have been so terrible.

All the Lucknow garrison came out here tonight. The intrenchments are evacuated.

November 23. James found out this morning to his horror and dismay that the box containing the church-plate and registers had been left in the intrenchment through the neglect and carelessness of Weston the clerk, who was left in particular charge, with orders to bring it out at any risk, if the place was abandoned. J. would not bring it away before, because, if Lucknow had not been given up, it must have remained there, and he would have had to return there himself, and stay there till relieved by another chaplain; he is so vexed about it.

Registers of course are of great importance, and it is shocking to think of the Communion-plate falling into the hands of the heathen enemy. The rebels went on firing as furiously as ever into the Residency till half-past eight this morning, before they discovered the place was deserted.

All the guns were brought away, except the very heavy ones. Poor Captain Waterman of the 13th was left behind asleep in the brigade mess, and did not follow the rest for more than an hour, but he got out all safe. James and Mr. Schilling walked to the Martinière this morning, Sir Colin's head-quarters for the day. They thought they might discover some debris of our property scattered about, but not a vestige of anything was to be seen, not even the leaf of a book lying about.

The clearance has been most complete; there is nothing left of the Martinière but the bare walls; every bit of woodwork, such as doors and window-frames, has been carried off, the beautiful marble pavement has all been dug up, and the place quite a ruin; no trace of course of the dear horses or carriage, or harp, to be found. General Martins tomb has been broken to fragments, and his old bones dug up and scattered to the winds. I went with Mrs. Dashwood this evening to poor Charlie's funeral; the boy lies, with several other officers who have died out here, under a grove of small trees near the Dilkoosha palace. We are to march tomorrow.

November 24, Camp, Alumbagh. Arrived this evening tired to death. We have only come about four miles, but have been the whole day on the road; starting about eleven, we did not get here till it had been dark some time. The enemy did not fire a shot at us the whole day, for which we cannot be sufficiently thankful; it is most surprising how they came not to molest us; no one expected we should get here without some trouble.

Mrs. Anderson, Miss Schilling, and I, started in the Fayrers' carriage drawn by bullocks, J. walking by our side; the road was frightful, and poor Mrs. Anderson very soon took refuge in a *palanquin* which somebody had lent her, or the jolting would have made her very ill; she is very soon expecting her confinement. The confusion of the march is perfectly indescribable; such a crowd of wagons, carts, camels, bullocks, elephants, loaded with baggage of every description, sick and wounded women and children, all moving along in one huge mass, without the smallest appearance of arrangement or order, could never be pictured by the wildest flight of imagination.

Every ten minutes we came to a standstill; and waited perhaps an hour before the mass was in motion again, without knowing what caused the obstruction; the dust was suffocating, the heat of the sun sickening, and when we reached the place appointed for encampment, where not a tent was pitched, and no prospect for the weary and hungry body presented itself, one felt inclined "to lie down and dee" from fatigue and exhaustion; only it seemed ungrateful and wrong to grumble now at any hardships after our merciful preservation, and before long our circumstances brightened; the camels arrived, and we found our tent, got it put up, and while that was doing received an invitation to the artillery mess, which made quite new creatures of us; and though the ponies with our bedding had not found us out, we were so tired that we slept very soundly on the ground, and had quite wraps enough to keep us from feeling very cold. Poor General Havelock died this morning of dysentery; he has been very ill for some days.

November 25, Camp. Breakfasted at the artillery mess, where they are most kind and hospitable, and asked us to dinner, which, as there was a delay in drawing our rations this morning, and we did not get them till very late, we accepted. J. has discovered an old school-fellow, a Mr. Bunney, who greeted him very warmly last night at the mess. John Coles and Mr. Ryves came to see me. We halt here today. The enemy continues marvellously quiet. I suppose they have not recovered the punishment they got at Secunderabagh, the day the junction between Sir Colin's force and the Lucknow garrison was effected. Our brave troops surrounded the building, which was full of the rebels; the wretches resisted to the death, and no less than 1600 of them were cut down, fighting like demons.

After they had buried 500 bodies, Captain Green told me the number seemed not at all diminished. Among those who were caught in the garden were sixty *sepoys* N.I. They were all made to stand up in a row, and a volley fired into them; twelve dropped dead, and then the officers and men rushed upon them, shouting out, "Cawnpore!" "Cawnpore!" and killed every man of them.

There are different reports about the unfortunate prisoners in the hands of the enemy:—Sir Mountstuart and Miss Jackson, Captain and Mrs. Orr and their child, Mr. Burnes, and one of the poor Christians' children from Seetapore. One report says they have all been beheaded, and Sir M. Jackson hung. Another rumour, which I pray may be the true one, is, that they are still alive, and re moved from the Kaiser Bagh to the Dowlat Khana. Mr. Jackson, the uncle of Sir M. J., and his sisters, has come out from England, and is with the force to try and recover them; but he is very out of heart about it, and fears the worst.

The eldest Miss Jackson, who escaped from Seetapore with Captain John Hearsay and party, has never been heard of, and they can get no trace of her whatever.

November 26, Thursday, Camp, Alumbagh. We halt here again today. Breakfasted, by Captain Green's invitation, at the mess of the Punjaub Infantry. Mrs. Polehampton, Mrs. Gall, and Mrs. Barbor have a beautiful tent lent them by Mr. Fisher, the second in command; so I spent the day with them, and we dined with the Punjabees again in the evening. Their mess is a very good one; they have everything of the best.

November 27, Friday, Camp at Bunnee. We were warned to start this morning at seven. I got up at five, made every preparation, as in duty bound: when we were nearly ready comes an order that we don't move till eleven—so we had time for a second breakfast at the artillery mess. Our carriage, by James's capital pioneering, got at the head of the ladies' column, immediately behind the advance guard of the infantry. We had a very tedious march; our progress necessarily so slow. We crossed the Bunnee bridge, and reached our encamping ground at sunset. The road, for India, was pretty. Oude is certainly much more fertile and pleasant-looking than any part of the country between Calcutta and Peshawur.

November 28, Saturday; four miles from Cawnpore, Camp near the Ganges. Started at seven this morning, and did not reach our place of encampment till nearly midnight. Our pace can have been little faster than two miles an hour. We were obliged to make a forced march of nearly thirty-eight miles today, as the commander-in-chief got news on the road of the Gwalior rebels being in force at Cawnpore. We have heard heavy and continued firing the whole day. A part of our force has been sent on across the river to the assistance of Brigadier Wilson at Cawnpore.

The enemy are in possession of half the city. There must have been a great deal of hard fighting today, to judge by the tremendous firing. This has been a very weary march: if James had not galloped off to the commissariat and seized some loaves, we should have starved. Mrs. Inglis gave us a tin of oxtail soup tonight when we arrived, so we did very well.

November 29, Advent Sunday, Camp near Ganges, opposite Cawnpore. After breakfast this morning we were ordered to strike tents and move on a mile and a half nearer Cawnpore. The firing is horribly close—we see the smoke of the guns plainly just across the river. All the troops have gone on, with the exception of one brigade, under Brigadier Inglis, left for our protection.

In the action yesterday poor Brigadier Wilson was killed, and we lost five officers and ninety men of the 64th: we took five of the enemy's guns. This encamping ground is very nice, on some beautiful soft turf. We are near the 9th Lancers' mess; so I mean to invite myself to John Coles for some dinner tonight.

November 30, Monday, St. Andrew's Day, Cawnpore. Here we are in this fatal place; and most thankful must we be to have arrived so far on our perilous journey in safety. We got the order to move onwards between 7 and 8 p.m. yesterday. The distance was not great, but it was past midnight before we reached the place of refuge appointed for us in the old dragoon barrack-yard, where we were so fortunate as to find our little tent pitched and ready, our servants having most cleverly managed to push on and get in advance of the rest of the baggage.

We had great trouble on the road; our carriage stuck fast in the sand; the bullocks lay down, and seemed as if they were going to die; and we were left miles behind everyone else, and were contemplating abandoning the turnout altogether; but at last, with the help of some sailors of the naval brigade, we contrived to get into motion again, and by a short cut rejoined the line, and by great good luck found Miss Schilling and Bobbie, whom we had lost in the confusion when we had to get out of the carriage.

Just as we were crossing the bridge of boats over the Ganges, a tremendous fire opened on the Cawnpore side. We were told it was principally our own men firing at the enemy afar off; but it sounded most awful, and I never, during the whole siege, more thoroughly realised such an extreme sense of nearly-impending danger, and how very close death might be: one felt as if the very next instant perhaps might be one's last. I shall never forget the crossing that river. The firing ceased as suddenly as it began. I suppose it did not last a quarter of an hour, though it seemed an age to us.

The enemy is all about in great strength: they say there are 17,000 in this Gwalior force, and an immense number of guns. They are in possession of the city and great part of the station, and there is no disguising the fact that our troops got the worst of it on Saturday. We have heard great guns and heavy firing all day: a round shot whizzed just over our tent this morning,—it is dreadful being again in the midst of war and fighting.

This place, with all its horrible associations, is a very painful one to be in. I trust we shall soon be sent off to Allahabad; but at present the enemy occupies the road, and posts are stopped both up and down, so I fear my letter to dearest mother I posted at Dilkoosha is lost.[8] There is not the faintest hope of our being able to get up to Dagshaie for ages to come.

December 1, Tuesday, Cawnpore, Artillery Barracks. We were all transferred from the dragoon to these barracks this morning at daybreak. Mrs. Edgell, Mrs. Anderson, and I, have a little corner-room, besides the tent; and I suppose we are likely to be here some days, as they will not send us on till the road is safe. We still hear constant firing, but no news of what is going on has reached us.

Yesterday there was a report that Sir J. Outram's force from Lucknow had arrived, but it has not been confirmed. J. tried to make his way this morning to the entrenched camp to see Mr. Moore, the chaplain, and inquire for letters at the post-office; but so many round shot were flying about, he thought it advisable to turn back. I never saw such a sad scene of desolation as this station. There is not a house left standing; it is enough to make one cry to look at the blackened ruins of what once were beautiful bungalows, and then to think of the awful fate of all those who so lately inhabited them—a fate too which

8. No, only delayed a mail.

we so narrowly escaped, and which even now we can hardly feel safe from; for with the enemy in such overwhelming numbers so close to us, there can be no safety until we reach Allahabad.

It is quite uncertain when we shall leave this, but the commander-in-chief is sure to get rid of us as soon as he can, for we must be greatly in his way. I went to see Emmie B. this morning. Charlie has been appointed brigadier-major to Brigadier Walpole. We have received no more letters since we came here, which is a dreadful disappointment.

December 2, Wednesday, Cawnpore. James rode to the entrenched camp before breakfast, and came back with beer, soap, ink, and other prizes he succeeded in getting there. We had to draw eight days' rations for the road, which looks as if we were to start soon. I wrote a few lines today to dearest mother in the faint hope of its ever reaching her. J. and I walked this evening with Mrs. Case and Miss Dickson to see poor Sir H. Wheeler's entrenchments, where he held out twenty-one days against the enemy. The only wonder is how a single person came out of them alive; and far better would it have been if they had all died there instead of suffering as they did a worse fate.

The barracks in which they took refuge are perfectly perforated with round shot. The unhappy creatures could have had no possible shelter either from the sun of an Indian June, or the murderous fire which never ceased day or night. It made one shudder with horror to think what their sufferings had been; and yet they were nothing in comparison of what the hapless survivors who left the entrenched position afterwards endured. I picked up the leaf of a Bible, and brought it away as a relic.

We saw some writing in pencil on some of the walls. In one place there was a cross drawn with a great number of initials underneath, and the date June 16th.

On another part a poor fellow had written, "Dear Jesus! have mercy on us, and deliver us not into our enemy's hands," and signed "James Tyrrel."

The entrenchments by way of a defence are quite laughable: a very narrow ditch, not knee-deep, and a low bank of earth, over which we stepped with the greatest ease, was all that divided them from the enemy, and yet the cowards never attempted to come over. We had a visit from J. Coles after we came home; he very kindly brought us some sherry, and James a few cigars, to console us on the march. The B.'s got some English letters today, and Emmie sent me one from Aunt Ellen to read, in which she mentions dear mother and all at home being well. I cannot think where our letters can be.

December 3, Cawnpore. We were warned last night that we should probably get the order to start before morning; however, none came, and here we are still, but may have to start at any moment. There seems to be a good deal of fighting going on today. The Gwalior force still holds the town, and the *Nana* is said to be with them. Yesterday three English officers were seen hanging outside one of the enemy's batteries, near the place where the women and children were massacred. J. Coles came to see us this morning, and brought us some delicious fresh butter. I have got my child Ally back. Mrs, D. sends him to spend the day with me whenever we halt.

December 4. We are 24 miles from Cawnpore, on our road to Allahabad. The order to march came last night, and we started at ten, and did not reach this place of encampment till between twelve and one in the middle of the day. We are to get to Futtypore (48 miles) in two marches; but how the poor tired animals will ever manage another journey of 24 miles tonight I know not. Our escort consists of the 34th regiment, two guns, and some native cavalry. We breathe more freely now we are out of that mournful place, Cawnpore; and as the whole road between it and Allahabad is lined with our troops coming up country, I trust it is pretty safe.

We met the 42nd Highlanders, the 38th, and some of the Rifles this morning, and yesterday the 85th and some artillery arrived at Cawnpore. C. Barwell is left behind as brigade major to General Walpole. It is very sad for him and Emmie being separated. I can't be thankful enough my dear J. is able to come with me. We were all very tired and knocked up when we arrived today, especially the gentlemen who had been riding all night and had no sleep; but after some breakfast, a wash, and a snooze, we are considerably better.

We have picked up another Madras servant, Peter by name, to help Chunia, who has turned out a regular trump on the march, and cooks and works most willingly for our whole party. J. has mounted himself on a lean old grey mare, about 100 years old, which he bought at Dilkoosha to carry baggage. It is a wretched old beast, but saves him walking. Dr. Fayrer has bought a buggy: so Miss Schilling goes in it now with Mrs. Fayrer; and Mrs. Anderson, who was obliged to give up her *palanquin* at Cawnpore, comes in the carriage with me. I make room for J. to squeeze in between me and one corner to get a sleep when he gets very tired. We start again tonight at nine o'clock.

December 5, Saturday. We came a march of thirteen miles last night, and got here about eight o'clock this morning. The camping-ground is very pretty, with a great many trees round it, which, as many people are without tents, is a great advantage. We have been mercifully protected on the road so far; not a shot has been fired, or an alarm of any kind given, since we left Cawnpore. If it were not the fear of enemies, which we cannot help feeling, I should enjoy this out-of-door, picnicking-life excessively, in spite of all the inconveniences and roughing it we have to put up with.

The fresh air and open country, and feeling of liberty, are so intensely delightful, after our six months' close confinement to Dr. Fayrer's small narrow strip of compound, with nothing to look at but a high stone wall, to remind us still more that we were prisoners. If it had lasted much longer, and I had not had plenty to do, I should have gone melancholy mad.

December 6, Sunday, Camp. We started last night at seven, halted this morning at ten; no adventure to record. Captain —— chose a horrid place for our tent—on rough dirty ground, with no shade. Everyone else is under beautiful trees, on turf, at a little distance; but when we arrived all the camels were unloaded, so we could not move.

The marching arrangements are very bad. J. found some wounded today, who said that they had not seen a doctor or had their wounds dressed since leaving Cawnpore. Then he met two doctors, who had been, they said, hunting the camp for two hours in search of their patients and could not find them. The sick are scattered about in all directions instead of being together in one place, and the confusion is extreme. We hear that the Gwalior rebels evacuated Cawnpore and made off for Bithoor the day after we left. We met more troops this morning on their way up. Sir Colin will soon have 14,000 with him, and be able to do great things.

December 7, Monday, Fort Allahabad. We reached the railway station at Lohunda this morning at sunrise, and were immediately requested to take our places in the train, where we sat in very uncomfortable 2nd-class carriages crowded to suffocation (with ten people in a place for eight) for at least two hours before starting, having had no breakfast or refreshment of any kind. When once we were off, however, it seemed delightfully home-like and natural to be once more on a railroad, and we came along at a good rate, arriving at Allahabad (40 miles) in about two hours, which was very quick for India, and the train was tremendously long and heavy.

When we arrived at the terminus we found it crowded with gentlemen and soldiers, who all cheered the poor Lucknow garrison most enthusiastically; and indeed the kind and hearty welcome we received at Allahabad—the first place of safety we have rested in for many a month—will not soon be forgotten by any of us. We found beautiful tents pitched in the fort for our accommodation. They are the governor-general's own tents. We share ours with the Edgells, but it is large; we have each a private bedroom, and large centre room to sit in.

We were regularly knocked up when we arrived; we had had nothing to eat since the night before; but Mr. Spry, the chaplain here, took us off to his quarters in the fort, where we were regaled with a luncheon that revived us considerably. Tonight, for the first time since the 24th May, J. and I enjoy the luxury of a room to ourselves. Nothing can exceed the kindness and hospitality we meet with here. Furniture, in the way of beds, chairs, and tables, is provided for our tents, and there is a *table-d'hôte*, at which we may all take our meals, furnished by the relief fund. Mr. Spry is the manager.

There are no steamers here yet to take us down to Calcutta, so we may be detained here some time, and the idea of rest in a place of security is very pleasant. Mr. Spry is very hard worked here, and has applied for a second chaplain; we may be ordered to stay here till we can proceed to Dagshaie in safety. Mrs. D. and Emily B. are gone to Dr. Irvine's in cantonments; they are the only ladies not in the fort. Nearly all the bungalows in cantonments here were destroyed. The Sprys lost the whole of their property. There has been telegraphic news of great successes at Cawnpore since we left; no particulars yet. No English letters for us here.

December 8, Allahabad, 4, G.-G.'s Tents, Fort. Mrs. Spry kindly sent her *dhobee* over to me this morning, and we gave him an accumulation of unwashed clothes. We breakfasted at the Sprys', and found Mrs. Forbes and Mrs. Polehampton there; after breakfast we assisted Mrs. Spry in distributing shoes, stockings, pocket handkerchiefs, combs, and hair brushes, &c, sent up by Lady Canning for the ladies of the Lucknow garrison.

We dined at the *table-d'hôte* at three o'clock, and had tea in our own tent; our camp is really very pretty, beautifully pitched in a square, with the large dining-tent in the centre, on a lovely piece of turf, with trees all around. Allahabad Fort is very strong, overlooking the Jumna. The station looked very pretty indeed as we saw it yesterday from the railway. J. telegraphed to Sir J. Colvile this morning to write home by the mail which leaves tomorrow, to tell dear mother of our safe arrival here.

The luxurious feeling of rest and peace and safety here is perfectly indescribable; one can scarcely realise it or know what to make of it after the excitement, anxiety, and turmoil of the last six months.

December 9. Mrs. Spry asked me and Mrs. Polehampton to assist her in the distribution of Lady Canning's gifts, so we were busy all morning going round to different tents and supplying people's wants. We dined today in our tent: the *table-d'hôte* is given up, the Khansamer having struck work, so people are now requested to cook for themselves.

J. walked to the post-office this evening and found the English mail just arrived, and coaxed the post-master to let us look over all the Lucknow letters, but alas, alas, in vain! After diligently inspecting two large packets we found not a single letter addressed to one of the Lucknow garrison: they were all to officers belonging to General Havelock's force. It seems evident that we have been given up for lost by those at home.

The kind way we are treated here is most touching. People seem as if they could not do enough for us: we have the most beautiful flowers, and vegetables and milk, and all sorts of good things sent us every morning.

Mrs. Fayrer had a little son this morning—prematurely.

James has undertaken to superintend giving out the rations, and was very busy this morning. We are fed at present entirely by the Relief Fund, but it is too heavy a pull on the charity, and I believe the Commissariat is to take us back again.

December 10, Fort Allahabad. Mr. Schilling dined with us. We luxuriated in a table-cloth, and presented such a wonderfully civilized appearance he was quite struck. The rest and comfort here is something too delightful; we seem as if we could not be thankful enough for the great mercy which has placed us once more in safety and peace. We only now seem realising all we have suffered If only now I could hear from home I should be so happy.

Two people of our old garrison died today. Mr. Gubbins has been dangerously ill, but he is better.

The news from Cawnpore is capital—27 of the enemy's guns taken.

December 11, Friday. Mrs. Polehampton and I went round the barracks and took down the names of all the widows belonging to the artillery and 32nd, for Mrs. Spry, who is going to give them each a black dress from the relief fund. Some of the poor things are in great distress, having come out of Lucknow with only the clothes they wore. Such numbers of children were running about wild, Mrs. Polehampton and I thought it would be a good plan if we could get them together and keep a sort of school while they are detained here.

We are going to ask Mr. Spry about it. Mrs. Fayrer's little baby died this afternoon. Mr. Schilling started for Calcutta by mail cart. We engaged Ramsay, Mrs. D.'s African servant, as she does not want him any longer; he attended Mr. Polehampton and poor Charlie Dashwood in their last illness. Dear old Bustle has arrived with the sweeper quite safe. We left him to come by the road when we took train.

December 13, Sunday. At eleven o'clock this morning we had service in the garrison chapel, where all the Lucknow refugees attended and returned public thanks to God for our merciful deliverance. The appropriate psalms were 34th, 71st, and 92nd; lessons *Exodus* 15, *Romans* 12, and a special thanksgiving prayer. Nearly 100 partook of the Holy Communion. The offertory was given to the asylum founded by Sir H. Lawrence for soldiers' children in India. The collection was 250 *rupees*.

After church I went with Mrs. Polehampton to the barracks and collected between thirty and forty children in a large empty room where we opened our school. We have no books or any school appurtenances to help us, so it is rather difficult to manage. We divided the scholars into two classes, those who could read, and those who could not. I took the big ones, Mrs. P. the little ones. Considering how long they have been running wild, they are more tractable than one could possibly have expected.

In the afternoon we drove down three in a buggy to the cantonments, which are extremely pretty. There are only about a dozen houses left. The bungalows were all destroyed by the mutineers, and no less than thirty-six officers murdered. The church is left standing, and is used for divine service, but all the interior fittings are destroyed.

December 14, Monday. J. has been on the sick list today. Mrs. P. and I kept our school and got on very well—began a home letter. Mrs.

Birch confined last night of a boy.

December 15, Tuesday. The Sprys lent us their buggy, and we drove out to see Emily B. and Mrs. D. Poor darling little "Chota Loll" is so dreadfully ill, I am sadly afraid he will not live; he is the colour of an orange, constantly sick, and no bigger than when he was born.

It is settled that we stay here till the roads are safe for us to go to Dagshaie.

December 18, Friday. Sent off our English letters. The steamer *Madras* started with a large number of wounded, and seventeen ladies, for Calcutta. Mrs. Dashwood came to see me this afternoon. The dear baby is better.

December 20, Sunday. Church in the garrison chapel at ten a.m. Mrs. B.'s baby baptised Frederic William. We dined at two. At half-past four went to church in cantonments. The interior was entirely destroyed by mutineers—seats, pulpit, altar, rails, &c, all torn up and smashed, and windows broken.

J. had the kindest letter I ever read from —— this morning. He begs us to make him our banker if we want money, and offers to do anything he possibly can for us. He says Dr. Leckie, secretary to the relief fund, has portioned me 1000 *rupees* to enable me to refit. I shall come out like a butterfly some fine day!

Thursday, Christmas Eve. We have given the school children a holiday till Monday. I walked round the ramparts this evening. Mrs. C. told me that the last news which had been heard of those unhappy prisoners at Lucknow was that Maun Singh had planned their escape, and had the ladies dressed as native women, and the gentlemen disguised in the same manner. They were on the point of getting away, when some *sepoys* discovered them, and they were carried off again to the Kaiser Bagh; and nothing has since transpired, so whether still alive or not is unknown.

Christmas Day, Allahabad. The services of the church are all we have to remind us of this joyful season. It is less like Christmas time than any I have passed even in India—not the least cold, and not even the ghost of a mincepie. That we should have been spared to see Christmas in safety is a great cause of thankfulness and joy; but it is good to fix all our thoughts on the real cause we have for rejoicing at this season, and one must do so to feel in any degree glad. The church was very full. Emmie and Mrs. D. came from cantonments. The poor widows all looked so sad and tearful, there will be little mirth anywhere this Christmas, I fancy.

We had a narrow escape from great danger coming home this evening from the cemetery, where J. had been for a funeral. The horse shied at something going over the drawbridge; his feet slipped on the iron nails, and he fell, with his head and forelegs over the side of the bridge. Had he been a few inches more forward, his own weight must have dragged buggy and all down to the bottom of the moat. We jumped out at once, and some European soldiers came to the rescue. With a good deal of trouble, the poor horse was got on his legs again.

December 28, Monday. The band of the 79th Highlanders played this evening in front of the barracks; it was quite a treat. Emmie and Mrs. D. came from the cantonments, and we walked together. A flaming order about J. has come out in General Outram's despatch, and he has received the warm thanks of the governor-general for the second time, which is very gratifying.

A writer of Dr. Fayrer's has made his appearance here; he says he has been a prisoner with the rebels during the siege, and just made his escape; his account of what went on outside among the enemy is very interesting; he says every single thing which occurred in the Residency was known outside; the rebels were thoroughly acquainted with all that occurred among us by our faithful (?) *Seikhs* and servants in the garrison. They knew everything about Sir H. Lawrence, and the exact moment of his death, and about Miss Palmer and Mr. Ommaney, only they mistook the latter for Mr. Gubbins.

The *Baboo* says rewards were offered for every European head; 100 *rupees* for an officer, and sixteen for a soldier; and that a head which the wretches gave out was that of Captain Carnegie (the cantonment magistrate), who is alive now and well, was hung up in one of the public gateways for a long time. There were strict orders to slay every man, woman, and child who fell into their cruel hands, and every servant caught was immediately killed.

Every native Christian, or person connected in any way with us, was murdered in the city. The wretches did not find out for many hours that we had evacuated the Residency. They have levelled it, houses, church, and all to the ground, and are preparing to make a tremendous stand there; but I think they will find we shall retake it very much sooner than we lost it, strong as they may make it. If they had had the smallest particle of courage, they could have walked in with the greatest ease; but God turned their hearts to water for our deliverance.

By the last accounts, Miss Jackson and Miss Orr were still alive, confined in a small den, where they could not stand upright; but Sir M. Jackson and the other gentlemen had been put to death.

Jan. 1858. Postscript.—The man in the 7th Cavalry who murdered his comrade was allowed his liberty during the siege, and behaved most gallantly; he was killed by a round shot at the Redan battery. One of his children was also killed, and poor Mrs. Eldridge's idiot daughter had her leg taken off by a round shot, and died in great agony. The D.s' cousin, Mr. Fane, whom I mentioned in a letter as killed, escaped, and is alive and well. Only one of the Miss Jacksons escaped, with her brother; the other was taken by a *rajah*, and has never been since heard of. Sir Mountstuart Jackson and his poor sister are still prisoners in Lucknow.

Here the Journal ends.

[*The following letters—by the husband of the writer—are added with a view of completing the narrative.*]

Allahabad, December 17.

A short time since I had little hope of ever writing to you again, but here we both are safe and sound, mercifully preserved through innumerable perils, and enjoying such rest and peace as has been unknown to us for six months past My duties, as you may imagine, were never-ceasing; and the trying part of all was that we got so little rest though so sorely fagged, until I reached this. I had slept in my clothes (rolled in a rug on the ground) for more than six months, and subject oftentimes to be roused two or three times in the night by a general call to arms, when an assault was either made or threatened by our fiendish foes.

In our small and open position no soul was safe from shot, shell, or musketry fire; and those whose duties took them out of their several posts and garrisons had to run the gauntlet of as murderous a shower of all as can be conceived. My preservation I look upon as miraculous, for I was more exposed than almost anyone in the place; but it must have been rather for the sake of others than my own deservings.

I buried some five hundred during the siege: many will, I fear, be bitterly disappointed who think their dear ones preserved.

The list first published was painfully incomplete, and numbers have fallen since Outram and Havelock forced their way in and were shut up with us. My poor brother chaplain was shot through the body, and died of cholera, just at the commencement of the siege. I was then left single-handed in my most painful duties. We stay here until the roads leading up country are safe enough to travel.

Allahabad is a nice place for the plains: the chaplain requires help sadly, owing to the number of wounded coming in, and the increased amount of duty arising from the accumulation of troops. It is not time to speak of losses, though ours have been heavy indeed—everything gone but a few clothes: carriage, horses, furniture, books, all. Our losses could not be repaired at the least under 1,200*l.* I grieve for my books: they are things one gets to love from old associations.

Allahabad, January 2, 1858.

My Dear Mother,

It never was intended that last mail should leave without a few lines from me to you. Dear G. promised to leave me room in her letter, but finished and sent it off before I knew of it. We had just arrived, and I was at the time incessantly employed with our poor wounded, and in distributing immediate and necessary relief from the fund available in this place. Thus it came about. But I am sure you will have attributed it to some such reason as this.

I rushed to the telegraph as soon as we arrived, and sent you a flitting message through Sir J. Colvile, which it is a comfort to us to know will have gladdened your anxious hearts long before you had a real letter. We have so constantly grieved about your imaginary trouble. What a mercy it is that we have been preserved amongst the few who lived to see the triumphant end of that dreadful siege!

I do pray it may have been so ordained in great mercy to both of us, and that we may henceforth be more earnest and faithful. It would be very dreadful if the lesson should be lost to us. My dear G. behaved splendidly—never gave in—and constantly occupied herself in doing acts of kindness to others less able than herself.

It pleased God to give us both good health: thus we were able to forget ourselves very much in going about our several duties. It was a painful thing that we never could be alone together all those weary months; but we managed to read the Psalms and Lessons together daily in a comparatively retired corner, and that was a great thing, for of course I was one of the few who had constantly to go about the position, leaving the cover, such as it was, of our several posts. I never did so without the chances being many against my ever coming back to her again.

But God's mercy has been great, and here we are safe and sound, and very happy, inasmuch as New Year's Day brought us a budget from all our dear ones. G. kept a sort of scrambling journal during the siege, which I hope to send you soon; it was written under difficulties, with little hope that you would ever see it. Not that we ever utterly despaired, for a protecting Providence was in so many things apparent that we felt it wrong to be distrustful; though as our garrison daily diminished, and help seemed ever farther off, the last resource of blowing up the magazine was talked of and tacitly resolved on in case we could no longer protect our women and children.

They never would have boasted of another Cawnpore. I rejoice now very much that I never took one of their wretched lives, although constantly under arms. I resolved not to shed blood unless in extremity; that is to say, unless the enemy actually got a footing in our position. This they never did, so they had their practice at me *gratis*. You may imagine what work it was, when I tell you that many of our little garrison have each, during an assault, to their own knowledge, killed their ten and fifteen men. Well, it is over now, and I think the neck of the mutiny is broken. Retribution is now the thing; and I trust the punishment dealt will be severe, but not merciless. The garrison of Lucknow are, here in India, perfect lions; and, really, it was a gallant defence. We have been stripped pretty bare, but shall no doubt be able to get on. They talk of distributing lots of rewards, but that can't come to me. I cannot look for more than the satisfaction of having tried to do my duty—imperfectly at best—but it was hard work singlehanded.

General Havelock's reinforcement relieved almost all but me, who had some 300 wounded added to my former cares. The appointment to Dagshaie is the best thing for us now; and if it please God to spare us, we shall, after service there, be brought close on our furlough, and hope to see you all again. Will you tell the rector of W. that I received his kind letter in the middle of the fight at Cawnpore, and was quite refreshed by his mention of old times and people, of which we had so often talked in our troubles. I will write to him soon.

Kindest love, &c.,

James P. H.

To my Sister.

Allahabad, January 3, 1858.

Who would ever have thought six weeks ago that I should now be wishing you a Happy New Year? Poor girl! I am so distressed to find by your letter, dated Oct. 17, that you have been so miserable about us. Well, indeed many a time did we despair of ever seeing any of your dear faces again; we used to wonder whether you really knew and understood what a position we were in; and now we gladly find you did not realise it.

Dear Aunt G. says it "was a comfort to you all to know that, although closely beset, we were in an impregnable fort!" We were in no fort at all; we occupied a few houses in a large garden, with a low wall on one side, and only an earthen parapet on the others, in the middle of a large city, the buildings of which completely commanded us, and swarming with thousands of our deadly foes, thirsting for our blood.

God gave us protection and pluck, the former in a wonderful degree, or not one of us would be here to tell about it. This you will see when you get G.'s journal. It is short, written under difficulties, but will give you some idea of our position. She put down what she could day by day as it occurred, just on the chance of its ever reaching you.

The Engineers calculated that all those months never one second elapsed without a shot being thrown in at us, and at times upwards of seventy per second, besides round-shot and shell. Every house was shattered; every single building seemed to be marked with severe smallpox; and yet, notwithstanding this, and the number of killed and wounded, the brutes never dared come and fight us hand to hand.

They tried hard a few times, but were killed round our earthworks by hundreds; so they took to shooting us down by degrees, and this they would have done, humanly speaking, if those brave fellows under Havelock had not come in. Even then, after losing 1000 out of 2800 in doing it, the rest were shut up with us for six weeks, fighting with us day and night, till old Sir Colin came with 10,000 more, and with great difficulty and loss got us out of it. Well, thank God! now we are all right.

We got your letter New Year's Day—a delightful gift—and truly thankful are we to find that my dear father and all of you were pretty well, except being bothered about us. Fred Baily came to Lucknow with Havelock's force, not looking well, poor fellow; he stayed with Sir J. Outram's force in the district of Oude—at the Alumbagh and the open plain—about 4000 men, and they have not been molested to speak of. He had left his property in Cawnpore.

I meant to have got it sent to him; but on getting there we just came in for the battle in which General Windham was defeated; and though Sir Colin's force soon set him right again, all the baggage, stores, &c.—amongst them poor Fred's belongings—had gone to the natives or been burnt. Your letter, and R.'s and W.'s, have just reached us. Poor things! how sad it was for you to hear, after all, that the relief of Sept. 25 was no relief at all!

They did relieve us, though, of incessant work and watching by bringing more to take the duty; and they also brought us some meat—precious tough too—for we eat all the old bullocks that dragged in their heavy guns. We had scarcely any provision left when Sir Colin came. Had he delayed a fortnight, we should have had to cut our way out, to the probable loss of all the lives of women and children, if not men: we were however saved that terrible alternative in God's great mercy.

[*Extract of letter from the Authoress.*

Allahabad, March 7.

It is too bad of people to raise such wrong impressions as that man must have done, who wrote about the ladies being so well dressed when they came out of Lucknow. How could people be well dressed who had not seen the sight of clean clothes for five months, and nearly all of whom had lost or left behind almost everything they ever possessed?

There was one lady, and only one, who certainly did come out dressed beautifully, as if she had been equipped for a drive in Hyde Park in the height of the season. She laughed about it herself, and it was a joke with us all. She had but one good gown saved in the world, with shawl and bonnet equally handsome; and said she did not see why she should not come out in them, rather than leave them behind: they had the advantage too of being warm, and we all thought her very wise.

There were three or four ladies who lived in the Residency houses, and, therefore, their property was not destroyed at the cantonment mutiny: so of course they saved their clothes; but I do not remember that any of them had anything on the least smart. As for me, on Mrs. Cowper's principle, I came forth in the only respectable dress I had, which had lain by, as too good and too warm, during the siege,—a black *barège*, trimmed with crape, and black silk jacket. Every one, for the same reason, wore the best they had.

One lady from our garrison staggered out under the weight of three silks and a velvet dress, rather than leave any one behind: some burnt the few valuable dresses and things they possessed, rather than let them become spoil to the enemy. Several widows, who had saved their wedding dresses from the cantonment fires, made bonfires of them before leaving Lucknow. I found Mrs. ——, and the two widows who lived with her, standing over the blackened ashes of their wedding dresses, veils, wreaths, &c, the day before we evacuated the Residency.

We were told at first that we must go out with as much only as we could carry, and it was only about an hour before we started that we knew we should be allowed carriage for any baggage: then those who had anything to bring away had scarcely time to get ready.

Day by Day at Lucknow

Contents

Preface

In submitting the following pages for public inspection, I have listened to the suggestions of my friends rather than to the dictates of my own judgment. They were written for the perusal of my relatives in England, and with no view whatever to publication; and it was not without a struggle in my own mind that I at last complied with their wishes. They represented to me, that but few journals had survived the siege of Lucknow and the wreck of the steamer which conveyed us from India, and that any particulars of that protracted and dreadful beleaguerment would be read with great interest by the friends and relatives of those who fought and bled in that ill-fated city.

I have not attempted, by subsequent additions, to produce effect, or to aim at glowing descriptions, but have given it as it was written, in the simple narrative form, which the dangers and privations of the siege alone permitted. As I do not aspire to the ambition of an author, I feel that I shall be exempted from that criticism which invariably attends works of a more pretending character. It cannot but fail (for no woman is equal to the task) to do justice to the heroism, or to describe in adequate terms the great sufferings, of the gallant defenders of Lucknow, but it will help to fill up, by particulars, the general outline of the contest, which has been heretofore published in official despatches, and partially gratify the curiosity of those who have sympathised with us in our severe trials, until some more able and more practised person shall undertake the task of favouring the world with a complete and detailed history.

Adelaide Case

June 5th, 1858.

Chapter 1

May 21st - June 1st

Thursday, May 21st, 1857.

For several weeks past much anxiety had been felt by us all at Lucknow, in consequence of the alarming rumours respecting the mutinous state of the Indian Army. The ladies scarcely knew that things looked so dark and gloomy as they really did; but I must confess my fear on the subject was more roused by the serious way in which I used to hear dear William, who was always bright and cheerful under any circumstances, talk over affairs with Colonel Inglis, than from what I read in the papers.

On Saturday, the 16th of May, there was a consultation amongst the senior officers as to what had better be done, as they were in doubt whether the *sepoys* in the station would be true; and if they mutinied, it was thought the city would also rise. The result was, that, in the course of the day, the 32nd Regiment received an order to occupy the Residency in the city, a commanding position, containing the treasury and all the public offices; and in the evening they sent in, as a support to the *sepoy* guard, 130 men and four guns, with all their sick, and women, and children. The following day, Sunday the 17th, the remainder of the regiment marched to cantonments, and encamped under some trees; the thermometer 110°, and a dust storm.

There had been a rumour in the night that the *sepoys* were about to burn and kill, and we afterwards heard that all the ladies had rushed to the Residency, but it was a false alarm. Sir Henry Lawrence had most kindly offered to put up the ladies of the 32nd Regiment (we were only four) at the Residency in cantonments; consequently we were busy packing up our things the whole of Saturday, and I was dreadfully knocked up, Caroline helping me with her usual kindness and activity. William, of course, was obliged to be attending more to his regimental duties than to us. We were told that we must be ready to mount our horses at three o'clock on Sunday morning, as we were to go with the regiment into cantonments.

I think it must have been twelve o'clock before I went to bed, as we had packed up everything but our furniture. I had not slept an hour, when I was roused up by Colonel Inglis's voice calling William, who instantly jumped up to see what was the matter. I felt very nervous and frightened, and when he came back I heard that a rumour was afloat that the regiment was to be attacked on its way into cantonments. William, of course, hastily dressed and went off to the regiment, leaving injunctions that Caroline and I were not to start till he returned. I went instantly to Caroline's room and found her getting up, as she had been restless owing to the great heat, and, like myself, rather nervous; for indeed it would be difficult for anyone to realise our sensations who had not experienced them on that dreadful morning.

We were soon equipped and ready to mount our steeds; our good and faithful servants doing their best to make us as comfortable as they could. The *ayah* had our tea and bread and butter as nicely brought in as if we had been going out for our usual morning's ride. When we had been ready some little time we began to get impatient that William did not return for us. At last I could bear the waiting no longer, so mounting my horse, and taking my *syce* with me, I went over to Mrs. Inglis in the next compound, but finding her not ready to start, I returned.

The scene at this time was truly curious. The moon was shining brightly, and all the servants were busily engaged loading the *hackeries* which were to take our things to the station. Several *chokedars* had been sent down to take care of the house, gardens, and property which we left behind us. They were all armed. Everything was carried on as quietly as possible, so as not to excite the suspicion of the city people. As all these preparations were going on, the sensations I felt as I sat quietly on my horse are perfectly indescribable. Caroline's horse was lame, so she could not ride him; but Colonel Inglis most kindly lent her one of his horses, "Waverley," and as soon as he was brought over she mounted, and we both went over to Mrs. Inglis. Still William had not returned, and the moments passed anxiously away.

At last Mrs. Inglis proposed our riding up the road in the direction of the city. The children were placed in her carriage, and my *ayah* went in ours; Mrs. Giddings, the paymaster's wife, went in a buggy. I confess that I was very much frightened, but my courage all returned when, after waiting for nearly an hour from the time when we were first ready, we saw dear William coming towards us, and then we all galloped up as fast as we could to the spot where our escort was. This consisted of an advanced guard of cavalry and the 32nd Regiment. The ladies were in the centre, and the 32nd in the rear. We reached the Residency in cantonments safely about 6 a.m., all tired and exhausted.

The time appeared long till breakfast, but as soon as William had seen all right in camp, for with him his soldiers were ever his first object, he came to the Residency, about ten o'clock, to see how Carry and I were getting on. Much to his horror, he found us in a dark room, without a window in it, the only light we had coming in from the bathroom. We were, however, soon afterwards removed to a very comfortable one, through the kindness of Sir Henry Lawrence, who, though so much occupied with weighty and important matters, thought nothing too trifling for him to attend to. He insisted on our going with him to the different rooms in his house, and gave us the choice of any we liked, provided we made ourselves comfortable, which he wished us to do before anyone else arrived; so Carry and I were soon settled in a very nice cool room, with a *punkah* and *tatties*.

The officers of the *sepoy* regiments turned out of their messes and houses to give them up to the 32nd men, and the camp is moved much nearer the European artillery. William came to breakfast and dinner, so I am as happy as I can be under the circumstances. With Mrs. Inglis and her three dear boys, we are a cheerful little party. In the evening, whenever we can, we go into the camp and spend, at any rate, one happy hour with our husbands, sitting in the cool *semianah*, where they generally have iced water and sherry for us, and dear Johnny amuses himself with looking at the different tents and the horses, &c., with the bearer.

Tuesday, 26th.

We have been subjected to constant alarms during the last few days. Sometimes it was a panic amongst the ladies in the station, who got frightened with the continual reports that the city was going to rise, when they rushed over to the Residency for safety; then it was an alarm of fire. One evening these wretches did set fire to a building behind the Residency just as we were sitting down to dinner, but most providentially the wind changed, and their intention, which had evidently been to burn the Residency, was thus frustrated. So constant, however, was the terror in which we were kept on this subject, that we always had a little bundle ready by our bedsides at night, for instant flight.

Yesterday morning Monday, I was awoke about three o'clock by Mrs. Inglis coming into our room, and telling us that we must immediately, get up; as, in consequence of Sir Henry Lawrence having received unfavourable accounts of the state of things at Cawnpore. it was deemed by him to be safer for us ladies to go into the city Residency. We were all to start as soon as possible, so I roused up Caroline, and we dressed as hastily as we could, leaving our few things to be packed up by my good *ayah*, who, with the rest of the servants, was to follow in the course of the day. As soon as we were dressed, William came over from the camp, and, as usual, on seeing him and hearing the cheerful sound of his voice, I was inspired with renewed courage. He could only remain with us a few minutes, as he did not like to be away from camp. Mrs. Inglis and the children started about half an hour before we did.

We drove into the city in our little carriage; everything appeared quiet. We reached the city Residency in safety between six and seven o'clock, and found Mrs. Inglis already located at Mr. Gubbins's. We drove to his house first, and found Mrs. Gubbins, who kindly offered to do anything for us that she could, but told us that her house was already full, and that Mrs. Inglis's room was too small to take us both in. She would most kindly have done so, had it been possible. We therefore went over to the Residency, accompanied by Mr. Edmonstone of the 32nd, where we saw Mrs. Ogilvie, whom we had known slightly, having met her at dinner at Sir Henry's. She said that there were no rooms to spare in the Residency upstairs, and ongoing below, we found it still more crowded.

Two ladies and seven children were squeezed into a very small room, having some tea, and every moment fresh arrivals drove up, in search of rooms also. While we were deliberating what we had better do, Mrs, Ogilvie sent word to us to come up again, and then offered us one of her own rooms, which was so filled with boxes, books, and papers, that it seemed almost impossible to turn round in it. At the same time she told us, that we must not mind the bearer passing through the room at all hours of the day for the iced water used in the house, and for all his candles and lamps; but of course we did not refuse her kind offer, considering ourselves fortunate in obtaining the smallest corner.

We immediately set to work to clean out the space allowed us, and the things soon coming up with the *ayah*, we succeeded in making ourselves as comfortable as the circumstances would admit of. Nothing could exceed the kindness of Dr. and Mrs. Ogilvie.

Friday, 29th.

Everything still remains quiet, Caroline and I join the Ogilvies' party at dinner. We see Mrs, Inglis every day, and she and I think of nothing but our happy evening's drive into cantonments, where we spend the only delightful hour during the twenty-four. She drives her buggy, and takes me with her. People say we are very foolish to persist in going to the camp in the present state of things; but so long as our husbands do not forbid our going out, we shall continue to do so, for I think we would both risk almost any danger for the sake of that one happy hour, which always appears so very short! Oh, how loath we always feel to return to the Residency again! How we linger before we turn our steps towards the city, till Colonel Inglis or William insists, for the sake of safety, that we will not delay.

Monday June 1st.

On Saturday last, the 30th, Mrs. Inglis, as usual, came, and asked me if I was ready to drive into camp. Of course, I was. So off we started about half-past five o'clock. The day having been hot, we enjoyed our drive exceedingly, and, as usual, found William and Colonel Inglis sitting on the *semianah* ready for us. We remained with them a short time, and on coming away Colonel Inglis said he would drive Mrs. Inglis part of the way home, and William drove me; but they could not go far with us, of course. When they left us, and we found it begin to get rather late, and towards dusk, we felt uncomfortable, especially as we passed the Iron Bridge, a place always very much crowded. We fancied the people we saw looked fierce and sullen. Mrs. Inglis drove a fast trotting horse, neither of us spoke, but she urged him on. I cannot express how thankful we felt when we drew up at the door of the Residency, and alighted in safety. It is really surprising that we did so, for the mutiny in cantonments broke out that very evening, showing how rebellious the prevailing spirit must then have been.

Just as we were all retiring for the night, guns were heard in the direction of the cantonments. All the gentlemen immediately armed themselves and disappeared, leaving us very anxious. On going out into the verandah, we distinctly saw the firing, and saw one bungalow after another set on fire, and blazing away with tremendous fury. The stillness in the city was very remarkable; not a sound was heard. The sight of the burning bungalows was awful, and we could do nothing but watch the flames with beating hearts, and listen tremblingly to the booming of the cannon.

About half-past eleven o'clock, the firing diminished, and a *sowar* galloped up to the Residency with a message from Sir Henry Lawrence, to say that all was nearly over. A few minutes later, Mrs. Inglis sent me over a line in pencil, which she had just received from Colonel Inglis, telling her of his own safety, and that of dearest William. Those only who experienced the anxiety and terror of that dreadful night can ever know the heartfelt gratitude we felt towards our Heavenly Father for preserving our beloved ones through so much danger. We then retired to our room, I cannot say to sleep, but anxiously to wait for the dawn of day. Mrs. Boileau and her eldest boy shared our room with us. They had come over with several other ladies from the Fayrers and Ommanneys' houses.

Poor little Charlie laid down on my bed, but the child was so restless from the heat and anxiety, that he could not sleep. The usual messenger from camp brought me, what I never failed to get every morning—a letter from dearest William. He told me that the *sepoys* had mutinied on the previous evening, and attempted to get hold of their officers, but failed. They then set fire to the bungalows and plundered them. Lieutenant Grant, of the 71st Native Infantry, was betrayed and cruelly murdered, receiving many wounds. Cornet Raleigh, a young officer who had only joined his regiment three days before, was cut to pieces by the cavalry, and Brigadier Hanscombe was shot dead as he went up to harangue the native regiment.

A careless shot from one of our own guns went through William's tent, and killed Caroline's beautiful horse "Lalla," and wounded the poor "Sahib" so badly, that he was obliged to be shot next morning. Three of our poor servants were killed, and William's and Colonel Inglis's tents were riddled to shreds. I cannot say how much I feel for poor Caroline having lost her favourite horse. Mine was only saved by the *syce* having the good sense to take him away to a neighbouring village, where he kept him for a whole day and night. The poor man looked so pleased when he brought up poor "Hira" to the door of the Residency and showed me that he was all safe. I am sure I was not the less pleased to see him.

Yesterday, Sunday, there was a report that the city was going to rise, numbers of people having been seen assembling together. About one o'clock the Residency was filled with all the ladies from Mr. Gubbins's, Ommanney's, and Fayrer's. They all assembled in the large room, where luncheon was prepared for them. Such a scene of confusion, talking, and rushing about, first for one thing and then for another, I never witnessed. The alarm turned out a false one. Most of the ladies returned to the different houses where they had been previously located, but some remained in the Residency, Mrs. Inglis among the number, and we arranged to give her and the three children part of our room, as well as Mrs. Giddings; so that the accommodation of our party in that small space was very limited.

Chapter 2

June 9th - June 15th, Break Follows Due to Colonel Cases's Death

Tuesday, 9th.

The heat is very great indeed. Mrs. Inglis, the children, and Caroline, always sleep on the roof of the house, and as soon as I awake in the morning I go up there, and we have our "*chota hagree*" brought to us, as it is so much cooler than below till the sun rises. The view from the top of the Residency is truly beyond description beautiful, and in the early morning, when the sun begins to shine on the gilded mosques, and minarets, and towers, it is like a fairy scene. The whole of this vast city spread out before one, and on all sides surrounded by beautiful parks and magnificent trees, forms a panorama which it would be difficult to see Equalled in any other part of the world.

We now form a little mess of our own, Mrs, Inglis having the management of it, and we are, in consequence, much more comfortable. Mrs. Boileau, Mrs. Radcliffe, and their children, join us, so that we sit down to dinner a party of twelve. I always long for four o'clock, when the messenger arrives every day with a letter from the camp for me. I write without fail every night to William; Agaib, the bearer, coming in for my letter before I am awake in the morning. He always finds it ready on the table, and the messenger starts with it before daylight, returning with one for me at four p.m.

I am not so fortunate as the other ladies, who often have a visit from their husbands; but William does not like to leave the camp even for half-an-hour, so I very seldom see him. He is now in command of the regiment, Sir Henry Lawrence having appointed Colonel Inglis, Brigadier. They are busy working at our batteries and intrenchments, and everything is being done to strengthen our position. Sir H. Lawrence is indefatigable, and tires out all his staff, who, I believe, have to take it by turns to go out with him. It is perfectly wonderful to see his activity. He never seems to take any rest, night or day, and appears to live in his saddle.

The noise of the children in this house is something dreadful, and there is not one hole or corner where one can enjoy an instant's privacy. The coming and going, the talking, the bustle, and noise, inside as well as outside, the constant alarming reports, and at times the depressed expression on some of the countenances, baffle all description. Dr. Ogilvie says, that where there are so many people in one house, the hot air is better than none, consequently all the doors and windows are wide open, and often the scorching wind which blows in while we are taking our meals in the large room is almost unbearable.

Our evenings are usually spent on the top of the house, and sometimes Mrs. Inglis, Carry, and I go down into the Ty Khana, and see the women of the regiment, and any other poor creatures who may have been brought in there from different stations in the district. Mrs. Inglis never goes down empty-handed. She is kind and considerate to everyone, and often takes down some pudding or soup, which may have been at dinner, to a poor sick boy. A little tea, sugar, or any old clothes we can find to take with us to them is always very gratefully received, and it cheers their spirits to talk to them a little. Mr. Polehampton reads prayers to us in Mrs. Ogilvie's room at half-past nine, and then we retire for the night, and the sentry's call of "All's well" is generally the last sound I hear before I go to sleep.

Monday, 15th June.

We continue to suffer a good deal from the heat. Constant reports of murders and horrors in the district are brought in every day, and fugitives who have made their escape from the different places continue to arrive; some come disguised in native dresses. The fall of Delhi is the one great event which we are all longing to hear of. Captain Orr has received a letter from his brother, giving a very sad account of the Shahjihanpore affair, I believe there were twenty-eight of them who reached Mohumdee in safety, only to be murdered afterwards, at Mithowly, in the most barbarous manner. Captain Orr, his wife, and child were saved, and are living in the jungle, exposed to the most dreadful heat and privations of every kind. We are very anxious indeed about the state of things, and the prospect before us is most alarming and gloomy. God in His mercy grant that help for us may be near at hand!

City Residency, Lucknow,
Oct. 30, 1857.

My Dearest Gabrielle,

How I long for the moment when I shall be able to send you a letter, feeling sure of its reaching you safely; but still more do I long for the time that, should it please God to spare us, will see us once more together. It is now nearly six months since I have been able to send you one line, and I cannot bear to think of the anxiety you must all be in about us. I shall endeavour to make this a sort of little journal between you and me, which when we meet we may read over together.

At present there is not much to relate; but I will go back to the month of May, and give you as good an account as I can of our doings since that time. They are trying to send out Colonel Inglis's despatch, which I have no doubt you will see in the papers, and a true and clear account it gives of the siege. I shall begin from the day we left our comfortable bungalows, which was on the 17th of May.

As for some time previous to this date there was cause for anxiety lest the 13th, 71st, and 48th Native Infantry, quartered in cantonments about half-an-hour's drive from the city, should mutiny, it' was thought advisable to remove the 32nd Regiment from the city, and encamp it somewhere near the lines of the native regiments. Sir Henry Lawrence, then chief commissioner, invited Mrs. Inglis, ourselves, and Mrs. Giddings, the paymaster's wife, to his house, the Residency in cantonments. The Residency in the city was occupied by a party of the 32nd Regiment and two guns; and the ladies, wives of the civilians and others, also took up their abode at Messrs. Ommanney's, Fayrer's, and Gubbins's, whose houses were all within a short distance of it.

I think you must have received my last letter, written from our bungalow, when I told you of a disturbance which took place on one of the first Sundays in May. Adelaide and I were going to church at six p.m., and as we were entering the church an artillery officer, Mr. Cunliffe, rode up and asked for Colonel Inglis, who had not yet arrived. As neither he nor Colonel Case came, we were sure there was something wrong. As the service began a large bird, the size of an owl, hovered over our heads in a melancholy way. As we drove away from the church, we were met by three of our servants, Azail the shepherd, and Adelaide's *syce*, who thought we should perhaps find it difficult to get through the city. The 7th Oude Irregular Infantry, stationed at Moosabagh, eight miles off, had mutinied. We met some of the 32nd Regiment, or I should say *all*, going. We found Mrs. Inglis, and Mr. and Mrs. Giddings anxiously waiting in the road for us. Our bungalows were all close to each other; Adelaide's good *ayah* was in a dreadful state about us, and we all felt very uncomfortable. There was some fear that the city might rise, and we were left with only a guard of the 32nd Regiment at Mr. Giddings's. Adelaide and I took our dinner to Mrs. Inglis's, and spent the evening with her.

After dinner we went to the top of the house. A more beautiful, clear evening, I never saw. The stillness all round was such as I shall never forget. Getting fidgety to hear some news, we strolled towards Mrs. Giddings's about eleven, and met Major Banks coming from the house. He kindly came to tell us that all had ended quietly. The *sepoys*, as soon as they saw our guns placed in position, ran away. Great was our delight when William on "Hira" made his appearance soon after; and we went home and gave him some supper. Adelaide was completely knocked up, and was obliged to go to bed.

The rising of the troops at Meerut, and the horrors committed there, hastened our move. On Saturday the 16th, we had to pack up everything but the furniture. We were occupied till one o'clock, only interrupted by dinner. Poor Adelaide was sadly knocked up. We were to be ready to mount our horses at three o'clock, so I got only an hour's rest,—I cannot say sleep, for I was so restless and hot, that for the first time I called for my *punkah Coolie*. At two I jumped up and dressed hastily. Adelaide was very nervous, having heard that we should perhaps be attacked on entering the cantonments. William had gone to see that the 32nd were preparing, and we were to wait until he came back. About three o'clock, or a little after, we mounted, a most beautiful clear moon shining. Mrs. Inglis lent me her bay pony, "Lalla" having been lame for some time. The carriage was ready for the *ayah*. There was a great hurry to get our things put into the *hackeries*. Mrs. Inglis joining us, we agreed to go a little on the road, where were assembled the carriage, with Mrs. Inglis's children, Johnny, Charley, and Alfred the baby; and her buggy with one of the *ayahs*. Here we waited nearly an hour on our horses, and had just returned to Mrs. Inglis's bungalow to quench our thirst with a glass of iced water, when William came for us, and we trotted up as fast as we could to our escort, which consisted of a body of mounted *sepoys* and the 32nd.

We arrived at the Residency at half-past five or six o'clock a.m. Never was I so thirsty. I could scarcely speak, my mouth was so parched and dry. It was a long Sunday, and we were all very tired. The 32nd encamped on a very good piece of ground in front of the 13th, 71st, and 48th Native lines. The unsettled feeling experienced during the week was very unpleasant. We drove out every evening, but there was no variety. There was always a large party at dinner.

On Tuesday, the 19th, we were much alarmed at a report that the 71st Native Infantry were going to rise, and also the city at two o'clock. Carriages were arriving every minute full of ladies and children, *ayahs* and servants hastening after them with any small bundles they could lay hold of. The house was soon full; but the report ended in nothings and many of the ladies returned to their bungalows. Among the ladies who remained were Mrs. Gall, Mrs. Barber, Mrs. Radclyffe, Mrs. Boileau, Mrs. Hayes, and some others. We used often to drive to the camp, and' spend the pleasantest part of our day with William. He generally came to dinner. The next alarm we had was a fire, which broke out somewhere behind the Residency, evidently the work of an incendiary; but it was soon put out.

On Sunday, the 24th, we were at church; the prayers were not quite over, when we heard one shot and then another. Two officers went out, but returned immediately, and Sir Henry Lawrence not moving reassured us, but I felt rather alarmed at the thought of going out. At last we recollected that it was the new moon, and it is the custom of the natives to fire when they get the first sight of it. On Monday I was awoke very early by Adelaide, saying that we must get up immediately to go to the Residency in the city. The news from Cawnpore was not favourable, and everything seemed in a very uncomfortable, uncertain state. Accordingly we dressed in haste, leaving the good *ayah* to pack up all we left behind, and everyone drove away quietly as soon as they became aware that they were to do so.

The following account of my faithful *ayah's* wonderful escapes was sent to me, after I arrived at Calcutta, by Mrs. Inglis, and it is so interesting that I quote her letter:—

Allahabad, 31st December, 1857.

Fancy my surprise, two evenings after you left, on returning from our walk to find your *ayah* and her family had arrived. Poor woman, she made double marches all the way from Cawnpore, in the hope of seeing you again, and was almost heartbroken when she found that she was disappointed in the object of her journey.. Had you remained at Benares, she would have followed you I am sure, and even now would go down with me to Calcutta, on the chance of seeing you, but this I dissuaded her from, for it would only be a momentary pleasure to you both, and she would find herself very lonely and friendless when we had all sailed. I have had some very long conversations with her, and the information she gives is most interesting. Upon leaving the Residency, that sad 30th June, she went immediately to our houses, but had not been there half-an-hour before the place was filled with *budmashes*, and city people, who ransacked the houses, cut up our gardens, &c., &c.

Most of our servants ran away, but the *metah's* children, who hid in a hole, in our garden, and covered themselves with manure, where they remained concealed till all the wretches had gone away, and at twelve o'clock at night got out by a hole in the wall, and made towards a village some miles from the city, where they were taken prisoners, brought back to Lucknow, and put in jail. They were kept for a week fed on grain. The king, a boy of about ten years old, came to see them with his mother. They told him that they were not gentlemen's servants, but only poor villagers, and, as they were almost naked, having been plundered of everything, he believed their story, and set them free. They then went to the same village again, and lived for some months in the jungle, begging for their food, and hearing daily that the Bailie-guard was to be taken immediately, and everyone killed.

The poor woman says that she used to dig a hole and hide her face in it all day, and pray to God to protect you, whilst her husband and my *ayah's* used to disguise themselves and go into Lucknow, to obtain information. When General Havelock's force arrived they again made an attempt to enter the Residency, but were seized by our own soldiers, and accused of being rebels; but your *ayah*, by speaking English, and giving the names of nearly all the officers of the 32nd Regiment, proved their innocence, and obtained their release. They again hid themselves, and when the commander-in-chief's force came, made their way to cantonments, there they remained, till they heard that we had all made our retreat. By a round-about way they came to Cawnpore. It was a sad disappointment to your poor *ayah* to find you had left Cawnpore, and she soon started for this place, where, as I have told you, she arrived two days too late to see you. Your dog 'Dandy,' is looking very well: he is, just now, my constant companion. I consider their having kept him in good condition speaks volumes for their faithfulness and attachment to you; for having a dog of that description naturally brought suspicion on them. They are good people, and I only trust that they will get good places, for they deserve to be happy.

We were fortunate to be among the first, for the difficulty of finding rooms was great. We first drove to Mrs. Gubbins's, where Mrs. Inglis was. Mrs. Gubbins offered to do what she could for us, if we could manage to find room. Mrs. Inglis's room was, however, much too small to take Adelaide and me in, so we went to the Residency, accompanied by Mrs. Edmonstone of the 32nd, where we saw Mrs. Ogilvie, a lady we, knew a little of before. She and her husband. Dr. Ogilvie, at first told us that they had no rooms to spare; but whilst we were looking at some rooms downstairs she sent us word to come up, and then offered us one of her own rooms, if we would not mind the servant passing through to get the iced water: I suppose he came through more than thirty times a-day. Of course we did not refuse her kind offer, thinking ourselves fortunate in getting even a corner to *ourselves*. So we set to work to clear it out, and the rest of our things coming up with the *ayah*, we soon made ourselves tolerably comfortable; and in a day or two a *punkah* was put up for us. Nothing could exceed the kindness of Dr. and Mrs. Ogilvie to us. For a time we joined their little dinner-party. Everything went on quietly till the 30th. Mrs. Inglis used to come over and see us, and we would drive over into cantonments, where we always found the half hour spent there too short.

On the evening of the 30th, Saturday, just as everyone was retiring for the night, guns were heard, and the gentlemen armed themselves, and immediately disappeared, leaving us very anxious. We went out on one of the verandahs, and there we distinctly heard the firing, and saw one bungalow after another set on fire. The stillness in the city was remarkable; not a sound was to be heard. It was awful to see the houses burning. About eleven, or half-past, the firing diminished, and a message came from Sir Henry Lawrence to say that it was nearly over; and we went back to our rooms. Adelaide and I took in Mrs. Boileau and her little boy, who had come over, with some other ladies, from Mrs. Gubbins's and Mrs. Ommanney's. Most of them returned. Anxiously did we wait till day dawned.

The usual messenger from the camp brought Adelaide a note from William, telling her the occurrences of the previous night. The *sepoys* had mutinied. They attempted to get hold of their officers, but failed. They then set fire to the bungalows, and plundered them. Lieutenant Grant, of the 71st Native Infantry, was betrayed and cruelly murdered, receiving many wounds.

A careless shot, from one of our own guns, went through William's tent, and killed my horse "Lalla" and the old "Sahib," I could not help crying over my poor horse "Lalla." Many a ride have I enjoyed on him, and he brings back to my mind many a pleasant moment. Now I do not regret that he is gone. Brigadier Hanscombe was killed as he went up to harangue the native regiments.

Chapter 3

Letters Continued

On Sunday there was a report that the city was going to rise, numbers of the people being seen assembling together. At one o'clock the house was soon full of people from Mr. Gubbins's, Mr, Ommanney's, and Mr. Fayrer's. They generally assembled in the large room next to ours, and lunch was prepared for them. Such talking, and such rushing about for this and that, I never heard. The alarm ended in nothing, and some of the ladies returned to their friends, but many remained. An old lady, Mrs. Halford, the wife of the Colonel of the 71st (since dead), and her daughter were glad to come to our room for a little quiet. The poor old lady seemed so upset, that we persuaded them to remain the night, which they did, and went back to the Fayrers next morning. Mrs. Inglis, with her three children, had come over, and we arranged to give her part of our room. From this, Sunday night, she and I, and the children, always slept on the roof of the house.

I shall never forget the beautiful moonlight nights and lovely mornings here! The view of the city all round was lovely. Adelaide and Mrs. Giddings, who also shared our room, used to come up and have their cup of tea; and then, when the sun began to be hot, I used, very unwillingly, to go down and dress. The heat was great, quite parching; and we often went to the ice-box for water. There were a number of children in the house, and a famous noise they made. They, the servants, and *coprawallahs*, about the two large rooms, formed a curious scene. Mrs. Ogilvie, Mrs. Martyn, Mrs. Polehampton, Mrs. Gall, Mrs. Barber, Mrs. Thornhill, Mrs. Radclyffe, Mrs. Boileau, Mrs. Orr, and Mrs. Anderson, all lived on the same floor that we did, and we saw them every day.

The days were sometimes dreadfully long. We spent our evenings on the top of the house. Everything was being done to strengthen our position; houses knocked down, batteries made, and trenches, &c. We used to see Sir Henry Lawrence go out to inspect the works every morning. The troops at Cawnpore mutinied soon after those here; and Sir Henry had two or three applications for help from Sir Hugh Wheler, but our force was too small to spare a man; and besides, there was no means of sending them across the river to Cawnpore, the insurgents having destroyed the bridge.

Sir Hugh Wheler and his little force held out twenty-one days, when, being no longer able to do so, they came to terms with *Nana Sahib*, who promised to let them go to Allahabad in boats: but what did the cowardly wretch do? They had no sooner got down to the boats, all had not embarked, when he opened fire upon them! Two of the boats were sunk; and all the ladies and those who were not drowned in them were taken and shut up for a fortnight, when, just as the troops under General Havelock arrived at Cawnpore, the very night before they got in, these savages murdered their prisoners in the most cold-blooded, cruel manner.

Poor Mrs. Moore, whose husband. Captain Moore of the 32nd, was in command of the party of the 32nd there, was among the victims. Many died during the siege, and their sufferings must have been dreadful, more than we can even imagine. We have seen Mrs. Moore's servant. His account was truly sad, and made one's heart ache for the poor sufferers. They endured great hardships; their food consisted only of *dhal* and rice, and of that not enough. Only one or two officers escaped. Captain Barrow, of the 90th (Queen's), told us that it was wonderful how they held out so long as they did. And so, my dear Gabrielle, the month of June passed in great anxiety, from the several reports that the enemy were every day getting nearer to us. At night we used to see large fires in all directions, which were no doubt generally signals.

After the rising at Cawnpore, it was difficult to hold communication with any place. Delhi was in the hands of the insurgents, who had murdered every European in the place. All hopes lay in this city being retaken. It was thought that this would have great influence, and prevent an attack upon Lucknow. It has, however, only fallen a little more than a month ago, since the arrival of General Havelock's force at Cawnpore. The month of June ended very sadly, and the 30th of June threw Adelaide into the greatest grief, for she that morning had to mourn the loss of him who had made her so happy for five years.

Colonel Case was killed in the disastrous action at Chinhut, of which by-and-bye. It is indeed a heavy trial for her. You should have lived with him to know his many good and noble qualities. I mourn for him as for a very dear brother. I miss his cheerful face and merry laugh, and if I miss, him, what must it be to dear Adelaide. The army, too, has lost in him a brave and gallant officer. He had a warm heart and a fine temper. He was beloved by all who knew him, and his servants, whom he had all the time he was in India, were much attached to him, and have proved themselves faithful by remaining with us now. He never missed a day, while in cantonments, writing to Adelaide, and she to him. He could seldom get away from camp, but when he did, he would come early in the morning; and how he cheered us up! I will insert here one of his notes, to show you how he always encouraged us:—

Who would have thought we should have been within four miles of each other, and yet not see each other for a week? and I fancy that I am the only one who has not been down, but I dare not leave even for a few minutes. Still I live in hopes that ere long I shall be able to pay you a visit. Truly these are sad times, and I think no nation was ever in such a fix as we are in just now; but don't despair, you'll see we will pull through with the Almighty's aid. The Psalms of this morning ought to give you every encouragement. I derive much every morning from one verse or another that I read, so applicable to our present condition. You know I have never been down-spirited about affairs, for I feel that no cause like that of the mutineers, supported by murder, fire, and everything that is savage and inhuman, will be allowed long to prosper. There must, and of course will, be many victories before we get the ascendancy again, but cheer up, look to the bright side of the picture, that will, I trust, ere long, be turned towards us, and pray that success may attend the endeavours of the loyal to restore peace and tranquillity to this land, now torn asunder by sedition and insurrection.

I don't know who could have seen me do anything, as what I

have done; but if I am cool and collected, darling, it is because my prayers to be so under all difficulties and dangers are answered, and I trust, finally, my other prayers will be heard too, and that we may all be preserved to talk over the past.

Such, my dear Gabrielle, were his cheering notes, which we used to look forward to with such pleasure.

On the 29th of June, the enemy having approached, it was said, within ten miles, William was ordered to strike the camp, and to bring the regiment into the Fort Muchee Bhawun, since blown up. That evening he came to see us as cheerful as ever. Mrs. Inglis was laid up with the smallpox. He had to pass through the room to come to the verandah where we sometimes sat; and as he said good bye to her on his way out he said, "I hope we may meet under happier circumstances."

I slept that night on the verandah, but could not rest for a long time, and often got up to look round me; one of those large birds I mentioned in the beginning kept hovering over my head backwards and forwards, and went several times into our room. I am not superstitious, but this bird made me feel uneasy. In the morning I was awoke very early by Adelaide, who came out on the verandah, looking anxious, and saying that there was something going on. The whole place was astir, cavalry outside the gate, guns going out, and an 8-inch howitzer drawn by elephants, and some of the 32nd, We all dressed as fast as we could, and Adelaide went to see if she could get any news. All she could hear was that a force had been sent out against the enemy. Alas! it was a most wretched day.

When they got some miles out. Sir Henry Lawrence sent to reconnoitre, and the party returned without seeing anything of the enemy. Sir Henry was on the point of returning to the city, but, unfortunately, he was persuaded to advance, as it was said the enemy could not be in great number. So the order was given, but when they came in sight of the mutineers, they proved to be very strong, 12,000 men, it was said. They closed in upon our little force; our native artillerymen ran their guns into *nullahs* and cut the traces of the horses and elephants. The howitzer fell into the enemy's hands. Desperate efforts were made to get it back, but the enemy's force was overwhelming and it was relinquished. William was shot through the heart whilst rallying his men. How one returned to tell the tale is a marvel. They came in one by one as they best could, looking more dead than alive. Poor Adelaide and Mrs. Inglis stood at a window watching the sad scene.

At nine o'clock Colonel Inglis got back, and then it was that poor Adelaide heard the sad news. She had no time, poor thing, to give way to her grief. Not a moment was to be lost in leaving our room for a safer place, and we had to hurry and put up our things. Oh, what a scene it was! Everyone had left before we had. Poor Mrs. Inglis, still very ill with the smallpox. We got down as far as where the artillery soldiers and their wives lived, and had to spend the day there. The firing was so great we could not get to any other place of shelter till evening. It was very close and hot. The poor soldiers came running in for a glass of water, and we had to barricade the windows on account of the bullets.

When the firing diminished a little in the evening, we managed to get across to the room Colonel Inglis had been arranging for himself. It was about ten minutes' walk from the Residency House, in a square surrounded by other enclosures, and the walls being high it was considered to be about the safest place. The room is just large enough to contain us three ladies and the three children. It is a most bare-looking place. Colonel Inglis had the place whitewashed. It looks like a room where provisions or something of the kind had been kept. We have a bathroom, where the grain for the goats is kept. Shortly after the siege began. Sir Henry was struck in the leg by a shot from that very howitzer we lost at Chinhut. He was sitting writing at the time, and only survived two days. He was deeply regretted by the garrison, and was a very great loss as an artillery officer. Major Banks succeeded, but was killed by a round shot at Mr. Gubbins's. Since his death Colonel Inglis (Brigadier) has had the entire command of the garrison.

I cannot give an account of each of the different attacks of the enemy. At first the fire was continual, night and day. To give you an idea how incessant it was, I must tell you, that when it ceased we quite missed it, and felt almost uncomfortable. Of course, I do not mean to say that when it did cease, after a time, it was not a great reprieve. The mutineers would then commence at different times, leaving you some days tolerably quiet. They would suddenly commence a heavy musketry firing, which might last about an hour or so; and how glad we were when we heard our guns firing away upon them. We soon learnt to distinguish our guns from theirs.

We have destroyed seven or eight of their mines. They never made a real attack; they were never bold enough, after the first commencement, to push their way on. These night attacks, for they were most generally in the night, and the mines, were very harassing to the men; then the rains came on, and they had to undergo the extreme changes between heat and cold, but they kept their health better than might be expected under the circumstances. Casualties occurred daily; not in the heaviest firing, when we expected to hear of many being hit, but by stray shots during the day. A mine of the enemy's killed seven of our drummers. We lost nearly every good officer before the arrival of reinforcements, particularly among the Engineers.

Great was our anxiety to hear of troops coming to our relief; it was most difficult to send any message out. The letters were sent in a small quill about an inch long, which I believe they hid in their mouth, hair, or ears.

Chapter 4

Letters Continued

On the 26th July, a messenger came in with a letter from Colonel Tytler, quarter-master-general, saying that two thirds of the force marching to our relief had crossed the river; that they had beaten the *Nana Sahib,* and his army had dispersed nobody knew where. Bithoor was in our possession, and they hoped to be in Lucknow in five or six days. The messenger went out again the same evening with an answer and a plan of the city, and he is to get 500*l.* if he delivers it safe. On the 16th of August, another letter arrived from Colonel Tytler, dated the 4th, saying they were on their way to Lucknow, but the messenger had later news, and told us they had had another engagement with the enemy, who were beaten with great loss. The relieving army had, however, returned to Cawnpore, to wait for the China force, which was coming out from England.

On the 29th August (last night) a messenger came in from Cawnpore with a letter from General Havelock to Colonel Inglis, as follows:—

Cawnpore, Aug. 24, 1857.

My dear Colonel,

I have your letter of the 16th inst. I can only say hold on, and do not negotiate, but rather perish sword in hand. Sir Colin Campbell, who came out at a day's notice to command, upon the news arriving of General Anson's death, promises me fresh troops, and you will be my first care. The reinforcements may reach me in from twenty to twenty-five days, and I will prepare everything for a march on Lucknow.

Yours sincerely, H. Havelock, M.-General.

This was disheartening news to hear the first thing in the morning: however, anything is better than their coming on with too small a force. The messenger told us that the Nana at Cawnpore had been twice beaten by our troops, but that fifty Europeans had been killed by falling into an ambush of the 42nd N. I. He added that the insurgents round us are about 11,000, that they have a council of war every day, and every day order an attack. On Wednesday, Sept. 23rd, arrived a letter from General Outram, dated 20th September.
On Friday the 25th Sept. the long looked for reinforcement came in. At 12 p.m. they entered the city. They had a hard fight to get through the narrow streets, the enemy inside the houses firing down on them, and the loss was very severe. At 6 p.m. great was the excitement inside the garrison, and great the cheering. Some of the troops had arrived,—the 78th Highlanders, the 1st Madras Fusileers, and some artillery and Sikhs. We hear that the loss coming in was between 500 and 600. The 90th Regiment did not come in until the next day, when they had a great deal of difficulty in making their way, they were so encumbered with baggage and ammunition. Every available man in the garrison, and the 32nd, were sent to their assistance.
General Havelock dined with us on the 26th, and there was much discussion as to future operations. At one time it was almost feared it would be necessary to abandon the guns, which were impeding the progress of that part of the 90th coming in, rather than sacrifice so many lives, now so valuable. All felt our force was not equal to the emergency. Never shall I forget the scene that day. We dined in a very large room, if you can call it a room at all; the walls were not even white-washed, and there was no matting or anything to cover the ground. The only light came through the large door, and near this we placed the table. The goats were kept at one end at night, and the other end was filled with Colonel Inglis's boxes. The confusion baffles description. The day General Havelock dined with us poor Colonel Campbell, 90th Regiment, lay wounded, a very little distance from the table.

Sunday 27th.

Everyone was today out of spirits; in fact, we felt we were not relieved, but only reinforced. A party, consisting of one hundred men, and eighteen of the 32nd, commanded by Captain Warner, went out to try and get some of the enemy's guns. The guns were not taken, but two were spiked. The portion of the 90th left behind with the baggage did not come in. They have intrenched themselves about four miles outside the city in a very good position, at a place called Alumbagh, and are doing very well and receiving reinforcements.

I felt more depressed on Monday the 28th than I had done since I have been shut up, but Hope soon rose again, and I cannot feel long desponding. We must put our trust in Him who has protected us so long; and although we have undergone much discomfort, we have much to be thankful for. Till the relieving force came in, we were not reduced in our rations; it is only now we are. Colonel Inglis had got in some supplies of his own, and with Mrs. Inglis's good management, I think that we shall not starve. Sugar and arrowroot have for some time past come almost to an end, but we still manage to have enough for the children, I cannot bring myself to drink tea without sugar, so I am treated as one of the children, and restrict myself to one cup a day at breakfast, and get a bit of sugar for it.

We have now no soap, and no *Dhoby*, so I wash Adele's and my things, and it is rather hard work. One morning I swept the room, the *ayah* being very busy with her boy, who was ill of pleurisy. The dust is dreadful, and though the room is swept twice every day, it is impossible to get rid of it. I dislike the half hour before dinner, particularly if it is at four o'clock, for just as one is *en train* for work, in comes the *ayah* with her broom, and we are driven out into the square, and even there you are pursued by the dust. Mosquitoes abound, and on account of them we are obliged to have the *punkah* at night, otherwise we should be cool enough without it. The moonlight nights are beautiful; so bright, it makes one long to be outside.

On the 29th September a party went out to take some of the enemy's guns, which was composed of men from the different regiments. They started at five o'clock in the morning, and, as usual, the brave 32nd leading, Mr. M'Cabe of that regiment having the command. This was his fourth sortie; and his last, for he was mortally wounded; he was a very good officer, and got his commission for bravery, having risen from the ranks. The party returned about ten, having taken seven guns, most of which had been previously spiked by the 32nd. On the night of the 30th Captain Harding, a very brave officer, made an attempt to go to Alumbagh with some of his *Sikhs*, but did not get far, the enemy's fire being too heavy upon them. The morning they went out to take the guns two men fell into a well; one of them was killed, but the other, belonging to the 32nd, escaped unhurt. He was three days in the well, not daring to call out till he heard European voices.

On Saturday, 3rd October, guns were heard in the direction of Alumbagh. They have there (at least then they had, for they have since been reinforced) 250 fighting men, and they have enough provisions to last some time. Sugar is not to be got now here, 25 *rupees* (2*l.* 10s.) were offered for two pounds, but in vain. Mrs. Inglis paid two *rupees* (4s.) for a very small piece of soap. You must pay a good price for anything you want to buy, if indeed it is to be got at all. Beer and porter are finished. I have made this letter very long! Oh! I wish I could get as long a one from you, it would be such a treat. I am sure there are some letters from you among those left behind at Alumbagh, and I should bear my captivity better if I could know that you knew something of us, for you must be so anxious.

Yours, &c.

City Residency, Lucknow,
Friday, 6th November, 1857.

My Dearest Gabrielle,

In my last letter to you, I brought up my long account of ourselves to the 1st November. I shall, however, in this, have to tell you some things which I forgot. I did not tell you that dear Adelaide was laid up for more than a week in July, and was very, very weak for two or three days. On the 20th of July I took the smallpox, and was in bed for ten days. It was fortunately slight, and has left no traces. One lady, wife to Captain Thomas, Madras Artillery, and also some children, died of this disease, but most of the cases were slight. We have been living upon beef and rice for the last four months; no vegetables. Now we do get occasionally some green herb resembling spinach, and a great treat it is. I like the rice, which I don't tire of.

The meat, with the exception of two or three times, has been good and tender. I hear people, however, complaining very much about it. This last week we have had some mutton. Our substitute for bread is *chupatties*, upon which the natives live. Since we have had reduced rations, and learnt that we must spin out our provisions to the 1st December, we have restricted ourselves to a certain number a day. We have enough to eat, and it is wonderful how long the provisions have lasted, particularly when one thinks of the addition the new force made to our numbers. We owe it all to the good management of the commissariat officer, Captain James.

It is quite wonderful to think how well our provisions hold out. How deeply indebted we are, under Providence, to Captain James, for his judicious management of all the stores at the commencement of the siege! It must have been very difficult *at first* to be careful, and required no common foresight to accomplish this so admirably. For our own rations we used at first to get rice, tea, *attah*, sugar, coffee, salt, and pepper. Now we get all but tea, sugar, and coffee. But we have plenty of tea of our own, and a little sugar. Mrs. Inglis says, that having to deal out things so sparingly makes her feel very miserly. She manages very well indeed. It will be a perfect luxury to feel clean again, for the dust is so great that it is really almost useless to dust anything in our room. We are overrun with rats and mice.

I cannot tell you of all the casualties which have occurred in the garrison since the commencement of the siege, but I may mention two; firsts Miss Palmer, whose leg was carried off by a round shot the first day of the siege, and she died. She was only twenty, and must be a sad loss to her poor father, Colonel Palmer. The other was Mr. Polehampton, the clergyman, whom we liked very much. He was first badly wounded, and afterwards died of cholera. We felt much for his poor wife. The children have suffered greatly, and many have died. There was very little milk to be had for them Mrs. Inglis fortunately had her goats inside. Her children, Johnny, Charlie, and baby, have kept, on the whole, very well, though they have had their share of sickness, in the way of fevers and bad colds. The nights and mornings are now cold; but we are obliged to have the *punkahs* on account of the musquitoes. The days are very warm. They have not been able to send off the despatch yet.

In the beginning of October General Sir James Outram published a most flattering order about the manner in which the

garrison has been defended by Colonel Inglis and the officers and men under his command. The whole affair he describes as being unparalleled in the annals of history. The troops at Alumbagh have been reinforced, and Sir Colin Campbell, the commander-in-chief, was expected at Cawnpore yesterday. Report says he is on this side of the river. The force from Delhi, under Colonel Grant of the 9th Lancers, is also close to Alumbagh.
Our army had hard work to take Delhi: and our loss was severe. Sixty-one officers and 2000 men killed and wounded. I hope that they will come up in sufficient strength this time, and that we shall be able really to get away. Since the arrival of Generals Outram and Havelock we have had very little firing. Once or twice at night there has been some sharp musketry, but all on the enemy's side. We have just had a visit from Major Eyre of the Artillery, who came with the reinforcement.

Wednesday 11th.
On Friday night a messenger came in with a letter from Cawnpore, from Major Bruce, stating that the force commanded by Sir Colin Campbell in person was expected to reach Alumbagh on the 10th (yesterday). It consists of 5100 infantry and 600 cavalry, and thirty-six guns. A salvo was to be fired at two o'clock yesterday, if they arrived. In the morning heavy guns were heard at Alumbagh: and they are expected to be here on the 15th. I trust they will not suffer so much as General Havelock's troops.
Our exit will of course depend much upon Sir Colin Campbell's success. Should the enemy not be entirely dispersed, we shall be all immediately sent off, and only allowed to take what we require in our hand. And should this be the case, we shall have to leave behind some things we value. This helps to make us regret the things we have lost, for it is more difficult to give up a thing than to lose it. However, I hope we shall get away better than that, and be able to take a box each. I dare say some of us will have to walk, as all the carriages, &c., will be taken up for the sick and wounded. The great difficulty will be getting away from this place.
Once at Alumbagh, I hope it will be easier. Colonel Inglis has not been at all well these three last days, but is better today.
When General Havelock's force came in, Colonel Campbell,

of the 90th, was wounded, and Colonel Inglis gave him up the large room at the end of our square, in which we sometimes dined. At first he went on very well, and his wound was considered slight, but fever ensued, and the wound in his leg getting worse in consequence, today at twelve the sad operation of amputation was performed. Fortunately, they had some chloroform left. He bore it wonderfully, and they say that he is going on well, though very weak.

I am very tired, my pen is bad, and the ink still worse, so I shall conclude.

Deil Cusha Park,
Monday, 23rd November, 1857.

My dear Gabrielle,

It is now a fortnight since I last wrote to you; I told you that poor Colonel Campbell was very weak. He rapidly sank, and on Thursday night, the 12th, he died. I must tell you a strange circumstance in relation to his illness. A white fowl had been brought to Mrs. Inglis for sale, but she thought the price, five *rupees*, was much too high. However, Colonel Inglis bought it. Its legs were secured, and it constantly hopped about before our door. Mrs. Inglis thought it was too bad that it should be eating our rice, and was just going to order it to be killed and cooked for dinner, when little Johnny comes running into the room,—"Mamma, Mamma, the white fowl has laid an egg!" This saved its life. Colonel Campbell was very fond of an egg—it was the only thing he could take well. The white fowl from this notable day laid an egg daily till Colonel Campbell died, after which it never laid another. We have brought the fowl away, and, may be, it will someday be in England.

I forgot to say in my last, that Mr. Kavanagh, head clerk in Mr. Cooper's office, volunteered to go out on the 9th inst. to Alumbagh, and conduct Sir Colin Campbell's force into Lucknow. This was a most gallant act on his part, and his safe arrival was announced the next day by hoisting a flag. He went out at night disguised as a native, taking a man with him as guide. He must have proved of great use to the force, as there was no one there who knew anything of this part of the country.

The enemy made an attack on Alumbagh on the morning of the 12th, but were repulsed with the loss of their guns. On

Tuesday, the 18th, sharp musketry firing was heard at Alumbagh. Since General Havelock's force came in on the 25th October, Colonel Inglis had 100 of his own garrison killed and wounded, and twenty-six of the 32nd killed.

Very heavy firing was heard on Saturday the 14th instant, between twelve and one o'clock, and our flag was seen flying from the Martinière College. Sir Colin had got possession of this park (the Deil Cusha) and the Martinière. Sir Colin did not advance on Sunday the 15th, as was expected by the garrison, who were in a great state of excitement, watching every movement. It was a very quiet day with us. We had the service read in the Brigade Mess-room, close to our room. On Sunday night at ten o'clock the enemy commenced a heavy firing upon us, but it lasted only a short time. I could not sleep much that night, as I could only listen to the distant guns I heard. Again, at four o'clock in the morning, they fired very heavily upon us. However, I believe it was chiefly blank ammunition. Sir Colin did not advance farther than Secundra Bagh, a palace with gardens.

On Tuesday the 17th, Sir Colin advanced and took possession of the 32nd Mess-house, and then Mr. Martin's bungalow. This effected a communication between the garrison and the force; and in the evening Colonel Berkeley, the new colonel of the 32nd, rode into our court-yard to see Colonel Inglis. On that Tuesday, the 17th, at dinner. Colonel Inglis told us that Sir Colin's orders were that the whole force was to leave Lucknow the next day. We were perfectly astounded. How the sick and wounded, women and children, were all to be moved so quickly we could not imagine. We got up very early on Thursday morning, as we had much to do, and the hour of our departure was so uncertain. I find now that we shall not leave the Residency till the 22nd. I am very busy, and can say no more at present, and so farewell!

(*End of Miss Dickson's letters to her cousin.*)

Chapter 5

July 5th - July 7th

(Recommencement of Mrs. Case's Journal)

Sunday, July 5th, 1857.

Caroline's letters which precede this will explain to you why I have not been able to write for some time past. Knowing how deeply interested you will be about us, I will endeavour to write down something every day, though I think it very doubtful whether you will see it or receive our letters. This is indeed a truly awful time: death seems ever before us, and I will not attempt to describe our sensations, because it would be impossible to do so, and indeed they could scarcely be understood by those who are enjoying the privilege of peace and quiet by their happy firesides in England. There is so much sorrow and suffering around us, that there is scarcely time to indulge in private grief, but deeply I know you will feel for me.

We are now under a heavy fire from the enemy night and day. Mrs. Inglis and her three children, Carry and myself, are all in a very small room, inside the square, near the brigade mess; but Colonel Inglis considers it safer than most places from the shot and shell, which fall about in all directions. We have two sofas, on one of which I sleep. Mrs. Inglis, Carry, and the children all sleep on mattresses on the floor. In the day time they are rolled up and put away, and we try to make our little room look as neat as we can, for it is used as a drawing-room, as well as for a sleeping apartment. We are, I believe, more comfortable than any other people in the Residency in one respect, for our servants and Mrs. Inglis's have remained with us. As we are four in number, besides the children, our rations go farther than they would do with a smaller party.

It is impossible to tell you how kind Colonel and Mrs. Inglis have been to us. They have insisted on our considering ourselves as part of their family, and in such times as these how doubly valuable are kindness and sympathy?

The firing is incessant night and day. The day after we were first besieged, it appeared to our ears, so unaccustomed to any thing of the kind, to be most awful. We did not know what was going on, and as every man who could carry a musket was at his post, we could get no information, and thought every moment that the place must be taken by storm; and we knew that if the enemy did get in a dreadful fate would have been reserved for us. Mrs. Inglis was ill in bed, just beginning to recover from the smallpox. We three offered up our prayers to Him who could alone protect us. I read the Litany aloud, and so wonderful was the effect of that heartfelt prayer, that it is scarcely too much to say, that we rose from our knees calm, and feeling ready for whatever might await us. The great terror which we experienced only a few minutes before seemed to disappear, and fresh strength to have taken its place. I am thankful to say that the enemy were repulsed in that attack.

A very sad event has happened to us; the death of that good and excellent man. Sir Henry Lawrence. On the 1st July he was hit while sitting in his room by a ball from the very howitzer which the enemy had taken from us at Chinhut. The wound proved mortal, and he died two days afterwards, regretted by the whole garrison. Poor Miss Palmer, the daughter of Colonel Palmer, of the 48th Native Infantry, a young girl of about twenty, had her leg taken off by a round shot entering her room. She died the following day. Some officers and men have been wounded, but, considering that day and night they are under such heavy fire, it is not surprising. Last night the rain fell in torrents, and the thunder and lightning were awful, during which time the firing never ceased. Oh, how glad we were when the first peep of dawn was seen: our courage feels renewed when daylight appears. I hear that the enemy's force round the Residency are in great numbers, and that they have a great many guns; but our brave little handful of Europeans, scarcely numbering 800, are holding out nobly.

Monday, July 6th.

Last evening there was a rumour among the natives that two regiments were coming in. I believe that there was some fighting going on in the direction of the Dil Koosha: it is supposed to have been among the natives themselves. This is the best thing that can happen for us, as it takes them away from the place. The enemy were very close to us yesterday, and burnt down a tent which had been prepared for Mrs. Inglis, when she was first seized with the smallpox. Last night was fine and light, and much quieter than the previous. Colonel Inglis breakfasted with us. Some nights ago the rebels looted the city, and the yelling and screaming were terrific. If they could only effect an entrance here, how dreadful would be our fate! Firing is still going on, but nothing compared to what it was during the past week. The natives in the garrison say that the insurgents are constructing a mine to blow us all up, but we have heard no real information to that effect. How long is all this to last? My poor heart is so weary and sad, that I feel truly desolate and lonely now in the world; and well indeed may I feel so, having lost one who was truly everything to me. Weather fine today: no rain. Captain Lowe came in whilst we were at dinner.

Tuesday, July 7th.

Some heavy firing during the night. Colonel Inglis came to breakfast. The Light Company of the regiment assembled in our square, and went to the top of the house to fire on the enemy. Officers and men look both very tired and worn. Day cloudy, close, and sultry. Major Francis badly wounded.

Wednesday, July 8th.

Very heavy rain last night; also after breakfast this morning. Firing still continues: very sharp about 1 p.m. Colonel Inglis came in at two o'clock, and told us that Mr. Polehampton had been shot through the body, but he does not know whether the wound is dangerous. I pray it may not be. A shell fell close to our cook-room door, quite near the *khansamah*, while he was making the soup: he must have had a narrow escape. Major Francis had both his legs shot off, and they say that his recovery is very doubtful. I think and fear that we shall hear of many more sad things before all this dreadful business ends. All at present wears a most dismal aspect. The rain makes everyone and everything look most miserable, and in the trenches it must be dreadful. My poor heart aches. I wonder what has become of my poor Hira? All the horses were turned out of this some days ago. Of course he fell into the hands of the insurgents. What an ending to such a favourite animal, one which had carried me so many happy miles on his back. Carry's Lalla shared a better fate with the poor old Sahib, being shot the first night of the outbreak in camp.

I forgot to mention that on Wednesday the 1st July, the day after we came in here, the Fort Muchee Bhawun was blown up by our own people, and the whole party came in bringing their sick with them; and all, to our surprise, in perfect safety. We heard the explosion: it was very loud. It took place between twelve and one at night. Yesterday a gallant charge was made by some of the 32nd and some *Sikhs*, about fifty men altogether, into Mr. Johannes' house, a position which the enemy had taken up, and where it was supposed they were mining. This turned out, however, not to be the case; and the brave little party returned with only two men wounded, having killed eight of the enemy. Major and Mrs. Banks came in to see Mrs. Inglis while we were at dinner, and Mr. and Mrs. Turnbull came to talk to her some time.

Thursday, July 9th.

Last night, or rather early this morning, the firing was very loud indeed, and the rain heavy at times. Heard a report again that the enemy were mining. We hear that they are going to offer Maun Sing five *lacs* of *rupees* (5000*l.*) to come and fight on our side, for he is said to be here, but as yet neutral. They purpose sending out six messengers, and they are to get 100*l.* each for carrying the message. I should think it doubtful whether even one will ever reach him. Colonel Inglis brought me yesterday my dear William's *Bible*, *Prayer Book*, and a little *Companion to the Altar*,' which I had given him. It was entirely shot through by a ball. These, with another *Prayer Book*, were the only things of his saved at the Muchee Bhawun.

Friday, July 10th.

Last night was quieter than usual; much less firing. We heard at breakfast there was a report that part of the force which had returned from Persia had arrived at Cawnpore, and would be here very shortly. Day fine but showery. Dr. Boyd came to Mrs. Inglis in the evening while we were sitting outside our door. He told her that he could not find any one to take charge of Mrs. Stephens's little boy while she was ill. She was confined last night, but the child was born dead.

Saturday, July 11th.

The night past appeared very quiet to us, but when Colonel Inglis came to breakfast, he told us that he had been called up in the night, for a man had come in with the intelligence that the enemy meant to attack us. It turned out to be a false alarm. There was, however, I believe, a good deal of firing on the other side of the Residency. Weather very hot and oppressive today.

Sunday, July 12th.

Firing much as usual during the night. Day fine but very close. Colonel Inglis read the morning service to us after breakfast. How little it appears like Sunday, that day which always used to be such a happy one to me! Heavy firing during the night, chiefly, I believe, from the enemy. There appears to be no news; indeed, nobody knows anything of what is going on beyond the precincts of this Residency. Surely there never was in the annals of history a more extraordinary state of things than this. When will it all end? The natives say they have heard that our bungalows have been looted, and all the servants who were left there killed. I trust this is not the case, for we cannot help hoping that the poor creatures would be able to get away to some village before these wretches commenced their work of plunder and destruction. How sorry I should be if anything were to happen to my poor good *ayah.*

Monday, July 13th.

Last night the firing was very loud indeed, but from what we heard at breakfast there does not appear to have been anything very particular going on. Day fine, but cloudy. When Colonel Inglis came in to dinner he told us that poor Mr. Charlton (32nd) had been badly wounded by a ball through his head, and that he did not think he would live. Heavy rain just after dinner, which prevented us from sitting outside our door as usual. Mrs. Need spoke to Mrs, Inglis and told her of some little child which had just died. We saw it carried past in the dark to its last resting place. We saw no Europeans with it, poor little thing! The *khansamah* told us just before we went to bed that seventeen men, including Europeans and natives, had been wounded, but I know not if it be true.

Tuesday, July 14th.

About nine o'clock this morning, just as we had finished dressing, there appeared to be a good deal of excitement. It seemed that the insurgents had collected in great numbers, and were intending to make an attack; but finding our force on the lookout for them did not then carry out their intentions, whatever they may have been. Mr. Charlton is better today, but I fear that there is but little hope of his life being saved. The enemy have been trying to annoy us a good deal. There was heavy firing just after our dinner, which must have frightened the ladies, as the verandah of the building where they are was hit. One of the officers, who was passing by while we were sitting outside our door, ordered us to go in, as it was scarcely safe to sit out while the balls were flying about in that manner. We saw a poor man carried by who had his leg shot off (one of the 32nd). Dr. Boyde came and spoke to Mrs. Inglis for a few minutes in the evening. The insurgents tried to effect a breach in the wall, but were unsuccessful.

Wednesday, July 15th.

Last night appeared to me very noisy, but it does not seem to have been much more so than usual. While we were dressing, a round shot fell close to our door; most providentially no one happened to be on the spot at the time. A bullet fell close to the *khansamah,* while he was cooking the breakfast, and one also close to the chick, near which Mrs. Inglis was sitting settling something in one of her boxes. For the first time, today the *khansamah* has complained of being short of wood for cooking. He has, however, found some. If things came to the worst we should have to break up our tables and chairs for firewood. Some of the poor ladies fare badly, I believe, in the way of provisions, many having laid in no private stores of their own, and are entirely dependent on their rations, which of course are but scanty.

Dr. Scott came to see us. I believe it is only the second time since his illness that he has been out. He looked very weak and broken down, but rather better in face than we expected to see him. I am sure he felt a good deal at seeing me. His recovery is wonderful, after so severe an illness. Dr. Boyde also came in the afternoon. He told us Mr. Charlton is wonderfully well, but I do not think any hope of his recovery is entertained, though Dr. Boyde said he had known an instance of a person recovering with a bullet lodged in the head. Came inside earlier than usual, for Captain Wilson told us as he passed by that it was not safe to remain outside, as they were going to send off a shell.

Thursday, July 16th.

When Colonel Inglis came to see us this morning at our early tea, he told us that his servant (Vokins, a 32nd man) had his leg struck by a round shot yesterday evening, while sitting in a chair under the portico of the hall door at the Residency. The leg was amputated, but the poor man was too weak to have chloroform administered to him, and suffered dreadfully. Colonel Inglis held him while they performed the operation; he is going on as well as he can be expected to do.

Today is little Johnny's birthday; he is four years old today, poor little fellow! It is not a very happy birthday for him. We must only hope that the next one may be in England.

I have been too ill to write for some days, so shall copy here what dear Carry has been kind enough to write for me.

Friday, July 17th.

Adelaide being too ill to continue her journal, I do so for her, till she is well again. She rose yesterday morning with a sore throat, and headache came on in the afternoon. Mrs, Inglis and I persuaded her to lie down, and see Dr. Scott in the evening.

On Thursday night there was a heavy fire of musketry, between eleven and twelve, from the side of the Cawnpore Battery, which lasted about half-an-hour. The guns continued firing all night. None of our people were hit. Yesterday was a very quiet day, which we paid for at night. Again at half-past eleven we were startled out of our sleep by a very heavy and furious firing, both of musketry and artillery. It was frightful, and seemed as if it were to be our last struggle. In half-an-hour it was over, and the rest of the night was quiet. Mrs. Inglis says that there was some loud firing early in the morning, but it was chiefly from our own guns. It was such a relief to see Colonel Inglis last night after the firing. He came to tell us that all was right. Poor Adelaide, who had taken, when she went to bed, a composing draught, and had fallen into a comfortable sleep, was roused by it, and did not get a good sleep again till after four o'clock. She was dreadfully weak.

In the night we had to give her port-wine constantly. Several very loud shots are to be heard. A man of the 32nd was wounded this morning, and a sergeant of the Artillery killed. No one hurt in last night's firing. Colonel Inglis is very kind. He brings Adelaide all he thinks will do her good. I must not forget to mention the escape he had yesterday morning. He slept in the Residency, which is a great mark for the enemy, and had left his room only ten minutes, when a round shot came through it, passed over his bed and tub, and through his portmanteau. He has now removed his quarters elsewhere. Mrs, Inglis had only the day before been saying, how wrong it was to stop there. It was a narrow escape indeed.

When he came into luncheon he told us there was a man just outside the gate with a stick in his hand, who had been killed by either our guns or the enemy's. They fancy he might be the bearer of some despatches, and are going to try and get him in after dark.

Chapter 6

July 9th - July 28th

Sunday, 9th July.

After dinner last night, Mrs. Thornhill came to see Mrs. Inglis, and Mr. Thornliill also, and brought the report that the Rajah of Cawnpore had been taken. About half-past eight Colonel Inglis looked in, and said they had got in the body which had lain at the gate; however, it turned out to be an *ayah*. At twelve last night there was some heavy firing, but nothing like the night before. An officer of the 7th Cavalry (Mr. Arthur) was killed this morning; he exposed himself too much. Mr. Harmer (32nd) had his leg much hurt by the splinter of a round shot which passed through the mess-room while they were at breakfast in the Residency, A carcase came into Colonel Inglis's room there last night, and set fire to part of it. Adelaide had a good night, but still suffers much from her head. At Dr. Fayrer's they have not a room which is safe, and they have no servants left, so they have to do everything themselves. How I long for all this to be at an end! Mrs. Inglis and I take a walk up and down a very small space. We are perfect prisoners, but are fortunate in being able to get out at all.

Monday, July 20th.

This morning, between eight and nine, we heard all the *cranies* in our square ordered to their posts. An alarm was given that the enemy were going to attack us. This proved true. They assembled in great numbers on the side of the church; the firing was very heavy for a long time, but they were repulsed. They appeared to be so sure of getting in, that they sent their standard-bearer to place their standard quite close to the gate; he was immediately shot dead. Mr, Edmonstone was slightly wounded. Firing still continues, but I fancy all is right for this time. The night was a very quiet one. Whilst we were sitting at breakfast, what seemed to us a large gun going off made the whole ground and building shake. It was a mine which the enemy had blown up close to the intrenchments, as their signal to commence the attack. It fortunately did us no harm.

It has been the severest attack we have had, and I am so thankful that it did not take place in the night. We heard yesterday evening that Mr. Polehampton was very ill with cholera, and I fear he can scarcely be alive now. A lady at the *Begum's* house (Mrs. Thomas) died a few days ago of smallpox. We had met her at Colonel Palmer's when she first came to Lucknow. Two soldiers' children also died of it. The firing of musketry very sharp at this minute. The day is cloudy. The flies here are a perfect plague; one can scarcely eat one's breakfast, dinner, or anything without being attacked by millions of them.

At four p.m. the firing ceased, and the stillness is quite strange. Mr. Cooper has just told Mrs. Inglis that the enemy have been well punished today. He says, that they were to be seen going over the bridge, carrying their dead and wounded in carts-full. They heard of the reinforcements for us being near, and were making a desperate attempt to get hold of the treasury and kill us all, and then make off. They also appeared to have received reinforcements; but whether they were regiments which they sent out to intercept the troops coming to our relief, and which report says were between this and Cawnpore, or a fresh body of men, is not known.

At all events, they were seen coming in from the Cawnpore road this morning. Mr. Healy, the veterinary surgeon, had his arm broken by a stray shot, whilst carrying a message. At two o'clock we expected another attack would be made. About twenty men got inside the palisades somewhere on our side, but were driven out. Only fancy being within only a few hundred yards of creatures, who, if they could but get in, would murder us in the most brutal manner, and commit horrors too fearful even to think of! God, in his infinite mercy, preserve us from such a fate, and soon send us relief. Our little garrison is holding out well, and they say we have provisions for a month longer.

(*Caroline ceases here, and Mrs. Case begins again.*)

Tuesday, July 21st.

Poor Carry has not been well for the last two days, and today she is very feverish. I (thank God for all His mercies!) am getting better, though not very strong; but am able to resume my journal again.

Not much firing going on today, though I believe they are constantly expecting something. Poor Major Banks has been killed this morning. His is a public loss indeed! He exposed himself too much, and it was only this morning that Colonel Inglis wrote to him and told him that he ought to consider how useful and valuable his life was, and begged him to be more careful. It is much to be regretted he did not follow this advice, for when he was killed he was firing, just as any private soldier, from the top of Mr. Gubbins's house. He was a most excellent man, and, I believe, a very clever officer. There is no one here qualified to fill his place.

I got up yesterday evening, for a short time, about five o'clock. I never remember in my life to have felt so weak as I did one night while I was ill, and I firmly believe I should not have lived, had not my two kind nurses, Mrs. Inglis and Carry, given me a quantity of port-wine. I feel as if my poor nerves, and indeed my whole frame, were much and severely shaken. The least thing makes me feel as if I should drop down.

Wednesday, July 22nd.

Very heavy rain this morning till about one, when it cleared up. Dr. Scott came to see us before breakfast. Carry still very unwell. She is very heavy and sleeps a great deal. Very little firing going on today. They must be preparing for something. Things do not wear a more cheering aspect. Nothing more heard of reinforcements for us. We got a few things washed today for the first time; the *dhobey* could not iron them, and though we gave him the soap he charged enormously. We can wash as well for ourselves, but we have nearly exhausted our soap, so what we shall do I know not.

A lady (Mrs. Dorin) was killed today while sitting in her room in Mr. Gubbins's house, by a bullet through her head. Poor thing! she had escaped from Sutapara, having seen her husband killed before her eyes. A party of the 32nd and some *Sikhs* went into a house near this, where they suspected the enemy were mining this evening, but they found nothing to confirm their fears. However, they set fire to the house. We lost only one man (32nd), and he unfortunately was shot in mistake by our own people.

Thursday, July 23rd.

Very good news, if true, this morning. A pensioner who went away before the siege began has returned with the news that a Queen's regiment, 500 Sikhs, and twelve guns were on their way here, and would be at Nawab Gunge today; that they had had two engagements with the enemy, in which they had beaten them well, and taken some of their guns. The *Nana* of Cawnpore has also been beaten by them, and that place as well as Bithoor is in our possession. Such is the information,—but the truth of it remains to be proved. The force coming to our relief is, according to this account, a very small one; but I trust and pray that the Almighty will make it sufficient to aid us in this our great need. The natives say that the insurgents are leaving this in numbers. At any rate they have been very quiet today. Part of a shell fell into the ground this evening *close* to where Mrs. Inglis and Mr. Baley were standing. Carry is easier today, but there is no doubt as to her illness being smallpox, and, as yet, it appears to be even in a milder form than with Mrs. Inglis,

Friday, July 24th.

Carry going on well. Dr. Scott is most kind, coming to see her every day, and says that she could not be doing better. No firing at all today. The insurgents must have gone away; at least, numbers of them. They say they are certainly mining. The rain was very heavy indeed last night, and Colonel Inglis was woke up by the intelligence that 400 of the enemy were inside our intrenchments. This was of course a false report, or I do not suppose that I should be sitting here to write it at this moment. Nothing more heard today of our reinforcements. After dark this evening Colonel Inglis had an examination of the Redan Battery, where it was believed the enemy were mining. It is not the case, fortunately.

Saturday, July 25th.

A very quiet day. Carry going on well. This morning, just after we were dressed, Mr. Need (a man who with his wife and two children had come here from Surora, and who live under a gateway close to us) was shot through the lungs while he was picking up a few sticks for firewood; he was taken to the hospital and is still alive. He had been over at our cook room about five minutes before. Dr. Scott told us a shell had hit one of the men of the 32nd on the wrist, and the poor man had been obliged to have his arm amputated. The balls are falling about and shells bursting in every direction.

Sunday, July 26th.

Last night between twelve and one Mr. Cooper came to the door of our room and asked Mrs, Inglis if she were awake: on her replying in the affirmative, he told us that a messenger had just arrived with a letter from Colonel Tytler, the quarter-master-general of the troops coming up to our relief, in which he said that two-thirds of the force had crossed the river be tween this place and Cawnpore; that they had beaten the *Nana*; and his army had dispersed no one knew where; that Bithoor is in our possession; that they considered their force quite equal to beating any number of the enemy they might encounter, and hoped to be here in about five or six days. This is very cheering intelligence, and the events of the next few days will be very momentous to all.

I fear the relief party will have to fight their way up, and will find much difficulty in getting in here. We know the enemy have sent out a force to meet them, and that there must be a desperate struggle before they reach the Residency. The messenger went out again this evening, and took with him a plan of the city, and directions as to the best road for coming in; and if he delivers all safely, he is to get 5000 *rupees* (500*l.*)!! They say that there are two Queen's regiments amongst the troops coming. Colonel Inglis says he shall be well satisfied if they arrive here on Sunday next.

Mr. Lewin, of the Artillery, has been killed today. Carry going on well, but of course feels uncomfortable. There was a short evening service in one of the mess-rooms, to which Mrs. Inglis went. The insurgents have been very quiet today, and we always suspect something is going on when that is the case. It is now known beyond a doubt that they are mining, but so are we, and I hope that we shall get in and blow them up.

Monday, July 27th.

Last night, about nine o'clock, while we were reading prayers, all undressed and ready for bed, we were suddenly stopped by heavy firing of musketry and cannon. It was preceded by a great shout, which we knew came from the enemy. At first we really thought for a moment they had got in. Mrs. Inglis knelt down and said a prayer, and our confidence was strengthened in that Almighty Power which in all our dangers is watching over us. The firing did not continue very long, and then succeeded a complete and deathlike silence, which was even more painful. It was frightful to hear the shells whizzing over our heads. Mrs. Inglis remained at the door for some time to see if any one might pass from whom she could hear what was really going on. I lay down and nearly fell asleep.

A few minutes afterwards Colonel Inglis came and told us that all was quiet, and that we might go to bed. So we finished reading our prayers and did so. The night was afterwards quite quiet. When Colonel Inglis came to see us early this morning, he told us that Captain Shepherd had been killed last night, and, sad to say, by our own people. He had gone too far out, it appears, and in the darkness of the night was fired at by mistake. We are all very sorry to hear this, for he was universally liked, and will be a great loss. How sad and depressing all this is, day after day Mrs. Need came before we were up this morning and told us that her husband had died in the night; and I have just heard that one of her children has got the cholera. Nobody could imagine all these horrors unless they witnessed them. Nothing we wash will dry, so our things are all damp, which is very distressing for the children.

Colonel Inglis told us this morning at breakfast, that one of the enemy's mines had fallen in. They seem to think the attack last night was only a ruse to divert our attention from the mining. Mrs. Inglis went this evening to see Mrs. Cooper, and there she heard that the enemy are mining just under the mess-room, close to where all the ladies are. It was first found out, I believe, by one of the ladies, who heard the noise when she was in her bath room, and called her husband to listen to the sound. But we are making a counter-mine there; so I hope we may get the best of it. The ladies are sadly frightened, and no wonder. Nothing can be more dreadful than the idea of mines. The weather is very damp today, and at times chilly. Carry going on well, but very sleepy.

Tuesday, July 28th.

A quiet night. Colonel Inglis looked into our room between twelve and one, as he was going his rounds, and told us that all was right. No news this morning. One of our servants said that guns had been heard on the Cawnpore road by some of them, but I think it must have been a mistake, as no one else seems to have heard it. The mining seems to be the engrossing topic today. At twelve o'clock Mrs. Need came and told us that her boy who had the cholera is much better; she also told us that everyone was under arms just then, and that they were expecting an immediate attack, and as we heard some heavy guns we thought it likely to be the case. Tuesday and Friday are the *sepoys'* great fighting days, I am sure they will make some desperate struggle to get in before the reinforcements arrive.

What a state to live in, never to know what these wretches are going to do! When our people were mining yesterday, they came close upon the enemy's mine, which they say was beautifully constructed, and a wax candle burning in it. They ran away as soon as they found we were near them; and in the evening we went in and blew the whole up, and completely destroyed it. As we heard the officers and men go by, they all seemed very much pleased with this affair.

In the evening Mrs. Inglis went to see Mrs. Cooper, and found Mrs. Martin sitting with her. They all had a consultation as to what they would consider best to be done in case the enemy were to get in, and whether it would be right to put an end to ourselves, if they did so, to save ourselves from the horrors we should have to endure. Some of the ladies keep laudanum and prussic acid always near them. I can scarcely think it right to have recourse to such means; it appears to me that all we have to do is, to endeavour, as far as we can, to be prepared for our death, and leave the rest in the hands of Him who knows what is best for us.

Chapter 7

July 29th - August 6th

Wednesday, July 29th.

There was a good deal of firing in the night, but it did not last long. I slept through it all. Why they make these attacks it is impossible to imagine. It must be to divert attention from something else. What an anxious time it is! We feel so very fearful about the reinforcements. We hear 6000 of the insurgents with twelve (some say sixteen) guns have gone out to meet them. I fear that they will have much difficulty in getting in. These mines are dreadful, and Colonel Inglis tells us that the enemy have regular Sappers. In fact, I think no one supposed they would have been capable of doing all that they have done. Another message was sent to the relieving force yesterday, with a duplicate of the plan of our position here, in case the first should not reach its destination.

Thursday, July 30th.

Yesterday, about six o'clock, while we were at dinner, the greatest excitement prevailed, the sound of distant guns being heard, and loud cheering from English voices. Everyone was rushing about in a frantic manner, exclaiming that the relief had arrived; and one would have supposed that they were actually at the gates, waiting for admittance. We all, like the rest, rushed out to see what it was, and went over to Carry, who, we thought, might be frightened; but she was quietly sitting up in her bed.

All the servants were calling out that the regiments had arrived,, and the *ayah* began to say her prayers. Colonel Palmer rushed up to Mrs. Inglis, shook hands with her, and congratulated her on the arrival of the reinforcements. For my own self, I must say I had no sooner got out of the room where we dined, than I began to think it was just as likely to be the enemy getting in. The excitement was tremendous, but lasted only for a few minutes, and then it subsided. Nobody knew what was the matter. The only thing that was quite evident was, that the relief had not arrived, and it was impossible to imagine what the guns in the distance, which sounded more like a salute than anything else, could be for. Some said that yesterday was the day on which the insurgents intended to proclaim a king, others supposed that a victory might have been gained by them.

Colonel Inglis made us all go to dinner again, and was very angry that there should have been such a frantic demonstration without any cause for it, as he thought it would do a great deal of harm when the reaction took place, and would greatly shake the confidence of our own few *sepoys*. It is impossible to help feeling disappointed after a thing of that kind, and today I think everyone looks more or less dispirited.

Whilst at breakfast. Captain Wilson came, and reported to Colonel Inglis that numbers of the enemy were to be seen in the direction of the Bridge of Boats, coming from the Cawnpore side; *palanquins* with quantities of men running alongside of them, and that tents and other appendages to an army had been seen with them. Colonel Inglis said that if they went over the bridge he should consider all was right; but if they went in the other direction, it would look suspicious. Captain Wilson said he did not know what to think, and looked, I thought, rather disheartened.

About twelve o'clock, Colonel Inglis came, and told us that they could see nothing more of these people, but that *charpoys* with wounded men in them had been plainly seen. What an anxious time it is! How one longs to know what it all can mean! If there has been an action fought, and our troops have been victorious, I think we *must* hear something of it this evening. On the other hand, I do think, if the insurgents had gained a victory over us, we should have heard noise and shouting in the bazaar.

Carry up today for the first time. Dr. Scott told us that Mr. Grant, an officer belonging to a Native Regiment, had died this morning from a wound in his hand. His wife and child also died (of fever, I believe) a few days ago, but he did not know it, poor man. Mr. Bonham, our best artillery officer, has been seized with smallpox this morning. Poor old Colonel Halford died yesterday from complete break-up, I believe. How sad for his wife and daughter! This morning has been very fine, but we had a heavy shower of rain about two o'clock. It is only wonderful that any one keeps well at such a time. The want of exercise and air, and the difficulty of keeping one's clothes or anything else even tolerably clean, are great trials to those who have never suffered from such evils before, but truly they are trifles in comparison with the great trials so many breaking hearts have lately had to undergo.

Friday, July 31st.

Carry sat up nearly the whole day yesterday, and did not seem weak or even tired, and it is quite wonderful how rapidly the marks of her illness are disappearing. No news whatever this morning; the night was quiet. Johnny still not quite right. Dr. Scott saw him this morning. This is a most lovely day; the air is quite delicious. What can have become of our reinforcements? There is a native report today that some bridge is broken down, and that they will have to go ten miles round. I have been washing a few things.

*Saturday, August 1*st

Last night was quiet, but this morning the enemy have been firing heavy guns, which they have brought over from the Muchee Bhawun. All the guns they had here have gone out with their force—at least so it is supposed—to meet our reinforcements coming in, and as nothing can be heard of them it is imagined that the insurgents have been cutting up the roads to prevent their getting in. Heard today that another lady, Mrs. Clarke, died yesterday. We also heard that Mr. Ommanney was dead, and Dr. Scott said there had been some fresh cases of cholera this morning.

Sunday, August 2nd.

This day last week we certainly expected that the relief would have been in or heard of today; but nothing whatever in the shape of news from them has yet arrived, so our prospects are less and less cheering. Colonel Inglis read the morning's service, but was interrupted by heavy firing. I believe, however, that it was blank ammunition which the enemy were firing, as this day is a great festival with them, which they call the *Buckra Eid*, the day the Mussulman have their sacrifices. Dr. Scott came and saw Johnny and Carry, the former much better. No smallpox; the latter he thought looking a good deal pulled down. At twelve o'clock Mr. Harris gave a short service, to which Mrs. Inglis went. Colonel Inglis returned after a short time, and finished reading the prayers to us when the firing ceased.

The rest of the day was quiet. The enemy, to the number of about 300, were seen going off in the direction of Cawnpore, but they have left quite enough here to annoy us with their shells and bullets. Carry came to dinner for the first time today. In the evening Mrs. Inglis went to see Mrs. Cooper, and just before we went to bed we walked outside the *Sikhs'* compound, close to the *Begum's* House. The night was most lovely, and bright moonlight, and though I do not suppose we walked above twenty or, at most, thirty paces, it is nearly five weeks since I have been so far.

We heard a good deal of shouting before we went to bed, and, as usual, the enemy's bugles, to which now little attention seems to be paid.

Monday, August 3rd.

Still nothing heard of our relief, and the days appear months while this dreadful state of things is going on. Colonel Inglis told us this morning that one man went out to our reinforcements four days ago, and that he is certain to return if he can. He has gone all the way round by Marian, and is to return by Chinhut. They seem to think he might possibly be here tomorrow.

It is now said we have only provisions for twenty days more. What is to become of us if our relief does not arrive before that time! By some negligence six fine bullocks were smothered in the *bousse* yesterday—a great loss at such a time.

The commissariat butcher came to ask for three of Colonel Inglis's goats this morning, to kill them for food, which looks as if we are beginning to run short of meat. In the midst of all this, it is scarcely possible to believe, but it is nevertheless true, that we have had today servants coming round with lists of ladies' clothes for sale, and a box with four very smart bonnets in it was also being taken round to see if anyone would purchase them. What a strange contrast do such facts present to the awful scenes around us and the feelings that we are impressed with! It is dreadful to think that we may be short of provisions.

Every morning before she is dressed Mrs. Inglis weighs out everything for our daily consumption with her own hands, and so good is her management that she is always able to give a little arrowroot or sugar to a sick child, and has two or three times succeeded in making little puddings for invalids without an egg and with but a very limited quantity of sugar. Mrs. Inglis paid her usual visit to Mrs. Case, but heard no news. We spoke to Mr. and Mrs. Martin as they passed through our courtyard; they told us poor little Tiny is very ill.

Tuesday, August 4th.

As usual, I begin with the same remark. No news! Nothing heard of the relief. The night was quiet, but I suffered so much from violent pain in my face and head, that I hardly slept at all. Colonel Inglis is not very well; he has been out too much this morning in the sun. We dined in our small room, and just as we had finished dinner, a shell burst in our courtyard, causing great confusion amongst the inhabitants. Our *punkah Coolie* left the *punkah,* and darted into the room. He had seen it coming. It made a great noise, but fortunately hurt no one. A short time before, one fell close to Mrs. Cooper and her children, but fortunately did not burst for want of powder. Of course she was a good deal frightened. Dr. Scott told us this morning that poor Major Anderson is very ill.

Wednesday, August 5th.

It is raining heavily today, and therefore it is lucky we did not wash, as it was our intention; there is so much difficulty in getting anything dry. Colonel Inglis is better today, but looks very tired.

Yesterday our servants came and told us about four p.m., that they heard guns in the distance. Mrs. Inglis and I went out and listened, and thought we heard them also, but as no one else did, I suppose we must have been mistaken. How weary one gets, hearing nothing of our relief! These wretches around us were shouting a great deal last night, looting the city again, I suppose; and the cries we hear must be often of those in distress.

A man of the 32nd was killed in the hospital today. He was taking something to one of his comrades, when he was shot through the heart! I believe he is the second or third who has been thus shot in the hospital. This must be very disheartening to the sick people. I have heard that since the commencement of this siege we have already lost 180 men of the 32nd *only!!*

Thursday, August 6th.

Last night, while we were at prayers, a shell burst close to our door, just behind the *punkah wallah.* It struck into the ground with a great noise, and made us all rush to the door to see where it had fallen. Not many minutes afterwards a bullet came close to the *ayah,* and with a tremendous clatter broke a plate, which she had beside her. This also was just at our door. Several other shots were fired into our little courtyard, and so near did they appear, that Mrs. Inglis began to think they must be taking particular aim at this place, thinking that Colonel

Inglis slept here. I believe that there was some heavy firing during the night, but I am thankful to say I slept well, and did not hear it.

This morning poor Mr. Studdy, of the 32nd, has had one of his arms taken off by a round shot in the Residency. I hear that he is likely to lose both, and that it is even doubtful if he will live. Poor young man! We were very sorry indeed to hear of this, he has behaved so well all through the siege. No news of any kind. It is now twelve days since we have heard anything from outside, and our relief was then supposed to be within three marches of us. Tomorrow we and the servants are to be put on half rations. How dreadful it will be when they are obliged to commence that with the fighting men!

Yesterday evening Mrs. Inglis and I walked through the *Sikhs*' compound and Begum Khotee. When one sees the walls and narrow roads within which we are enclosed, *escape* seems an impossibility if these wretches were to get in! I would give much to know what has become of my poor *ayah*; she would be a treasure to us here. A very warm, but fine day.

Chapter 8

August 7th - August 15th

Friday, August 7th.

Last night about eleven o'clock, just before we went to bed (for we were later than usual). Colonel Inglis told us that two messengers had just arrived, bringing news of the reinforcements. One of the men had been sent out about ten days ago with a letter to the officer commanding the relief. It appeared that he had been in our neighbourhood four days without being able to get in. He brought a letter with him, which, unfortunately, he lost just before he arrived. He states that there are four European regiments, besides artillery, sappers and miners, and *Sikhs*.

They are only able to march about three miles a day, as they intrench their camp every night, and the enemy have done all they can to break up the roads and impede their progress. He says that there have been two actions fought, and both times our troops were victorious. One man says we have taken twenty-three, the other eighteen, guns from the enemy. He says a retrograde movement had been made by our troops; the reason is supposed to be that the *Nana* was collecting a force in their rear, and they had gone back to attack them. From the account of their position and distance from us, it is possible they might be here in two or three days; but Colonel Inglis says he shall feel very thankful if they arrive in eight. The man says that in the city here the insurgents talk of blowing us up by mining, or starving us out.

This morning, two sergeants of the 32nd (both good and useful men) have been mortally wounded. A shell burst, and they rushed out to see where it had fallen, when another burst at the spot where they were, and wounded them both dreadfully in their right arms. Dr. Scott says, Mr. Studdy is going on well. His arm (the right one) was amputated, but he was able to bear it, and they do not think now, as was at first supposed, that he had received a severe inward bruise. They gave him a bottle of champagne before the operation, as he was too weak for chloroform, and he bore it, poor fellow, without saying a word.

Mr. Thornhill and Captain Hardinge came in while we were at dinner. A report had just before been made to Colonel Inglis, that a body of men were seen gathering in the direction of Mr. Innes' house, and they came to say that it was a false alarm. After dinner Mrs. Inglis read us the deposition of the messenger who came in last night; and certainly there is a great stamp of truth about it; especially from one or two quite native and original statements which he makes. One was, that when the enemy fled, they left behind them thousands of *shoes!* It puzzles us all very much to imagine how our messengers carry the letters about with them, small as they are, for they wear so little clothing, that it must be most difficult to secrete them; one was brought in a quill, and another, I believe, in a shaving brush; the man passing for a barber among the insurgents.

Saturday, August 8th.

Everything going on as usual. A very warm day; not much firing going on. The servants have begun today to grind their own food, a process which Mrs. Inglis says they do not like at all. We have just seen a letter which is about to be sent out to the relieving force, and certainly it was a curiosity. The whole thing was not larger than this  ; indeed, I do not think it was quite so long. It was a piece of a quill sealed at each end, the letter rolled up inside. One could scarcely have imagined it possible that it could have been made up into such a tiny thing, but yet the letter contained 253 words, and some of them very long. I should like to know where the man will carry it; he might put it in his ear. I am very glad I saw it, as otherwise I could not have had an idea that it *could* be made so small. A private of the 32nd was killed at Mr. Gubbins's today, and a poor *ayah* was badly wounded.

Sunday, August 9th.

Poor Mr. Studdy died this morning. The severe inward contusion which he received appears to have been the chief cause of his death. He is much regretted; a very promising young officer, and had behaved so very well during all the siege! One of the sergeants who were wounded on Friday, died this morning also. Divine service in the mess-room at twelve: Mrs. Inglis went. A quiet day.

Monday, August 10th.

When we went to breakfast this morning, we saw a *Sikh* sitting in the room, who had come in last night; I believe he had not been beyond the city, but his deposition has not yet been taken. About twelve p.m., as I was sitting at the table writing, Carry washing our things, and Mrs. Inglis working, we were suddenly alarmed by what appeared to us a great shaking of the earth, followed by a *dreadful* noise, such as I never wish to hear again. It was indescribable, and sounded as if the whole earth was coming against us; it was a mine exploding without doing any harm. We thought it had been in the ladies' room, especially when we saw Mrs. Cooper, her nurse and children, and Mrs. Radclyffe with hers, all coming over to our room as fast as they could. Poor Mrs. C. was dreadfully frightened.

We laid her on one of our couches, and gave her some wine. A fierce attack followed the explosion of the mine, and a round shot fell close to our door; half a yard nearer, and it must have been into the room. It sounded altogether very frightful, as these attacks always do. In about twenty minutes Colonel Inglis came and told us that we had better all go into the large room, as we were safer there from the round shot, so there we all adjourned, each of us seizing hold of a child. I got hold of little Charley. For about an hour and a half the firing was loud and frequent. When the mine exploded our servants all rushed into our room, and for a moment appeared alarmed; but it is quite wonderful to see them sitting outside while the firing is going on, washing their clothes and pursuing their occupations as usual, just as if nothing was going on.

Colonel Inglis had a wonderful escape; one of the orderly-room clerks of the 32nd was shot down and mortally wounded as he was standing between him and Colonel Palmer; I believe the man actually fell against him. Poor Sergeant Campbell (32nd) was killed today, a most excellent man. I used to see him very often when we were coming down from Peshawur, and always heard him spoken of as being a very good and superior man. Mrs. Ouseley had a little boy this morning, and Mrs. Barwell yesterday.

Tuesday, August 11th.

Last night about nine o'clock, just as we were preparing for bed, there was another attack. We were sitting outside our door, as usual, when we observed what a complete lull there was, and how wonderfully quiet everything appeared to be. We had hardly said the words, when a tremendous fire of musketry and round shot began. The noise was fearful; the attack lasted about an hour, and during that time the firing was the sharpest and loudest we have yet had. We did not undress till it was over, when Colonel Inglis came and told us that all was quiet, and not one of our men had been hit. There was an attack while we were at dinner, which they say was the most fierce of all, though it did not sound so to us.

The enemy made a tremendous rush, and got so near that they seized hold of some of our men's firelocks. They seemed determined to get in, but I am sure they will not do so without a most desperate struggle. I cannot help thinking that they must have heard something about the relief being near, and that is the reason why they are making such desperate attempts. I hear that they say that in less than a week they will have murdered all the "*Sahib logues.*" Captain Hardinge told Mrs. Inglis last night, that just before the attack was commenced yesterday morning, two guns were distinctly heard in the distance by two or three people. What they were we have not yet heard. Three of our men have had a most wonderful escape. They were blown up by the mine, and actually thrown among the insurgents in the midst of the heavy firing, but got back again quite safely,—one of them being only a little singed.

A dreadful accident has happened this morning. Part of the Residency has fallen in, and five or six men of the 32nd have been buried in the ruins. When Colonel Inglis was there a short time ago, two of the poor men had been extricated as far as their heads only, and could just speak, with the help of brandy being poured down their throats. Their sufferings must be dreadful; and they, as well as those who are digging them out, are under fire the whole time. It certainly is the most dreadful thing that has happened to us since the siege began; and now when the life of every man is of such value, one cannot sufficiently lament such a loss. Poor Major Anderson is dying. It is just reported that guns have been heard towards cantonments.

Wednesday, August 12th.

A good deal of firing went on during the night. The enemy were as usual making an attack somewhere. The nights are dreadful; one looks forward so anxiously for the first ray of daylight. Then the day arrives with no news of our relief. One's heart sickens at all this delay, and knowing nothing of what is going on outside these gates.

They say that we might, with very great difficulty and pinching, as far as provisions go, hold out one month longer, but after that there will not be a hope for us; and now the natives have a report that the reinforcements will not be here for two months. If such should be the case, what a fate is before us! May God, in his infinite mercy, grant that we may be prepared, through the merits of our Saviour, for whatever is to happen to us! An attack is going on while I am writing, and I cannot help thinking what would be the feelings of any lady suddenly transported from quiet, peaceful England to this room, around which the bullets are whizzing, the round shot falling, and now and then a loud explosion, as if a mine were blowing up, which I think is almost worse than all the sharp and fast fire of the musketry. It is an awful time; and words could never make any one understand all that we have undergone during now nearly three months (ever since the 17th of May).

Poor Major Anderson is dead. He was a great favourite, and is universally regretted. The attack yesterday, I believe, hastened his end. His death has made poor Dr. Scott very ill again. His head has become quite affected. Some of our people went out today to blow up a house near this, but unfortunately failed in the attempt, as the enemy were prepared for them, and this was the cause of all the firing we heard. I am thankful to say that we had not a man of ours killed or wounded, which to us appears almost incredible, after such a heavy fire. Little Ada Radclyffe died this morning; she had been ailing for some time, and at last it turned to cholera. An *ayah* also died of cholera close to this yesterday. We had a few potatoes for dinner yesterday, a thing we had not seen for more than a month. They were found in one of the rooms. Mrs. Inglis is not looking well; the want of air, exercise, and proper nourishment begins to tell more or less on everyone.

Thursday, August 13th.

A very hot day. After breakfast our people blew up the house which they attempted yesterday. The explosion made very little noise, which surprised us, as we expected it would be very loud. There was very little firing on the part of the enemy; but this is a fast day with them, so, perhaps, not a fighting one. Mrs. Cooper's nurse, with the two children, came over to our room when they expected the explosion. She told us that little Tiny Martin died this morning, also a little child which Mrs. Pitt had the care of. I heard this morning that Captain Power died four or five days ago.

Friday, August 14th.

I felt very unwell yesterday, and went to bed early, but was awoke soon after by heavy firing. It lasted but a short time, and the night afterwards was quiet. We are still without news of any kind, and the enemy are painfully still this morning. They must be plotting mischief. A great many children are suffering dreadfully from want of proper nourishment; it is so very difficult to procure milk.

Yesterday afternoon a very respectable-looking person, with a little baby in her arms, came to the door of our room, and after asking Mrs. Inglis if she was "the brigadier's lady," said she had come to beg a little milk for her child, as she was afraid she should lose it if she could not get proper nourishment for it. Her simple story, told in such a genuine honest manner, affected us all, though one hears sad things every day. She said that her little baby was born the first day of the attack; her husband (whose name was Beale, an overseer of the works) was shot through the lungs, and died almost immediately.

From grief and fretting she had lost all her milk, and had nothing to give the poor little thing. She told us that she had lost three children—one she described as being a beautiful child, and was very anxious if she could to rear this one, to take it to her friends in England. Mrs. Inglis asked her where her home was; she said, in Kent, and that her father is a clergyman there, and her husband's father was an officer in the army. She said she had everything she wanted but nourishment for her child, and though many in this place are doubtless in the same sad plight, her plain tale, told without the slightest appearance of wishing to excite pity, made an impression on me I shall not easily forget. Dr. Scott paid us a long visit this morning; he was quite out of spirits, We are all very anxious he should come and live in our large room, as we think it would be more cheerful for him.

Saturday, August 15th,

Yesterday a *metah* belonging to a native doctor of the 7th Cavalry came in. He had been shut out on the first day of the siege, and therefore had been in the way of hearing something of what is going on outside. His deposition agreed with other native reports which we had heard. He said our reinforcements are still at Mhow, waiting for the China force to join them; but that 900 (we suppose an advance-guard) had come on to a place much nearer, and had an engagement with the enemy the day before yesterday, and captured two guns from them. He describes the *sepoys* round this place as getting disheartened, but still in great numbers. Dr. Scott came over this morning, and took up his abode in the large room in our courtyard. We think it will do him good being with us all. The rain was very heavy last night, and the lightning vivid.

Chapter 9

August 16th - September 25th

Sunday, August 16th.

Last night the pensioner who went out to Colonel Tytler with Colonel Inglis's letter of the 8th instant returned. He brought with him a few lines from Colonel Tytler to Mr. Gubbins, dated 4th August, saying that the reinforcements were on their way to Lucknow, and expected to be with us in three or four days; but the deposition of the messenger stated they had had another engagement with the enemy and had returned to Cawnpore, so when they will be here is as much a matter of conjecture as ever.

I hear that the longest time we can now hold out, as regards provisions, is to the 10th of next month. The messenger states that he delivered Colonel Inglis's letter and plans to Colonel Tytler. He describes the insurgents as being very numerous, and says that they have proclaimed some child "king." There is a story that the messenger was asked by some of the people with the relieving force, "If the *Sahib logues* here were able to take rides every evening and morning!" If that is true, they have not the slightest idea of our position, which is dreadful to think of, but we must keep up hope.

Monday, August 17th.

Everything is still very quiet, indeed far too much so, for the insurgents must be plotting mischief when they are not busy with an attack. Azaib and Din Mahomed went to the Residency today, to see where our few remaining boxes are. They gave a miserable account of them. A round shot has been through one of them, and, of course, everything inside was broken. They are all used for barricades, and some are in water. I would give anything to have one of them, which contains some precious letters and some of our favourite things, nearly all presents. I fear there are but few of them we shall ever see again.

Mr. and Mrs, Thornhill and Mrs. Barber came and sat out here in the evening. Mr. Thornhill was looking very ill, having had fever and been hit by a spent bullet a few days ago.

Tuesday, August 18th.

This morning about six o'clock we were all roused by the explosion of one of the enemy's mines. Six drummers were buried in it; three have been got out, the other three still remain. It is to be hoped that the poor fellows are dead; for they say it is impossible to extricate them, as the place is so completely under the enemy's fire. Two officers had a wonderful escape: one was in bed at the time, but they were both blown up in the air and came down again without being hurt. The enemy have certainly gained an advantage today. It is only wonderful that they do not get in altogether, so numerous as they are; but they advance by two and three at a time. It appears that their leader came on quite close this morning waving his sword and beckoning on his men, but he was shot dead at once, as well as the few others who came after him. 3 p.m.—Just heard that we have retaken the position which the enemy got possession of this morning, and we have not lost a man.

Wednesday, August 18th.

Yesterday was a most successful day for us; for not only was the position which the enemy had taken in the morning retaken by us in the afternoon, but Johannes' house was blown up, and our people got out farther than they have hitherto been, and some fresh mines were discovered. I should like to be able to give an account of the proceedings of the day, but do not sufficiently understand the different positions of the place to do so. Colonel Inglis was much pleased with his day's work, but was dreadfully knocked up in the evening, and did not return to dinner till past seven. We all thought we should have a very quiet night, but at nine o'clock, just as we were going to bed, the enemy commenced an attack.

It lasted only a short time, but the firing for the time was very loud. Mrs. Pierce was so frightened that she came over here with her little child and remained till it was over. A man of the 32nd was killed yesterday. There is an old woman, a resident of Lucknow, living now in this compound, who is most anxious to go out as a spy, and says that she will undertake to take a letter to the reinforcements, or even to go to Calcutta if it were necessary: but to judge by the way she walks about here, she would be a long time getting there. She says that she could disguise herself so as to be able to pass out among the insurgents. A round shot fell in our courtyard today, close to the head of one of the goats, but fortunately did not hurt anyone.

Thursday, August 20th.

Colonel Inglis was very much knocked up yesterday; indeed, I do not think he can stand all this wear and tear much longer. It rained heavily last night, and we could not sit out as usual. Dr. Scott had his tea with us in our room. We all fancied last night had been very quiet, but Colonel Inglis says that there was a great deal of shouting and noise of *tomtom*, and that he had a disturbed night. A good deal of shelling has been going on this morning, but it is mostly our own. Captain Lowe and Mr, Browne came in while we were at dinner. It rained in the evening a good deal. A poor little child next door to us died of cholera; it was only taken ill about one o'clock and it was dead before seven. The poor mother was in a dreadful state just before it died, and afterwards perfectly calm. While we were undressing she came and asked if we had an empty box we could give her to bury the poor little thing in. We had not one long enough.

Friday, August 21st.

Just after we were in bed there was a great deal of firing, but it lasted a short time. There was a second attack during the night, I am thankful to say, however, that I did not hear it. I was awoke (it was scarcely daylight, and our lamp still burning) by Mrs, Pierce, with her little child in her arms, standing at the foot of my bed; she said she had spoken, but we were all asleep and none had answered her. She appeared very much frightened, and awaking in that confused way, I really at first imagined the insurgents had got in. I tried to awaken Mrs. Inglis, but she was so sound asleep that I could not make her hear. Mrs. Pierce then told me that our people were going to blow up Johannes' house, that the explosion would be very loud indeed, and that 100 men and Colonel Inglis and several officers had just passed by on their way towards the ladies' square.

I succeeded at last in awakening Mrs. Inglis, and soon after the mine exploded. It shook our room, but the noise was not loud. When it was over Mrs. Pierce went away, but she appeared very much frightened. We soon heard that the whole thing had been very successful. We had one man killed, one mortally wounded, two severely, and two slightly. It was sad to see the poor creatures carried through our courtyard before we were up. Another child of the poor Dedmans was seized with cholera this morning, and is not expected to live. Captain Barlow died this morning, he had been ill for some days. Captain Lowe was slightly wounded today; he had a very narrow escape of his life. A shell burst close to the bed on which he was lying, and took off the arm of a man beside him.

Mr. Edmonstone came and paid us a visit yesterday evening. He is looking much better. This has been a very quiet day, scarcely any firing at all. While we were at dinner Captain Wilson brought in a boy about eleven years old who had come over from the insurgents. He had been picking up bullets, and came near our sentry, who laid hold of him and got him in. He said that the enemy had been stealing some arms belonging to us at the Redan. It really is a perfect wonder to me that they do not get in altogether. He did not appear to give any particular information, but he describes the enemy as being in great numbers, and says that they intend going out and fighting our reinforcements in the open field when they arrive. Carry not at all well yesterday, but better today.

Saturday, August 22nd.

Last night was very quiet. Yesterday a sergeant of the 84th was killed—a very good man. From what he said before his death it would appear that he was well connected, and had a relative in this garrison. He had enlisted under the name of Allen. Dr. Scott left us today, as he considered it necessary to be at the hospital. Dr. Boyd having been taken ill. In the evening we walked up to the end of the road past the Ommanneys' house, farther than we have ever been since we were shut up here, and yet it is but a few paces. We lost three men yesterday.

Sunday, August 23rd.

There was Divine Service and the Holy Communion in the mess-room this morning. It was a melancholy Sunday indeed; three more men killed! While we were at dinner Mr. Foster came to say that the back verandah of the Residency had fallen in: fortunately no one was hurt. Dr. Scott came and had a cup of tea with us in the evening. He told us that distant guns had been heard from different places, but one gets weary of hearing reports which never come to anything. The Dedman's child is better, its illness is not cholera.

Monday, August 24th.

A man came from outside this morning and brought intelligence that our reinforcements are still at Cawnpore, the China force not having yet joined them, so that in fact they were nearer to us this day last month. Our people here seem to think that the man is a spy, and no great reliance is placed on what he says. He represents the insurgents as having suffered a good deal, and says that ninety were killed in the explosion of the mine the other day. The man was once a *kitmaghar* of Mrs. Hayes, and lived afterwards with the Coopers. So many children are sick now that one hears nearly every day of someone dying, and many children and grown up persons too are suffering from boils and eruptions on the skin.

Tuesday, August 25th.

Another sergeant of the 84th was mortally wounded yesterday, and one of the 32nd died of cholera. Mr. M'Crea, an officer of the engineers, was also wounded in the arm yesterday. Last night at twelve o'clock we were awoke by tremendous firing. The enemy made a sharp attack, but it only lasted a short time, and all the harm they did was slightly wounding two men of the 13th. To us, lying quietly in our beds watching the flashing of the guns and listening to the loud report of the cannon and bursting of the shells, it seems almost impossible to think otherwise than that they are rushing in upon us.

Today a suspicion seems to be afloat as to the fidelity of our *Sikhs*, but merely, I believe, because they were overheard saying they wanted their pay. Dr. Scott came to see us, but would not remain for tea.

Wednesday, August 26th.

When the *ayah* came in last night, she arrived with a very melancholy face, and told us that the insurgents had been knocking a hole in some place near the ladies' rooms, and having already made a good road to it, they were sure to get in there in three or four days. She also said she had heard that our reinforcements would not be here for three or four months. I wonder that we are not all getting more disheartened than we appear to be. I did not sleep well last night, and really to hear the firing going on the whole night long whenever one happens to awake is most wearing.

Nothing new this morning. Dr. Scott came to pay us his usual evening's visit. We thought him looking ill. He told us that Mr. Webb of the 32nd had just been killed. About eight p.m. Captain Wilson with a native came to Colonel Inglis's room. We at once imagined that a letter had been received from the relieving force, and remained in anxious suspense for some time, but we soon found that he was only a spy from *inside*, who had come to report on the feeling which pervades our native troops in the garrison.

Thursday, August 27th.

Colonel Inglis had a most merciful escape last night. He was standing on the bastion at Mr. Gubbins's house, close to Mr. Webb when he was killed. They saw the round shot coming, and went down to avoid it, but it hit Mr. Webb, and a native who was with him, killing them both instantaneously. It makes one shudder to think how death is hovering about and around us all; busy indeed has he been amongst this little garrison.

Mrs. Thornhill had a little girl last night. Sir Henry Lawrence's things are being sold today; heard of a ham being sold for 7*l.*, and a tin of soup sufficient only for one day's dinner for 1*l.*, 5s.!!! Money has ceased to be of any value, and people are giving unheard-of prices for stores of any kind—one dozen brandy, 20*l.*; one small box of vermicelli, 5*l.*; four small cakes of chocolate, 2*l.* 10s.!!!

At Mr. Gubbins's house, today, one man was killed, and another mortally wounded, both 32nd men. This evening has been very hot, and we could not sit out at all. The day has been very quiet.

Friday, August 28th.

A quiet night. Our people appear to think there will be another attack on the 31st, or perhaps sooner. They have been taking down the large doors in the room where we dine, to form barricades. A man of the 32nd killed today. We have not heard much firing.

A lovely moonlight night. Mrs. Inglis and I walked up and down the little space we have for nearly an hour; our topic—the only one from which we derive support at present and hope for the future-religion.

Saturday, August 29th.

A messenger came in last night from Cawnpore, bringing a letter from General Havelock to Colonel Inglis, as follows:—

Cawnpore, August 24, 1857.

My dear Colonel,

I have your letter of the 16th inst. I can only say, Hold on, and do not negotiate, but rather perish sword in hand. Sir Colin Campbell, who came out at a day's notice to command, upon the news arriving of General Anson's death, promises me fresh troops, and you will be my first care. The reinforcements may reach me in from twenty to twenty-five days, and I will prepare everything for a march on Lucknow.

Yours very sincerely,

H. Havelock,

Major-General.

Colonel Inglis, H.M. 32nd Regiment,

I fear that this will sadly dishearten all the natives inside, and with the weak state of our garrison, how are we to hold out a month longer? Faith and confidence in our Heavenly Father's protecting care will, I trust, support us under all the trials and difficulties which are before us. The messenger states, in his deposition, that there are three Indian regiments at Cawnpore; that the fall of Delhi was expected in twenty days; that we have a very large force surrounding it.

The insurgents had ceased to fire on Agra. The *Nana* at Cawnpore had been beaten twice by our troops, but fifty Europeans had been killed by falling into an ambush of (I think) the 42nd Native Infantry. He says that the insurgents are very numerous about us (11,000); that they have a council of war every day, and every day order an attack, but tomorrow and Tuesday are the great days they talk of. He says the rebels *say* the *Sikhs* and men of the 48th and 71st Native Infantry in here are in league with them, and will desert us, but he does not believe it. He says that they hear from people who go in and out everything that goes on inside, and he represents Lucknow as being a most difficult place to get to, or have any communication with. The worst of all this is, that if the siege continues as long as we should of course suppose it will, what a loss of valuable life there must be before it is raised!

A mine has been blown up by our people most successfully this morning, close to the ladies' room. They needed something to put them all in good spirits today. This morning has been very wet. Mrs. Bankes moved from Mr. Gubbins's house to some room near Mrs. Cooper's. She gave Mrs. Inglis a dreadful account of the number of round shot which went into the upper story of Mr. Gubbins's house. One came in while Mr. and Mrs. Gubbins were in bed; it struck the foot of the bed, and made them jump up a good deal frightened. Another poor soldier of the 32nd was killed last night.

Sunday, August 30th.

Heard this morning that twelve of our people from inside had deserted,—three drummers and their wives, a *kitmaghar* of Mrs. Cooper's, and other servants. The Gubbins's confidential servant, taking 400 *rupees* with him, and some others belonging to the same establishment, went off a few days ago. The Martins' youngest child died on Saturday. This day has been very quiet, and no attack as was anticipated.

Monday, August 31st.

Mrs. Inglis is not feeling well today, and does not look at all herself. This want of air and exercise, and prison life, tells more or less on all of us. Very hot. One of the 32nd men killed at the Gubbins's.

Tuesday, September 1st.

Last night about nine o'clock some heavy firing commenced, and we of course imagined it to be the signal for an attack, so carried off the three children into the large room, but did not remain there more than half an hour, as it turned out to be nothing. Colonel Inglis came in for a moment, and said that he did not think it would be much. I am always sorry when he gets so disturbed at night. He has not slept with his clothes off since the 16th of May! Today up to four o'clock very quiet. It is now stated that upwards of 300 *Europeans* have been killed since the commencement of the siege.

Wednesday, September 2nd.

Yesterday passed off very quietly, but two men of the artillery were killed at the postoffice in the evening, and a very serious loss they are, our trained men of this arm being so few. There was a good deal of musketry between ten and twelve last night. We had all our boxes and furniture moved out of our room this morning; carpets taken up, and all cleaned; day very hot. When Mrs. Inglis went to see Mrs. Cooper this evening, she heard that five babies had been buried during the night.

Thursday, September 3rd.

A sad thing has happened. Mr. Birch, an engineer officer, was killed by mistake by one of our own sentries last night. He was out on the fortification reconnoitring the enemy's ground, and the sentry, not having been warned, fired and shot him. He lived three or four hours, and was quite sensible to the last. He has left a wife, sister, and brother, all dependent on him. Poor Vokins died yesterday. We managed to get four tablecloths washed, but they do not look much better than they did before they went. Carry is washing our clothes today. Very hot. Got two of our boxes from the Residency, but there is not much in them that is of use to us now. Nearly everything we have is, I fear, lost in the Serah Roti. I have just been grieving over Carry's nice dressing box, besides a variety of other things endeared to us by fond associations, which I never expect to see again.

Saw Dr. Brydon out this evening for the first time since he was wounded; also saw Dr. Boyd, who is quite well again. Day quiet.

Friday, September 4th.

Quiet last night; but one man (32nd) mortally wounded. Nothing going on this morning, except a native report that our force was to cross the river today. If we could only hear for a certainty that they had actually started for Lucknow it would cheer us up a little; and, indeed, we need it. There is a native report that Maun Sing is here with 6,000 men. A man of the 32nd killed today. Major Bruce also killed while we were at dinner. He has left a wife and large family. The native soldiers of his regiment would not allow anyone but themselves to touch him after he was dead, and carried him to the grave, which is a great mark of their affection, as it is against their caste to touch a Christian after he is dead.

Saturday, September 5th.

Mrs. Inglis was called up at three this morning to Mrs. Cooper, who was taken ill: and she was brought over to our large room. She had a little girl about five o'clock, and is doing very well. About ten a.m. the enemy blew up two mines. The first was the most severe shock we have felt, but I am thankful to say they did no harm. An attack succeeded in which it appears the insurgents got well punished, though they had been preparing for it some time, and today I hear brought up their cavalry. I have not heard of any one being wounded, except one poor boy of the 32nd, who has lost his hand. I believe the enemy were more determined in their attack today than they have ever shown themselves before. A great part of the wall in the ladies' room was knocked down by a round shot yesterday while we were at dinner. A pensioner and a *sepoy* were killed today.

We have now to dine and breakfast in our little room. The only change we had in the twenty-four hours was going into the other room for our meals; so we are greater prisoners than ever. The cooing of some doves belonging to the servants, and a green tree before our door, are the only pleasant things that we have in our captivity!

Sunday, September 6th.

While Colonel Inglis was reading the morning service there was a good deal of firing, but the rest of the day has been quiet. An artilleryman killed. Weather very hot now. Dr. Scott came to see us yesterday evening; he looked ill. A native report says that the king is to leave this place tomorrow.

Monday, September 7th.

At ten last night, what appeared to us a fierce attack in the direction of the Brigade Mess commenced, and the firing was so loud that, each of us taking up a child, went over to Mrs. Cooper's room. Never saw such a small child as hers in my life. We did not stay there long, as the firing soon diminished. It appeared that the attack was only a blind, and that the insurgents were trying to burn down the Residency gate going out to cantonments, which was an unsuccessful move on their part. Reported this morning that a number of men, *hackeries*, and camels, were going over the bridge of boats, perhaps the king going off. Soap is become so scarce an article now that little square pieces are selling for seven *rupees*!!! Paid our servants today one month's wages, minus a *rupee* each. Two artillerymen wounded today. C. and T. went, after dinner, to look at the place where the wall in the ladies' room had fallen in.

Tuesday, September 8th.

Heard a good deal of firing during the night, and more bullets fell in our courtyard than have ever done before. Some of the bricks of the wall also came down. We thought we saw someone in the bathrooms in the night and were all frightened, and sent the *punkah Coolie* to see who it was, but it turned out to be the shadow of our own figures in the moonlight. Got a present yesterday of three pieces of soap from Dr. Scott. I forgot to mention that on Saturday last an officer committed suicide by shooting himself. Captain Simons (Artillery) died this morning.

Mrs. Inglis and I looked into the ladies' square in the evening. It seemed very wretched and miserable. Nearly all the ladies have moved out of it. We were saying to each other yesterday, how surprised people in England would be to hear how long we have been without bread, butter, vegetables, or eggs. Now and then one or two of the latter are procured for eight *annas* or one *rupee* each!!! *Many* people without milk or sugar, and all seem to be suffering from a scarcity of soap, which is worse than all, *I* think. A *dhoby* came this morning and said he would wash our things for ten *rupees* (1/.) the dozen, but without ironing them, and of course without starch and soap; so, as we can wash quite as well ourselves, we declined his services. We shall soon be reduced to our last cake of soap!

Wednesday, September 9th.

We blew up one of the enemy's mines this morning. The shock was very severe, and made much noise in our court-yard, as a good deal of plaster and mud fell down; a piece of a shell fell close to our door. None of our people were hurt, but I do not believe the explosion was so successful as was expected. It took place while we were at breakfast.

Captain Carnegie came and told Colonel Inglis this evening that the insurgents are fighting among themselves, and that they will not let the king go away from this. That he has not paid his troops, and that they are desirous of coming to terms with us, and even talk of a flag of truce; but it is evident that not the least reliance can be placed on these reports. All, however, are unanimous in thinking that the enemy are getting disheartened, and well they may, as hitherto they have been unsuccessful in everything they have undertaken. A great number of people seen about this evening.

Thursday, September 10th.

There was a good deal of firing during the night, and at times there has been a good deal this morning. The brass gun, which one would say was actually firing into our courtyard, is something dreadful in sound, and shakes one's whole frame. Nothing particular going on today. Carry and I walked for a long time this evening in the adjoining courtyard, and as there had been some very heavy rain previously, we found it cool and pleasant.

Friday, September 11th.

This morning at eleven o'clock we blew up one of the enemy's mines. It appears to have been very successful, but I believe there were several of the wretched creatures outside very badly wounded. The shock was extremely severe, and if Colonel Inglis had not insisted on every one of us remaining inside, someone would most likely have been killed by the large masses of brick-work which fell close to our door. The whole courtyard was full of them, and of branches of the trees which were knocked off in the crash. Carry has been washing all the morning, but it has been so rainy and windy that the things have all got wet again. Dr. Scott came this evening to see the children.

Saturday, September 12th.

Two men of the 32nd were wounded yesterday. A second mine,

somewhere near the church, was blown up by our people in the afternoon of yesterday, also with success. Poor little Johnny was very unwell last night. As all the three children are ill, our room is more like a hospital than anything else. Just as we were in the midst of dressing, washing, and having our room swept out, an old Frenchwoman, to whom we had given some clothes before the siege began, came to see us, and asked for some tea and old clothes, if we had any to give her, as she had lost those we had given her; but of course nothing of that kind do we possess beyond what we have for daily use.

Sunday, September 13th.

Last night a *grassent* belonging to the insurgents came in, and we read his deposition. He states our force to be 4000 strong and a regiment of *Sikhs*, and that they crossed the river on this side of Cawnpore four days ago; that Maun Sing is at Chinhut, waiting orders from our troops; that hitherto he had remained neutral, waiting, no doubt, to see which side will be victorious. If this be true it is good news for us, and I do trust ten days more will see our relief in Lucknow. Colonel Inglis appears more sanguine than I have yet seen him since the siege began. Captain Mansfield (32nd) was seized with cholera last night about twelve o'clock, and died before twelve this morning. As a man and an officer he will be universally regretted. Alas, the poor 32nd! how few remain now.

Monday, September 14th.

We hear that there is a great deal of excitement in the city today, and that a good many people are to be seen about this place. I believe that an attack is anticipated tomorrow. A man came in today from outside, supposed to be a spy. He represents himself as being the servant of some lady in the garrison. His story is that our reinforcements have *not* crossed the river. He says that there is to be an attack tomorrow, at least he had heard so, and that the *Nana* is here.

Tuesday, September 15th.

Captain Hutton, of the Engineers, was killed last evening about seven, on the top of Mr. Gubbins's house. He will be a dreadful loss, as he was most useful and active in his duties, and was very much liked. Mrs. Inglis and I went to see Mrs. Pearce yesterday evening. The weather is very *hot* now; Johnny not so well today; we have all colds, and most people are looking very ill. A man of the 32nd killed today, and one wounded. Little firing, and the day passed off very quietly. Heard yesterday that some men had been cutting a hole to get at the

Treasury.

I spoke to one of the drummers' wives of the 48th in the next square this evening, and she told me that she had heard that the murders at Cawnpore had been most brutal; that little children had been cut up and their bodies stuck on poles. One man, whose name she mentioned, they had tortured horribly; and had asked him, while they were killing him, "How he would like his mutton chops and bread and butter now?" She also says it is reported that these savages have murdered every Christian resident in Lucknow.

Wednesday, September 16th.

Day very quiet. A letter is to be sent off to our relieving force tonight, and if the messenger brings an answer he is to be most handsomely paid. We hear that there is a native report to the effect that Maun Sing as well as the *Nana* is here, that he has been ordered here by our force, and if such is the case it would lead us to believe that they are not far off. They also say that the insurgents wanted him to join them, and his reply was that he would show them how to take the place if they would give him up one side to himself, but this they refused to do, fearing he might be in league with us.

Thursday, September 17th.

Scarcely any firing during the day, but at about six o'clock this evening one of our own shells burst, and the pieces came back into the ladies' square, killing one child and wounding another, and also wounding two poor sweepers, one in the foot and the other in the hand. I saw the latter pass through our courtyard to the hospital, supported by two men, and he seemed to bear his pain wonderfully. A 32nd man was killed at the church by a round shot this evening.

Mrs. Inglis bought some coffee yesterday, and is to pay three *rupees* (6s.) a pound for it; tea is selling at *sixteen shillings per pound*! I went to see Mrs. Cooper this evening, and Carry and Mrs. Inglis went to see Mrs. Radclyffe.

Friday, September 18th.

Last night, about twelve o'clock, there was some heavy firing, but it soon subsided. This morning, while we were dressing, one of the enemy's shells or shrapnells burst, and brought down a quantity of brick in our courtyard, pieces of which hit the *khansamah* and *ayah's* boy, touching them, however, very slightly. At eleven a.m. there was a partial eclipse of the sun. Gave some of our clothes to a *dhoby* to wash; he charges fourteen *rupees* per hundred, without soap or starch! An enormous piece of wood, three feet three inches in circumference, and thirteen inches long, was sent over the house and fired into the ladies' square this afternoon.

No one could believe such a large mass could have come in in that way, unless they actually saw it. It is now supposed that the insurgents have 18 and 32 pounders. Carry and I walked for some time this evening in the next square, but were driven in by a bullet falling near us.

Saturday, September 19th.

Nothing worth noting has taken place. The day has been quieter than usual. Captain Mansfield's things were sold today, prices enormous, 55 *rupees* for an old flannel shirt; 21 *rupees* for one bottle of brandy! I think people are desponding and dispirited at getting no news from our force. It would almost seem as if they had neglected us altogether, and forgotten that such a place as Lucknow exists in the world.

Sunday, September 20th.

Heavy firing last night, and the guns sounded fearfully loud. Today, while Mrs. Inglis and Carry were at church a piece of shell fell deep into the ground close to the cook-room. Most fortunately none of the servants were sitting there at the time. Carry went to see Mrs. Polehampton this evening.

Monday, September 21st.

A good deal of heavy firing again last night. A bandsman of the 32nd was killed today. Several bullets have fallen in our courtyard. It began to rain before daylight this morning, and continued till three p.m. Evening quite cool and pleasant. Heard today for the first time that Mrs. Green was dead. She died three weeks ago.

Tuesday, September 22nd.

Very heavy rain last night; it poured down into our room, and we were obliged to get up and move the boxes and chairs, &c., to another part of the room. It continued without ceasing till three p.m., so our room became like a lake. Everything is damp and wretched-looking. Some desertions have occurred today; some *grassents* went away this morning, and some mess cooks in the evening. In consequence of the rain there has been little firing. Mr. Cunliffe, of the artillery, died today from fever. He had been ill some weeks.

Wednesday, September 23rd.

When Colonel Inglis came this morning, he brought us the delightful intelligence that his messenger had returned from our reinforcements during the night, and brought a letter from General Outram, who is coming here in command of the force. His letter was dated 20th September, and stated that they had nearly all crossed the river, and hoped to be with us very shortly. Indeed, had it not been for the very heavy rain we have had the last two days, they might have been here today. As it is we hope they will arrive by Sunday next. The force is said to consist of five European and one *Sikh* regiment. Captain Hardinge also got a letter from his cousin, who is with the advancing troops, and says that a great many regiments are on their way out from England, and that the sensation which all this terrible business has caused at home is something tremendous. The Crimean War, he says, was nothing to it. The Madras Presidency all quiet. In the Bombay, a few disturbances on a small scale.

We cannot be sufficiently thankful to find that our relief is so near, though no doubt there will still be some hard fighting before they reach the Residency gates. A round shot, a thirty-two pounder, came into our court today, knocking down a great piece of the wall, and lodging in the top of an archway. A bullet fell *close* to where Azaib was sitting. Spoke to Dr. and Mrs. Brydon this evening, as they passed through on their way to see Mrs. Cooper.

Thursday, September 24th.

Distant guns have been heard during, the day, but whether they are our reinforcements or the insurgents fighting among themselves, nobody knows. Some say they sound nearer than yesterday, and that even the smoke was seen. They have been firing a good deal into our courtyard. Two round shots came in, and the hall has been more knocked about during the last two days than during the whole siege. Mrs. Cooper moved back into her friend's room yesterday evening.

Friday, September 25th.

What a day is this to be remembered for life with gratitude towards our Heavenly Father, for his great mercies, by all those who have lived through this siege! Our relief has arrived! Firing was heard all day, and at times very heavy. About noon our force was entering the city, and at four p.m. the firing in the direction of the old bandstand was said to be very loud, though we did not hear it in our courtyard. At six we were sitting outside our door, when cheers were heard; great excitement prevailed; servants and soldiers passed by at the most rapid pace, and Ellicock came up to us looking as pale as a sheet from excitement, and saying that some of the troops had at last arrived at the Residency.

They consist, I believe, of the 78th Highlanders, and some of the Madras Fusiliers, besides Artillery; Sir James Outram and General Havelock both with them. They left Cawnpore on the 18th, and their losses coming here have been *very severe.* We hear that they have had 500 killed (a good many officers), and a number of wounded have been brought in. They have come up without tents through all the heavy rain, and with scarcely any provisions. The insurgents had cut trenches in the streets, and loop-holed the houses, so that they could fire down upon them, and shoot them like dogs. It is described as having been a most *murderous* affair!

The bodies of two young ladies were seen lying dead in the street, as if just killed, but who they were, or where they came from, I cannot learn. Sir James Outram has been slightly wounded. I have also heard that the young king who was placed on the throne a short time ago has been wounded. The rest of the force are expected in tomorrow. Captain Radclyffe has been badly wounded in the arm today.

The horrors these brutal wretches committed at Cawnpore are beyond description. Two officers only, we hear, escaped, *all the rest, with the women and children,* were butchered in the most fearful manner; many, while their bodies were still warm, were thrown into a place which was used in the barracks as a bath for the women. Little children of all ages were *cut up* into pieces and roasted before their parents' eyes; and poor old Sir Hugh Wheler was treated in some horrible way after they had killed him. Such would have been our fate, had it not pleased a God of Mercy to send us relief in time. The noise and excitement consequent on the arrival of the troops is dreadful; and how we shall get any sleep I know not.

Chapter 10

September 26th - October 10th

Saturday, September 26th.

General Havelock breakfasted with us this morning, and said he considered their losses yesterday must have been nearer 600 than 500. Brigadier Neill was killed by one of the last shots fired. The servants and natives were looting all day long and bringing in all kinds of things. Mr. Birch tells us that the scene outside is beyond description. Bullocks, camels, baggage of all description, and wounded men, being brought in; natives and soldiers plundering all they can lay their hands on. Ellicock says it is more like Donnybrook Fair than anything else.

The 90th Regiment have been trying hard all day to make their way in, and every available man in the garrison (all the 32nd I believe) has gone to their assistance. They will encounter great difficulty in getting the baggage and ammunition across the river. The latter is to be brought over on camels, and orders are given that two Europeans are to be at the head of each camel as they cross, to prevent accidents. This has been a sad day from the great anxiety entertained about the safety of the remainder of the force. The casualties are expected to be very numerous.

Three mines were discovered today, which the enemy were just prepared to blow up. Colonel Campbell of the 90th, who was wounded yesterday, was brought into Colonel Inglis's room just before dinner, and is to remain there, as it will be quieter. The scene while we were at dinner today, the appearance of the room, and the whole circumstances, we can never forget! Mr. Thornhill is badly wounded, also Mr. Joly (32nd) and Captain Hughes, who is attached to them, yesterday. I dread to hear of the casualties there will have been today. Colonel Inglis has been appointed to the vacant Brigade. He has dearly earned any honours to which he may succeed by all the wear and tear and responsibility he has undergone during this dreadful siege.

Sunday, September 27th.

After all this has been a very painful day; everyone is depressed, and all feel that we are in fact *not relieved*. The fighting men we have are too few for our emergency, and too many for the provisions we have in the garrison. A party went out today to try and take some of the enemy's guns (100 of the 5th Fusiliers, 18 of the 32nd, Mr. Warnal commanding). The latter led the sortie; they had three men killed and four wounded, and the Fusiliers one killed and one wounded. Did not take any guns, but spiked two.

Captain Barrow called and gave a fearful account of the massacre at Cawnpore, which took place the very day that General Havelock's force marched in to relieve them. Poor Mrs. Moore was the only lady of the 32nd who was *killed*, the others died of the hardships they had to undergo. When the people from Futtyghur arrived there, these savages took all the officers and separated them from their wives. They, poor things, declared that they would die with their husbands, and rushed to them, but they were all with the exception of one torn from them, and shut up in the place where the other women were, after which they were all murdered; and they and all the children, some of them their bodies still warm, were thrown into a well. Horrors indescribable were committed. We saw Dr. Scott this evening; he looked fairly done up, and said he had never been so hard-worked in all his life. He really looked so changed, that I should hardly have known him.

Monday, September 28th.

Captain Hughes died this morning, and Mr. Alexander, of the artillery, was wounded and died in the course of the day. A party was to have been sent out this morning to try again to take the guns, but it is put off till tomorrow. The 90th Regiment, with the baggage, have not yet arrived in the Presidency, but have entrenched themselves about four miles outside the city.

This has been a sad day. I have never felt more weary or more depressed since we came into this place. I do not know how we are to get on much longer. An attack is anticipated tonight. The 32nd and 5th Fusiliers are the only regiments inside; the others are located in houses close by. Saw Mrs. Boileau this evening. I gave up taking sugar today, and we are using our last piece of soap.

Tuesday, September 29th.

Awoke this morning about four o'clock, and saw the party assemble in our court to go out and take the guns. It made my heart sad to see them, knowing that so many of the poor fellows would not return alive. They started shortly before five, composed of parties from the different regiments here, the brave, gallant 32nd, as usual, leading, commanded by Mr. M'Cabe, who has distinguished himself greatly. This was the fourth sortie he has led, and is his last, for he fell mortally wounded, and cannot live through the day. He will be a great loss, for he was a right good officer; had got his commission for bravery, and now he has died a soldier's death.

The party returned about ten o'clock. They took seven guns, most of which had on previous occasions been spiked by the 32nd. Mr. Lucas was mortally wounded, Mr. Edmonstone slightly, and the officer commanding the 5th Fusiliers was killed. The total amount of killed and wounded we have not yet heard. The 32nd behaved, as they always do, *nobly*. We hear that Colonel Brooke has exchanged with a colonel from the Guards, who is supposed to be at Calcutta by this time.

Captain Moore's poor old faithful *khitmaghar* came to see us this morning, and confirmed all we had heard of the horrors of the Cawnpore massacre. He remained with them to the last. Captain Moore was killed in the boat in which the treacherous *Nana* agreed to allow them to escape, and Mrs, Moore was taken out and confined with all the other ladies, women and children. The hardships they underwent were fearful. The only food they had was rice and *dhal*. Many ladies died before they got out of the fort, and those who survived to that time were all murdered. The poor old *khitmaghar* was himself imprisoned, and the rope to hang him was actually round his neck, but he contrived to escape. Two days before she was killed, poor Mrs. Moore gave him a letter to her friends in England, and Captain Moore's picture, to try and send home if he could. They were found on his person, and torn before his face into atoms.

The gallantry of the devoted 32nd in the affair of today, as well as throughout the whole siege, is now the topic of conversation. One man of the regiment, Webster by name, went out alone and spiked one of the guns. Mr. Edmonstone behaved nobly. I hear they talk of carrying the stone bridge tomorrow or next day, on which occasion the 32nd are again to lead the way, Colonel Inglis himself going out, I believe, with them. Our rations are to be reduced from tomorrow, wine and beer are nearly all finished, and we shall have to grind our own "*attah*."

Nothing seems to be settled as to what is to be done about the sick and wounded, and women and children. Mrs. Gall came to see us this evening, and I found that they had often, like ourselves, consulted together as to whether it would be wrong to put an end to our own lives if the insurgents were to get in. Different opinions entertained on the subject.

Wednesday, September 30th.

This has been a very quiet day. Nothing particular going on. Colonel Inglis has been very unwell, and not able to leave his room. Weather very hot. Heard this evening that there is a report that Nana Sing has been murdered. This is not unlikely if he wished to declare himself on our side. Captain Hardinge is going tonight on what must be a very dangerous expedition. He proposes to go with his *Sikhs* to the place where the remainder of our force are with the baggage, four miles from this, in a garden on the Cawnpore road, and to try and establish some communication between them and this place. I trust he will return in safety, for he is a brave, good officer; but the risk seems great when we think of the sad fate that has attended so many who have gone out on similar expeditions.

Thursday, October 1st.

Colonel Inglis better this morning. Captain Hardinge could not get out to Allumbagh with his *Sikhs* last night. They were fired on as soon as they were seen, and obliged to come back and give up the attempt. I spoke to a man who came in with the force from Cawnpore; he is a tailor, belonging to the regiment. He gave an alarming account of the *numbers* outside; he said he thought that there were about 100,000 men about this place, and that the *Nana* is with them. He had seen our poor old bungalows, and says that they are occupied by *sepoys*. I could hear nothing of our servants from him.

A party of men from different regiments started today, about four p.m., to take possession of some houses near this. They have not yet returned, but, I believe, have been getting on well, and we have just heard they have taken one of the Bazaars. So I hope some provisions may be procured. Mrs. Inglis bought half-a-pound of common sugar today, for which she gave four *rupees*! We spoke to Mr. Browne, Mr. Foster, and Captain Bessano, as they were standing in our court with their mess. They tell us that there are now only four officers and about 250 men of the 32nd fit for duty. Alas! the poor 32nd; how I grieve to think of them.

At this present time, there are 800 wounded in this garrison, and 410 women and children. When we do get away, what an undertaking it will be! Mr. M'Cabe died this morning. Poor Captain Radclyffe is sinking fast, Mrs. Cooper's baby died this evening. Mrs. Inglis's baby has been ill today.

Friday, October 2nd.

Poor Captain Radclyffe died last night, about half-past ten. A party went out this morning and got possession of some of the enemy's guns. I believe they have now no guns just round the Residency. They took them away last night, while they made a feigned attack. The firing, to us, sounded loud and near. When our men went out, on Tuesday, to take the guns, two of them (one 32nd and the other Madras Fusiliers) fell into a well, and there remained till this morning. The former was killed, but not the latter, who, however, was afraid to call out, till he heard European voices, go by. They threw him a rope down and pulled him up, none the worse, only suffering, as may be supposed, from the most ravenous hunger. Truly he had a wonderful escape!

Saturday, October 3rd.

A very quiet day; scarcely a shot fired. There appears to be a perfect stagnation of everything; but I suppose they must be doing something towards advancing matters. Distant guns have been heard in the direction of Allumbagh, where the force with the baggage are. They have with them 250 fighting men, and provisions for the whole force here for a fortnight. Everything is now getting very scarce: sugar, almost impossible to be got for any price; 25 *rupees* was offered today for a *seer* (2 lbs.), and without success; 25 *rupees* for one bottle of brandy. Mrs. Inglis bought some soap; 4 *rupees* for a very small cake of *common* brown! I got one of my boxes from the Residency; it was so knocked about by shot and shell—having formed a barricade—that I should not have recognised it, and everything inside was ruined. Tomorrow I am going to examine another through which a round shot has been.

We certainly have been very unfortunate as regards our things; but I would have cared for nothing, could I but have preserved my Bombay box with all my precious letters and William's picture. But all are gone, and regrets will not recall them.

Sunday, October 4th.

Read the colonel's despatch, which is going to be sent to Calcutta. It gives a very clear and good account of the whole siege. Went to Morning Service, and received the Holy Communion. Afterwards I went to see Mrs. Radclyffe, who looked very ill. Poor thing I how I feel for her! This has been a quiet day, till about nine p.m., when the enemy made some noise; and four bullets fell in our courtyard in a very short space of time.

Monday, October 5th.

A most flattering Order published by Sir James Outram about the manner in which this garrison has been defended by Colonel Inglis and the officers and men under his command. The whole affair he describes as being unparalleled in the annals of history. I hope Colonel Inglis is certain of being made a K.C.B. A letter has been received today from the troops at Allumbagh. They had made a sortie, and had got in some provisions. Ours are rapidly diminishing; and today we have begun to restrict ourselves to two *chupatties* each a day; and soon, I fear, we shall have to eat horseflesh; but as yet we have beef and rice. I have been hungry today, and could have eaten more, had I had it. Seven men and three officers came in today from the Fureed Bux, badly wounded. Mrs. Roberts came to see us this morning, and told us the chloroform at the hospital is all gone. Mrs. Omiley's two children both died in one hour a day or two ago.

Tuesday, October 6th.

This morning, between eight and nine a.m., the enemy blew up a mine, and commenced an attack which lasted nearly three hours. They regained the position which our people had got possession of yesterday. A serjeant of the 32nd was killed and one man wounded, and two of the 90th slightly injured in the explosion. From what I heard, it appears that the attack had more plan and system in it than the former ones. I went this evening to see Mrs. Radclyffe. We had a visit from Mrs. Giddings.

Wednesday, October 7th.

Our people have been blowing up houses this morning. Little firing during the early part of the day; but between five and six o'clock, just as we were sitting down to dinner, the enemy commenced a heavy fire on the Cawnpore Battery, and they have been pounding away ever since till the hour I am now writing—nine p.m. I got 100 *rupees* today from Mr. Giddings, and gave the servants a little money each towards their wages; Azaib and Din Mahomet have had eighteen *rupees* each, and the two *Coolies* eight each. Mrs. Cooper came to see us in the afternoon. The weather still continues very warm.

Thursday, October 8th.

A quiet day. Heard that 250 men and twenty cartloads of provisions had reached Allumbagh yesterday from Cawnpore. Decidedly our people in the garrison seem in a brighter mood today, and talk of the strong force coming up, and which is said to be now between Calcutta and Cawnpore; though the general opinion is that a month at least must elapse before more troops will be here. Captain Barrow came to see us today. He said that from the time they left Cawnpore up to this date there have been 24 officers and 240 men killed, and 44 officers and 772 men wounded.

A man of the 32nd, while walking out near some of the works this morning, saw something like a garment of some kind lying on the ground, and on going to pick it up, found two bags of *rupees*, each containing 500 *rupees*. An easy way of making 100*l*.

Captain and Mrs. Orr came to see us this evening. Mr. Edmonstone also paid us a long visit. He told us that he had heard a report had gone to England some time ago that our garrison here had been cut to pieces! Mrs. Orr mentioned a very narrow escape she had some time ago. She was sitting on a chair outside her door, and was in the act of leaning forward to pick up something for her child, when a round shot came in and broke the chair she was sitting on, without touching her.

A gentleman, a few days ago, had half his pillow carried off by a round shot whilst he was lying on it, and it did not even awake him. These wonderful escapes are so frequent here that one hears them related without feeling much astonishment; but I think that should we ever find ourselves once again in safety, and able calmly to reflect over what we have heard and seen during the siege, it will surprise even our own selves.

Friday, October 9th.

Day quiet. Mr. Cromelin, of the Engineers, whom we formerly knew at Peshawur, came to see us. A letter has been received by Sir James Outram this evening from the officer commanding at Cawnpore, stating:

> that Delhi has positively fallen at last; that our losses there have been sixty-one officers and 2000 men killed and wounded; that they have had an addition to their force at Cawnpore of 300 men; and that at Allumbagh they have now 500 men, and have been able to go out and scour the country and get in some provisions.

There is a report in the garrison that Maun Sing has offered to take charge of the sick and wounded and women and children, if a force is sent out from this, but I cannot vouch for the truth of it, nor do I think, after all the treachery we have heard of on the part of the natives, that many would be anxious to entrust themselves to his care, though he has saved the lives of some ladies, whose names I have heard mentioned.

Saturday, October 10th.

The more this siege is talked of, the more wonderful does it appear how the insurgents around us have been kept at bay so long, when our garrison was so weak and our position was such a bad one. At one time we were so much in want of artillerymen, that the men who manned the guns had actually to run from one to the other as they were required to load and fire. We heard that at one time the enemy had made a breach large enough for a regiment to march in in perfect order, and yet they did not take advantage of it.

It appears quite marvellous. Maun Sing has been wounded they say. An attack seems to be anticipated tonight; and all the sentries are to be doubled. A good many people have been seen today about the bridge of boats. More going away than coming in. Several artillery horses, all harnessed but without guns, came in this direction. Dr. Scott came while we were at dinner, and mentioned the names of several people who had died or were killed at Delhi; amongst them, Brigadiers Halifax and Reid, General Barnard, Colonel Chester, and others whom I cannot remember; but their losses have been small in comparison to ours since the relieving force left Cawnpore.

Chapter 11

October 11th - November 3rd

Sunday, October 11th, 1857.

This has been a quieter day than usual. We went to Divine Service in the morning. The enemy blew up two mines, but, as usual, they were unsuccessful, though a soldier of the 78th was killed by one. Mrs. Brydon came to see us this evening, and gave us a melancholy account of the death of Captain Beecher (of the Artillery) who was wounded in the arm coming in with the Relieving Force, and died of lock-jaw. She also gave us a sad description of three days at the Gubbins's, when Mrs. Dorin and Major Banks were killed, and Captains Forbes and Grant wounded in the early part of the siege, also Dr. Brydon, while sitting at the dinner table. It made one's heart sick to listen to the sad details.

Monday, October 12th.

Last night letters from Major Bruce, at Cawnpore, were brought in by a messenger. They stated that a force from Delhi was moving up towards this place, and was expected to be at Alleyghur on the 5th instant, which would bring them to Cawnpore about the 20th. More troops are arriving every day at the latter place. Captain and Mrs. Barwell came to see us this evening. Mrs. Inglis has been writing a very tiny letter to her family, and a messenger has been found who, I believe, will take it out this evening. It is addressed to Brigadier Wilson, at Cawnpore, who is to forward it to Colonel Birch, at Calcutta. I trust it may arrive safely, as at such a time news will be beyond any price to those who have friends here.

Tuesday, October 13th.

Day very quiet. No news of any kind. The mornings and evenings are now delightfully cool, but the days hot. Mr. Thornhill died yesterday afternoon. The enemy have been so quiet during the last few days, that they must be meditating plans of mischief, and when they do make another attack I fear it will be a sharp one. Captain Barrow, Mrs. Giddings, and Mrs. Orr came to see us this evening.

Wednesday, October 14th.

Another quiet day; the enemy made a *demonstration* last night, and fired a good deal. While we were at breakfast this morning a message was brought to Colonel Inglis, reporting that some Sikhs from outside were anxious to come in, and wished to know whether they would be pardoned if they go out and fight on our side with the force which is coming up. The reply given them by Captain Harding, was to "go and do their best." Maun Sing has made an offer to protect us all and fight on our side, if the authorities decide on coming to terms with him, which if they did would, probably, end in our being sent off sooner than we at present expect; but I should feel very doubtful and suspicious of even Maun Sing's promises now, after the fatal Cawnpore business; I fear there is treachery somewhere!

Poor Mr. Harmer came to see us this evening, walking on crutches, and looking very different from the fresh rosy boy he was when at Kurrachee with us, just out from England, little more than twenty months ago! I fear he will always be lame. It made me quite sad to see him. Mrs. Giddings, Mrs. Orr, and Mrs. Boileau passed through our square this evening. Colonel Inglis sent his tiny English note off at last, addressed to Brigadier Wilson, at Cawnpore.

Thursday, October 15th.

Another quiet day. Colonel Inglis brought us some *beautiful* jewels to show us. An old pensioner who came to see Colonel Inglis this evening, talked much over the present state of affairs. He mentioned the names of some of the great men who are fighting against us. Captain Barrow came while he was here, and acted as interpreter. I have been so lame all day that I can scarcely put my foot to the ground.

Friday, October 16th.

I believe an attack was expected today, but up to this hour (nine p.m.) all has been quiet. Caroline went to see Mrs. Polehampton and Mrs. Gall and Mrs. Barber this evening. The evenings and mornings are quite cold now, and I think it is very chilly with the *punkah.*

Saturday, October 17th.

A great deal of firing last night, but it does not appear that the enemy did any mischief, though from the sound, round shot and bullets seemed to fall close to our courtyard. No news of any kind today, except that distant guns were heard yesterday. Heard the bagpipes this evening for the first time.

Sunday, October 18th.

Carry and I attended Divine Service this morning. Three men came in from Cawnpore last night; they say troops are coming in every day to that place. The 93rd and 23rd Regiments, and four troops of Horse Artillery are on their way from Calcutta. A *Sikh* came in with a message from Maun Sing, saying that he had always served our government and still wished to do so; that he was willing to withdraw and that he would protect us and give us assistance whenever our force marched out of this place, but that he has only 10,000 men that he can positively depend upon.

Mrs. Giddings came to see us this evening; she does not appear the worse for the siege, but looks in better health and is better dressed than any one I see. We have been out of soap for some days and are now obliged to wash with what is called "*bason*" (ground grain made into a paste with water). It is a nice clean thing, and the best substitute for soap.

Monday, October 19th.

A *Home News* was brought in last night from Allumbagh, date "26th August." Quite an event, and everyone in the garrison most anxious of course to have a look at it. We got it here for an hour. They had heard, in England, of Sir Henry Lawrence's death, but do not appear to have had any account of the Cawnpore massacre or Lucknow siege, as no mention is made of either. Got in some sugar and, I believe, a few other provisions, into the garrison last night. Between eleven and twelve last night the enemy commenced one of their unmeaning attacks. The musketry was very sharp indeed for a short time, but they did us no mischief.

A letter has been sent from Sir James Outram to Maun Sing today, but the contents I have not heard. Probably it tends rather to negotiating; and to have him as an ally would no doubt be a great thing for us, as we should then be enabled to get in provisions for the sick and wounded, who are very badly off for everything. I am so lame from an inflamed foot that I can scarcely walk a step. Captain Barrow came to see us this evening. I went to see Mrs. Radclyffe. In consequence of Colonel Inglis having laid in a small store of provisions, we are better off than most people in the way of food, but beef, rice, *dhal*, and *chupatties* are the only eatables ever seen now, and even a small quantity of sugar coming into the garrison is quite an event.

Yesterday, while Johnny and I were walking in the next square, a *Sikh* officer passing quite close to us was shot in the arm by a bullet. Captain Barrow had a very narrow escape a few days ago, a bullet passing through his hat without touching him.

Tuesday, October 20th.

A messenger arrived last night from Cawnpore, bringing word that troops were daily coming up to that place. A native reports in the garrison today that the Delhi Force is at Futtyghur (seven marches from Cawnpore). A child near the Residency had half its head carried away this morning by the bursting of a shell, and another was badly wounded. Captain Gordon of the 6th Native Infantry, acting here as Judge Advocate General, called on Mrs. Inglis today. He had been *Aide-de-Camp* to General Neill. He told us that at Allahabad fourteen officers, out of seventeen who had sat down to mess, were murdered by their own men, when the *sepoys* rose there; one poor ensign escaped murder, but died of starvation. Also that the *Rajah* of Gwalior is not fighting against us, but that he cannot restrain his men, who with thirty-one guns have joined the other mutineers.

I find that Sir Henry Lawrence's death was made known in England by a letter which Mr. Gubbins wrote to the Governor-General very soon after the occurrence. 10 p.m.—We have just heard that a letter has arrived for Sir James Outram, from Maun Sing, and that the purport of it is that Maun Sing will fight for us if he is pardoned and his life spared. He has a force of 10,000 men.

Wednesday, October 21st.

A quiet night, but a good deal of firing this morning. When Colonel Inglis came to breakfast, he told us that a young boy (an apothecary belonging to the 32nd) was killed by a round shot while asleep in his bed at the hospital this morning, poor fellow!

From what we hear, Maun Sing appears to have made strong professions of his willingness to assist us, in his letter of last night, and negotiating with him will, probably, be the order of the day. Much confidence does not seem to be placed in any good that he can do us, for they say he has very little power, and the fidelity of his followers, when once he joins us, is, after all, doubtful.

What a state this country is in. Scarcely a native regiment has remained entirely true to us, and every day one hears some new tale of horror of the past massacres which makes one's heart sicken. The enemy blew up two mines today, but did no harm. One of the 78th had both his legs taken off by a round shot while standing in a room, talking to some of his comrades. I went to see Mrs. Radclyffe this evening, and found Mrs. Clarke with her, who told me some more dreadful things about the poor people at Cawnpore, which she had heard from one of the two officers who alone escaped from that fatal place.

Thursday, October 22nd.

Distant guns and musketry were heard this morning while we were dressing; supposed to be the enemy making an attack on Allumbagh. It did not appear to last very long. A quantity of shawls, chiefly Umritsur manufacture, were brought for us to look at. I did not see one I admired. Mrs. Pearce came in the evening to show us her baby, and Mrs. Need brought in her children. Some people complain of the want of provisions, but most seem to have enough, though, of course, no variety; and I must say, I am beginning to get very tired of beef and rice every day for so long. I am more weary than I can ever express of this sad captivity. I feel at times so melancholy.

Friday, October 23rd.

No news today of any kind, except the pleasing intelligence that we are better supplied with food than was supposed, and now they say we can hold out for thirty-three days longer as regards provisions. A great sale has been going on in the Brigade Mess-room. We hear that two bottles of champagne have been sold for twelve *rupees* each, and a bottle of brandy, thirty *rupees!* Three *rupees* can be got any day for *one cigar.* Mr. Charlton paid us a visit this evening; he looks dreadfully ill, and very weak. Mrs. Giddings also called this evening, and Mrs. Cooper came in just as we had finished dinner.

Saturday, October 24th.

This morning, at breakfast, Colonel Inglis informed us that arrangements had been made that our provisions might last till the 1st of December, and in consequence our rations (with the exception of the meat) are to be reduced tomorrow. They do not appear to think that Maun Sing has any intention of assisting us, in consequence of which we must make up our minds to wait till our relief comes in, and go on as we are now doing. The evident intention of the insurgents is to try and starve us out. Sir J. Outram gave a man the other day 1000 *rupees* to go and bring in some sugar from some place in one of the enemy's positions; but the man never returned. Colonel Campbell is very unwell today. I went to see Mrs. Radclyffe, and found Captain Barrow sitting with Mrs. Inglis when I came back.

Sunday, October 25th.

Carry and I attended Divine Service and Holy Communion this morning. Maun Sing's *vakeel* came in with a message from his master, the particulars of which I have not heard. Captain Wilson, Colonel Napier, and Captain Birch, came to drink tea with us yesterday evening, which was quite an event in our quiet life. Mrs. Inglis has been suffering a good deal from her foot, but her patience is wonderful.

Monday, October 26th.

A messenger Came in last night with the news that a force, under Colonel Greathed of H.M. 8th Regiment, had gone out from Agra, had an engagement with the enemy, beaten them, and taken twelve of their guns; and also had had a fight with the rebels at Bithoor. Troops are said to be coming in every day to Cawnpore from Calcutta. Heard today that Maun Sing had proposed having an underground passage into this place, that he and his followers might come in and out as they liked; by no means a pleasant idea!

At times, how very dark and gloomy our prospects appear. Now that the insurgents are getting well beaten at Delhi and elsewhere, I fear they will all make for this place. A good many *sepoys* have been seen today coming over the bridge, and it was remarked, as an unusual thing, that they stopped and spoke to those they met going out. The enemy have been getting two guns into position this evening to bear upon the Brigade Mess. It is thought that they will do us a great deal of mischief.

As expected, our rations have been reduced today, with the exception of the meat. We are now commencing on two *attah chupatties* each a day, and two made of *gram* between us all. I am more distressed about the want of soap than anything else. The weather just now is very pleasant, and a *punkah* quite unnecessary, except to keep off the mosquitoes at night. Mrs. Cooper came in for a few minutes today, and appeared very desponding about the reduction of the provisions. Colonel Campbell called today: he has been improving ever since Dr. Scott took him in hand.

Tuesday, October 27th.

Another messenger came in last night with a letter for Sir James Outram. Five hundred men with provisions have arrived at Allumbagh, and 1000 more troops at Cawnpore, so that altogether the news is good, though at times our little garrison seems depressed. It is reported that a good many of the Delhi rebels have gone to their homes, which I hope is true, and then we shall not have them adding to the numbers against us here. Captain Barrow came for a few minutes this afternoon.

At eight p.m. this evening another messenger from Maun Sing came in, but not the man they wanted. Evidently some plan for negotiating is thought of. The messenger who came in states that Miss Jackson and her brother were brought into Lucknow yesterday in irons and are under the care of Maun Sing, who has hitherto protected them.

Poor young girl! who knows what misery and suffering she may have undergone. Her fate, with that of her brother and sister, has caused great interest ever since the commencement of the outbreak in the district. I have not heard what has become of her sister, but no doubt some diplomatic reason has caused Maun Sing to bring these two individuals to Lucknow just now. Mr. Graydon (44th Native Infantry) has been mortally wounded today. A very good officer, and a great loss he will be. Colonel Inglis says.

Wednesday, October 28th.

News came in last night that the force from Delhi has arrived at Cawnpore. Another messenger in today from Maun Sing. He said that his master did not like to send the man we wanted, as he fears to risk his life coming in. I suppose he is one of his chiefs. He says Maun Sing is ready to obey General Havelock's orders, and will send in another man tomorrow. I hear there are some other fugitives with Sir M. Jackson and his sister—Captain Orr's brother among the number. It seems that they have not been under Maun Sing's protection, but that he has offered large bribes to get them made over to him. If the general comes to terms with Maun Sing it may perhaps enable us all to get away from this place sooner than we at present expect. Mrs. Inglis better today, and Dr. Scott has not paid us his usual visit. Mr. Birch came and sat with us for a short time after dinner. I went over to speak to Colonel Campbell this afternoon, and was glad to find him better.

Thursday, October 29th.

A messenger came in this morning from Allumbagh. Our troops there have got provisions to last them for some time. The enemy are constructing a battery close to them. Some anxiety seems to be felt regarding the Gwalior troops, who, it is thought, are marching towards Lucknow, having with them a siege train, so if they were to come here they would be by no means a pleasant addition to the numbers outside. Thc losses at Delhi have been very great. I hear sixty-one officers have been killed and wounded.

Captain Barrow came to see us for a few minutes today: he said he thought our force might be here on the 10th of next month. Saw Colonel Campbell for a few minutes this afternoon. He is better, but still looks very ill.

Friday, October 30th.

No news today of any kind. Went to see Mrs. Cooper this morning, and also Mrs. Banks. Saw *The Friend of India* for a few minutes. The whole country appears to be in an unsettled and disturbed state. Every paper one sees, and all one hears, tends to confirm this. The enemy blew up a mine this morning near the place where the 78th Highlanders are quartered, but it fortunately did no harm. Dr. Scott called this evening, just for a few minutes, on his way to Colonel Campbell.

The state of our garrison here, as regards the 32nd Regiment, in numbers was, on the 29th June 651, and on the 25th. September 401! A sad list of killed in all this sad business.

Saturday, October 31st.

A messenger has been in today from Maun Sing. He has stated, I believe, that he is willing to withdraw, and the general has given him four days to do so. We shall be anxious to see the result. A letter has been received from Captain Orr's brother; it is signed by all their party, and says that they are well treated, and very happy. It is likely that they may have been forced to write it, but such, I hope, is not the case, and trust that their statement is true, poor things. Several bullets have fallen in our court today. Captain Barrow and Mr. Birch came this evening, and had some tea with us. There was a great sale yesterday, and I believe one again today.

Sunday, November 1st.

A very quiet day; no news of any kind; attended Divine Service. Went to see Mrs. Radclyffe before dinner. Captain Barrow dined with us. The nights are now most lovely, and I believe tonight is full moon. An 18-pound shot went into the Fayrers' house yesterday, into Mrs. Barwell's room, and hit the place where she always sits; but most fortunately she was out spending the day with a friend.

Monday, November 2nd.

There have been several casualties today; Mr. Grant, an officer of the 41st Native Infantry, and five Europeans and seven *Sikhs* wounded. A messenger came in from Allumbagh this evening, with a letter stating that Sir Colin Campbell is expected at Cawnpore today with an additional force of 1000 men, which, if true, is very good news. He states that a large force of ours is at Bunnee, but that is only a native report. He adds that, as he came through the city, he saw a great many *sowars*, and they gave him this piece of intelligence; also that the enemy intend making an attack tonight.

Captain Birch came and had tea with us. Our evenings and mornings are now quite cold. Got our rations today. If everyone gets the same rations we do, I am sure no one need be starving; for *we* have plenty, owing to Mrs. Inglis's good management in always weighing out the exact quantity of *attah* required for the *chupatties* we use each day.

Tuesday, November 3rd.

Nothing particular has been going on today. There was no attack last night. I do not think Colonel Inglis expects the reinforcements to arrive here before the 20th or 30th. I talked to Colonel Campbell for a short time this afternoon, and found out that he had known my dear brother when they were together in the Crimea. Colonel Campbell had command of the party which held the "Quarries" the night of that fatal 8th of June, when dearest William was killed. What a fatal month June has been to me! Mr. Birch came and had tea with us this evening. He told us a good deal about the dreadful doings at Cawnpore, and one tale seems more dreadful than another.

Three officers only and one man escaped the massacre. Fifteen Europeans took refuge in a mosque near the river, which the enemy surrounded, and then set fire to the brushwood to prevent their escape. A consultation was held as to what would be best for them to do, when it was found that only three officers and two men could swim; and in order to save these, the remainder of the party agreed to make a sally and create a diversion, and thus enable them to get away. Accordingly, those who could swim, jumped into the water.

One officer has since died, and one man was killed in getting away; the others swam down the river six miles, when they saw some natives who took off their turbans to them, and laying down their arms, beckoned to the poor fugitives to come on shore. They did so, and were taken by these people, who belonged to some *Rajah*, and treated with great care and kindness. Captain Moore appears to have acted through the whole Cawnpore business with the greatest gallantry. Distant guns were heard today.

Chapter 12

November 4th - November 18th

Wednesday, November 4th, 1857.

No messenger in last night. One man coming in two nights ago was taken by the insurgents, and two *Home News*, which he was bringing with him were lost, which is provoking. As we were sitting down to breakfast this morning. Captain Hardinge came to report that Mr. Dashwood had just had both his legs wounded by a round shot. He has since had them both amputated just above the ankle; and as there is no more chloroform, I fear he must have suffered a great deal, and from having been so long laid up previously it is hardly to be expected that he will get over it.

Caroline and I went to see Mrs. Ogilvie before dinner, and sat with her some time. Mrs.Vokins came to speak to Mrs. Inglis this afternoon about going home with her, but she seems to have changed her intention of going to England. So Mrs. Inglis will be rather at a loss who to take home as a servant. Two of Colonel Inglis's kids, and a fine large goat of Mrs. Cooper's, were killed by some of the Fusiliers who were on guard. An attack has, I believe, been expected today. A great many people have been seen about the Baillie Gate, but I dare say, as has frequently been the case when anything of the kind is expected, nothing will come of it. The days are now getting so short, and the evenings so long, that it is very wearisome and gloomy, and we long more than ever for change of scene and air.

Thursday, November 5th.

There was a good deal of musketry fire last night, between nine and ten o'clock. An artilleryman was badly wounded. Colonel Campbell was very unwell indeed this morning, and I fear the doctors have a bad opinion of his case. Colonel Inglis bought some pretty little cups and saucers at the prize agent's today, and gave Carry and me each a very pretty cup. Distant guns (supposed to be at Allumbagh) were heard today, and there is a report in the garrison that Sir Colin Campbell was at that place, but we hardly believe it. We spoke to Captain Orr today. He told us that he had not heard from his brother, who is a prisoner here, since the 30th *ult.*

The letter he then wrote represented them all as being well taken care of, as far as their bodily wants, such as food and clothes, went, but Captain Orr thinks that the letter must have been dictated, as it said so little, and was brought in by one of Maun Sing's men. The party of prisoners consists of Sir Mountstuart Jackson and his sister. Captain and Mrs. Orr, their little girl, six years' old, and a sergeant-major. When they were brought into Lucknow the gentlemen were on a bullock *gharry* in irons, and the ladies in *dooleys.* They must have undergone great hardships. I understand that they are now under the care of the king's *sepoys.* There is a report today that Maun Sing has gone away, but I believe no one knows whether such is really the case.

Mrs. Giddings came just before our dinner, and remained some time. She brought some bread which she had made with only *attah* and water, and it was very good, but I prefer the *chupatties* to eat every day. We are going to content ourselves with one *attah chupattie* each a day, making out the rest with gram, now that food is becoming more scarce. Poor Mrs. C—— comes to see us every day. She is so desponding and melancholy when she talks of provisions being likely to fail, that it is quite sad to hear her.

Friday, November 6th.

Distant guns heard today, and musketry reported by the officer on the lookout. Maun Sing is reported to have gone to Chinhut, and taken about 3000 or 4000 men with him. Major Eyre, of the artillery, came to see Mrs. Inglis today. He told us, among other things, that a conspiracy for taking the fort at Calcutta had been got up by the rebels; fortunately, however, without success. It appears that at the very commencement of the outbreak in Bengal, just before the mutiny at Barrackpore, the Rajah of Gwalior (generally called Scindiah) was to have given a magnificent fête at Calcutta to the Governor-General and all the great people there, in some gardens. They were to have had waterworks and all kinds of amusements, but it was put off in consequence of a violent hurricane which came on suddenly.

It is stated that the rebels intended murdering the Governor-General, and all the people in authority, and taking possession of the fort. It is supposed that the plan was unknown to the *Rajah*, but previously he paid a visit to the *Nana*, acknowledging him as *Peishwa*, which looked rather suspicious. However, he has hitherto been favourable to us, and has kept his men in check longer than it was supposed he could do.

Colonel Campbell is going on better. I went to see Mrs. Radclyffe before dinner. We were told that some of the soldiers belonging to the new force are so hungry that they will do anything to obtain food, and constantly run into the kitchens whenever they see cooking going on, seize on a *chupattie*, and leave a *rupee* in its place!! Poor fellows, it is indeed sad to hear of their being upon guard or duty of some kind all night long, especially now the mornings are so cold and keen, and that without enough to eat.

Saturday, November 7th.

Last night, just as we were going to bed. We heard that a messenger had arrived from Cawnpore with a letter from Major Bruce, stating that the army commanded by Sir Colin Campbell in person was expected to reach Allumbagh on the 10th instant. It consists of 5100 infantry, 600 cavalry, and 36 guns—a fine force; and if it does not effectually release us, I do not think anything will. Colonel Inglis appears to think they will reach this place on the 13th, and unless the rebels retreat on their arrival, the women and children and the sick and wounded will have to be sent off at once, taking with us merely a change of clothes, and carrying only what can be taken in bundles in our hands.

Those who are able will have to walk to Allumbagh, as all the carriages, buggies, and carts will be occupied by the sick and wounded; it will be a dreadful affair getting us off. Mrs. M'Bean has, I believe, promised to lend Colonel Inglis a *palkie gharry* and a cart for us all to go in and take our things. It is just possible that the enemy may go away, and affairs may take a better turn, and we may not have to be hurried off so rapidly; but at all events, I do not think there will be much delay in our departure after the force once comes in. The enemy blew up a mine this morning, but without doing any harm. The mornings and evenings are very cold now, and everyone is busy getting warm clothing made up, for the children especially.

Sunday, November 8th.

Colonel Inglis was very unwell this morning, and obliged to send for Dr. Scott after breakfast. Carry and I attended Divine Service, and remained for the Communion. Mr. Browne (32nd) was slightly wounded today. Colonel Campbell not so well, and I do not think the doctors think favourably of him. I went to see Mrs. Radclyffe before dinner, and found her looking forward with dread and anxiety to our move from Lucknow. I am certain it will be a terrible business getting us all off. Once at Allumbagh, I imagine that we shall be over the most difficult part. Everything very quiet here today.

Monday, November 9th.

Colonel Inglis better this morning, but had a bad night. When Dr. Scott came to see us he said he thought that we should be away from this before the 20th, and advised us to begin at once and prepare for our move. They say that we shall have to leave a great many things behind us, which we never can expect to see again. We hope to begin tomorrow and settle a little.

A great deal of firing has been going on from the enemy today. Two European artillerymen and one native were wounded this evening. Captain Barrow came to see Colonel Inglis, and remained to dinner with us, which he seemed to enjoy, for he had made a very early dinner; and though people may have enough, no one seems to have too much to eat just now. We have not seen Colonel Inglis, as he has been confined to his room all day.

Tuesday, November 10th.

Colonel Inglis better today, but not able to breakfast with us. Guns were heard in the distance, and the "Union Jack" was seen flying from Allumbagh, which all seem to think means that Sir Colin Campbell has reached that place with his force. Mr. Kavanagh, the head clerk in Mr. Cooper's office, volunteered to go out last night to Allumbagh, and conduct our force into Lucknow. It was a most gallant act, and all were delighted when the signal agreed upon to announce his arrival (the hoisting a flag) was spied from the top of the Residency about twelve o'clock this morning. Mr. Kavanagh went out about eight o'clock disguised as a native, with a man with him as a guide.

Captain Dodgson, assistant-adjutant-general to the force here, called on us today. He is related to or connected with our dear friends the Scotts of Brotherton. We are so grieved to hear that there is every chance of poor Colonel Campbell being obliged to have his leg amputated. He is not so well today, and when Colonel Inglis went to see him he was wandering a good deal. I scarcely know why, but this has been to me a wretched day; some days one feels more especially depressed, and to me this has been one of them.

Wednesday, November 11th.

No messenger has been in today, and I have heard no news of any kind. Poor Colonel Campbell had his leg amputated today. Fortunately they were able to get some chloroform from Dr. Fayrer. We hear that so far he is doing well, but he is very weak, and I fear that there is much danger of his not getting over it. We have had a visit from Mr. Harmer. His leg is getting much better and he is now able to put on a slipper and can put his foot to the ground. In the afternoon we arranged some of our things, separating those we were anxious to keep, and those we wished to part with. Mrs. Roberts came for some work to do for me, and Mrs. Campbell came and finally arranged to go to England with Mrs. Inglis. She brought home some little warm jackets she had made for the children.

Thursday, November 12th.

The telegraph, which works from the top of the Residency, and is replied to by the one from Allumbagh, announces that Sir Colin Campbell has arrived there. He is to advance with his force on Lucknow tomorrow, and is expected to arrive here on Sunday. They are to come in by the Dil Khoosha. Most fervently is it to be hoped that their entrance into Lucknow may be successful, and that this time we really may be released from our captivity. The enemy made an attack on Allumbagh this morning, but our troops got possession of two of their guns. There will be some more hard fighting before they get in.

Colonel Campbell is so weak and ill that he is not expected to live till the morning. He is quite insensible, but does not appear to suffer much. Captain Barrow and Captain Dodgson came to see us this evening. We did not dine till very late. I hear that an attack is expected tonight; they are certainly firing a good deal, but as yet (ten p.m.) nothing like an attack has commenced.

Friday, November 13th.

Sharp musketry was heard in the direction of Allumbagh this morning. The telegraph has been at work, and from it we learn that Sir Colin Campbell is to march tomorrow morning at seven. An important letter from him to Sir James Outram has been lost; but another has been written, which may come in tonight. The insurgents appear to be increasing in numbers round this place. The rebels who have escaped from Delhi have come here, and are, it is said, holding the outposts. They still seem to think that there will be an attack made upon us, and all are in readiness to meet it.

Colonel Inglis told us today, that since General Havelock's force came in (October 25th), 100 of his own garrison had been killed and wounded, and twenty-six of the 32nd killed. Captain Barrow dined with us. Poor Colonel Campbell died last night about eleven o'clock. Mrs. Giddings came to see us this evening; and told us it is reported that the enemy wanted Captain Orr (their prisoner) to show them how to make shells and the way to take the Baillie Gate. Gave the servants some warm clothes today.

Saturday, November 14th.

Very heavy firing was heard this morning between twelve and one; and our flag was seen flying from the Martinière College. Sir Colin's force has got possession of the Dil Khoosha Palace; and we are told that the officers were seen through a telescope smoking their cigars on the top of the house. Tomorrow will be a most anxious day, as they will have to come through the city. A sortie is to be made by some of the troops in garrison in the morning, in order to take the Kaiser Bagh Palace, and so divert the attention of the rebels. All must feel most deeply for the poor prisoners whose fate is in the hands of these wretches; but as we have prisoners also, it is to be hoped this may be a check on any bad intentions which may be entertained by the insurgents.

Mrs. Giddings came to see us and told us that poor Mrs. Ouseley died this morning, which shocked us much, as we had not even heard that she was ill. She was only laid up for a few days with dysentery and fever, and sank, from complete exhaustion. It is sad to think of all the distress poor Colonel Palmer has gone through during this siege; and now his little boy is so ill, that it is doubtful whether he will recover. Mrs. Roberts came this evening with some things she has been making for us; and told us she had sat up all last night with poor Mrs. Ouseley. I went to see Mrs. Radclyffe and as usual found Mrs. Clarke with her. She's a kind little creature. This has been a very quiet day. No firing till towards evening.

Sunday, November 15th.

Sir Colin's force did not advance yesterday as was expected, but remained stationary at the Dil Khoosha, and a great deal of excitement pervaded our garrison, all being on the lookout to watch the movements of his troops. The day has been very quiet, with the exception of a gun of the enemy's occasionally firing near Major Banks's house. Attended Divine Service. This is Colonel Inglis's birthday; Captain

Barrow dined with us, and gave us an account of the wonderful escape he, his wife, and family had, in getting away from Salone, where he was commissioner, just in time to save their lives; and, strange to say, the very man who saved them is now fighting against us; the account of his adventures interested us very much.

The extraordinary infatuation of officers in native corps never choosing to believe it possible that their regiments could prove faithless, is one of the most remarkable features in the whole of this mutiny. Everything is said to be quiet at Delhi and Agra, but it is strange that a regiment (the 50th I believe) has mutinied after everything had settled down there, and after they had been held up as patterns of fidelity and loyalty. We had a fruit-pie for dinner today, a thing we have not had for four months, and the poor children enjoyed it greatly.

Monday, November 16th.

Last night, about ten o'clock, the enemy began to fire heavily. It did not last very long; but was again commenced and was very loud indeed about four o'clock in the morning, after which it gradually subsided. Distant guns were heard, and we fear that there must have been some fighting during the night. We have had a very anxious day, and much firing has been heard during the whole morning, and till about three o'clock p.m., when it ceased. Sir Colin's force has now advanced some distance on this side of our old bungalows, and will not get here till tomorrow.

They have come only a short way today, but that is all the better, and they seem to be getting on well so far, though it is impossible to say whether there has been much loss of life on our side. A party was sent out from the garrison this morning to take some houses, three were killed, and twenty-one wounded: too many for what they accomplished. This will be a most anxious night. The garrison is, I believe, to be reinforced, and everything made ready to repulse an attack, should there be one. Captain Birch has had a most narrow escape. A bullet just grazed his ear and entered his hat. Fortunately it is a mere scratch; but this is the second time since the commencement of the siege that he has been hit.

Tuesday, November 17th.

We were much surprised that last night passed off so quietly; indeed scarcely any firing was heard. Sir Colin's force was seen to advance very slowly, that is to say, artillery only were visible, *no infantry*. About two o'clock we heard that "red jackets" were in the 32nd Mess-house, and soon after that they had possession of Mr. Martin's house. About four o'clock, a sight we had not seen for a very long time caught our eyes; two officers, each leading a horse and coming into our courtyard inquiring for Colonel Inglis. We at once saw that they belonged to the advancing force, and we were told that one of them was Colonel Berkeley, the new Colonel of the 32nd. Just before dinner, Colonel Inglis brought him up and introduced him to us.

Colonel Napier has been wounded today in the leg, but not dangerously I believe and hope, for so useful an officer can be ill dispensed with now.

When Colonel Inglis came to dinner he told us that Sir Colin Campbell's orders are that we are all to leave Lucknow tomorrow evening! Our consternation may be more easily imagined than described, and I think our faces when we looked at each other wore an expression of the most complete bewilderment. How all the wounded and sick people and women and children are to be got off in such a hurried manner, at only a few hours' notice, I cannot imagine.

Wednesday, November 18th.

It was found impracticable to get the women and children off today, so only the sick and wounded were sent, and we were told that we should not have to move till tomorrow. We were busy packing up the whole day and trying to compress our few things in as small a space as possible, not knowing for how much we should be allowed carriage. Our linen we sewed up in pillowcases and took as pillows; the other things which we absolutely did not want to leave behind us we put into boxes. We contrived to take a good deal of our plate among our clothes, but all our glass and crockery we were obliged to leave behind us, besides many other things we should like to have saved. We had some visitors in the evening, and I went over to see Mrs. Cooper and Mrs. Radclyffe. We went to our beds very late, for we could not help talking over our strange situation and the probable events of the following day.

Chapter 13

November 19th - November 30th

Thursday, November 19th.

We were up early this morning to finish all we had to do, and were several times interrupted by visitors; General Grant, Colonel Berkeley, and Captain Lowe were among them. Several of the ladies left the Residency as early as ten o'clock, and people were going out the whole day long. Colonel Inglis thought it better that we should start later, and it was arranged that four p.m. should be the hour. We got some Coolies to carry our *charpoys*, and procured a *hackery* for our boxes. They all preceded us by a couple of hours. We had some soup before starting, and were, I believe, about the last to leave the Residency. Strange indeed were our feelings on leaving our courtyard and that confined space where we had spent so many wretched hours.

Mr. Birch (A.D.C.) was sent by Colonel Inglis to escort us as far as Secundra Bagh, as he could not go with us himself; we knew not if wc should remain there the night or go on to the Dil Khoosha. We three ladies and Captain Birch started on foot, and the children and *ayah* in our shattered little carriage drawn by Coolies. Had we not known that it really was our carriage, we scarcely could have believed what a wreck it had become. A round shot had gone through the head, it was pierced with bullets, and in fact it was tattered to pieces; a wretched horse which could hardly walk was the only thing to be found to draw the buggy which followed empty.

The scene of ruin, devastation, and misery which presented itself to our eyes when we got out I *never, never* shall forget. To describe it would be impossible; but the horrors of war presented themselves with full force in the mass of shattered buildings and dilapidated gateways through which we passed. Three short bits of road were dangerous, as the enemy could, from the top of a mosque, see people going along, and fire on them. At these places we had to take the children out of the carriage, and have them carried,—and all our party ran as fast as we could. I am thankful to say that we arrived safely at Secundra Bagh, about half-past five o'clock. Mrs. Inglis and Caroline walked the whole way; I, the greater part.

The scene at Secundra is a most strange one; it is a garden enclosed within high walls. On Tuesday last Sir Colin's troops had an engagement with the enemy, and killed, some say 2000, others 1500, of them in this very place: they were all buried yesterday. Here were now assembled all the ladies, women, and children who had left the Residency. We had our *charpoys* carried inside, and seated ourselves upon them. The officers were going about, most kindly bringing wine and biscuits to those who wished to take anything; and numbers were busily employed in arranging about the conveyances to take us all on to the Dil Khoosha, whither, we were told, we were to proceed in two or three hours. Many kindly inquired whether we had all we required, and Sir Colin amongst them. Major Ouvry, of the 9th Lancers, offered us a bullock *gharry* of his own to go in, of which we gladly availed ourselves, and we three, and the three children, with another lady and child, all got in, and, as Mrs. Inglis said, were packed as closely as a box of sardines.

We had an escort of 1500 men to go with our column, which was a very long one. We were ordered to proceed very quietly, and silence was constantly enforced, so that the enemy's attention might not be attracted towards us. We had proceeded some distance, when the column came to a halt; and we imagine that the advanced guard must have heard some noise which caused alarm, for they sent back to Secundra Bagh for a reinforcement.

We reached the Dil Khoosha about midnight, and among all the camels, wagons. *Coolies*, and people moving in every direction, it was difficult to know where the tent was situated to which we were to proceed; but Colonel Little, the Brigadier, to whom Mrs. Inglis had brought a note, came to our rescue, and took us to a large tent where there were a great many other ladies. It was not enclosed, but we were only too glad of shelter of any kind; and Azaib soon put up the beds. Colonel Little, and several other officers of the 9th Lancers, kindly brought us tea, bread and butter, and pudding, which we enjoyed very much,—four months having elapsed since we had seen anything of the kind.

By the time we had made ourselves comfortable for the night (lying down under the *rezais*, without undressing), it must have been two o'clock. However, tired as I was, I slept well for two or three hours. I was the first awake, and I could not help thinking, as I lay there and looked around me, what a strange position we poor unfortunate creatures were all placed in. But we might have been in a worse condition; and the longest life will not be sufficient to pour forth our gratitude for our merciful preservation through all the dangers of the siege.

Friday, November 20th.

We got the large tent, which Colonel Inglis brought from Dr. Fayrer, pitched early this morning, and were delighted to change our quarters, and be able to wash and dress comfortably. There is a nice division in it, and as we had plenty of room in one half, Mrs. Inglis most kindly gave the other to Mrs. and Miss Birch, the former being an invalid. Very grateful they were to be allowed to share a tent so much more comfortable than the one they had been in during the night. After we were dressed, we went over to breakfast with the 9th Lancers. The table was laid out under the trees, and the whole thing looked very cool and pleasant. We enjoyed the bread and butter and jam, and a cup of coffee very much, for they were things we had not tasted for a long time. Our chief occupation during the day was arranging our things, and Mrs. Inglis had a great many visitors. I did not go out this evening; Mrs. Inglis and Carry strolled about the camp.

Saturday, November 21st.

Today we all got a great many English letters, and very sad they were to receive. The anxiety in England is heartrending to think of, and public sympathy seems indeed to be bestowed upon us to the very highest degree. The latest dates of our letters were 11th September. Captain Edgehill, who seems to have the management of the carriage required by the ladies, has been constantly during the day with a pen and paper at our door. We find that each lady is allowed a camel and a cart. I am sure even the few things that we have, and all the servants' bundles and pillows stuffed with their property (most of which they looted in the Residency), cannot possibly be taken if we do not get more carriage for them.

No order yet about our move, but we should not take long to be ready. No one seems to know when we shall march. I suppose they do not wish the natives to know anything about our movements. In the evening Carry and I strolled about, and walked some time with Mrs. Brydon and Mrs. Clarke. The ladies all seem very comfortable. Heard today that Dr. Derby and young Mr. Dashwood were dead; both, no doubt, having been the worse for the move. We dined late outside our tent.

Sunday, November 22nd.

While we were dressing this morning the enemy made an attack. The musketry did not last very long. The 9th Lancers went out, but soon returned. They killed some of the enemy in a village, and among others a *metah*, at which our servants were very indignant. The rest of the day was very quiet. Still no order to move. We are very anxious tonight, knowing that the whole force was to leave the Residency today. They began to move out about one o'clock p.m. Colonel Inglis, who was with the rear-guard, did not leave till midnight. We heard a good deal of musketry during the night, which gave us some alarm; but it turned out to be the enemy firing on the Residency after the whole force had left. However, all our people arrived at the Dil Khoosha quite safely, without having seen one of the insurgents.

One officer (Captain Waterman, of the 13th Native Infantry) was very near being left behind. He had fallen asleep, and awoke up suddenly much surprised to find everything so quiet all round him. He jumped up, found everyone gone, and ran as hard he could till he overtook the force some little way beyond the Residency, It would have been far from a pleasant fate to have been left alone to the mercy of those whom he knew would rush in as soon as they found we were gone. Musketry was still heard when we went to bed, and Colonel Inglis had not arrived at eleven o'clock. Mrs. Inglis did not undress, in order that she might be ready to get up at any moment.

Monday, November 23rd.

Colonel Inglis arrived this morning about six, having been out all night, and all are now safe at the Dil Khoosha.

Wednesday, November 25th.

All was confusion and bustle this morning. To know what a camp such as ours is when getting ready for a start, it must be seen. The *hackeries*, camels, elephants, vehicles of all sorts, servants rushing about, every one looking after their boxes and baggage, presented a most extraordinary scene. We were up very early, being told that we should march at eleven o'clock. When we had settled our things we sat down to some tea and bread and butter, having decided that we would not make a regular breakfast. Mrs. Giddings came and staid for a long time. Not being able to get bullocks for the carriage and buggy, we got a native *hackery*. Mrs. Inglis, Carry, myself, and baby went into it; Johnny,

Charlie, and the *ayah* going in a *doolie*.

It was some time before we got fairly off, for we were very much in the rear, and found ourselves among the baggage and camels. The dust was something fearful, and at times the heat very great. We get on slowly, having constant stoppages. We did not reach our encampment, which is about a mile from Allumbagh, till nearly six o'clock; so that it took us nearly six hours from the time we started till we were on the spot where our tent was to be pitched. The *hackeries*, with our things, and everything on which we had depended for dinner, were anxiously looked for for a long time, without making their appearance.

Being so late we had the small tent belonging to Colonel Inglis pitched instead of our large one. I do not know what we should have done had it not been for the great kindness of General Grant, 9th Lancers, who himself brought us a bottle of beer, some tongue, and some excellent bread and butter; and not satisfied with *that*, returned a second time, bringing us some tea. We were very tired, and as soon as we had finished our repast we lay down on the ground in the tent, and rolled ourselves up in the blankets and *rezais*, and slept soundly, hard as was our bed. Just as we were starting this morning we heard of the death of poor General Havelock: this is a hard fate, just as he had so well earned all his honours!

Thursday, November 26th.

Finding we were to remain at Allumbagh we had the large tent pitched. Sir James Outram and all his force arrived here today. Captain Barrow came to see us as soon as he arrived. We have our large tent all to ourselves, so we enjoyed the luxury of a bath, and spent so much time over it, that it was very late when we breakfasted. Colonel Inglis was with us. We strolled out a short distance, but did not see any one. Colonel Inglis dined with us.

Friday, November 27th.

I felt so unwell that Mrs. Inglis and Caroline insisted on my remaining the greater part of the day in bed, as we had a prospect of so much fatigue before us. I got up about four o'clock in the afternoon. Colonel Inglis dined with us. As we were told we should march at seven tomorrow morning we only took off our dresses and laid down on our beds.

Saturday, November 28th,

Got up very early and prepared all for a start at seven, but just as we were dressed. Captain Edgehill came and told us that we should not go till eleven o'clock. We are very well off for conveyances, Captain Probyn having lent Mrs. Inglis his bullock *gharry*, and Mr. Jackson insisted on our taking his carriage with a couple of mules. The children and the *ayah* go in the bullock *gharry*, and ourselves and baby in the carriage. We started about half-past ten o'clock, and had a most tedious day's march. I think we were one hour and a half sitting in the carriages without moving. To imagine the sight of so many *hackeries*, camels, carriages of all kinds, riders, camp-followers, &c., is quite impossible without having been an eyewitness of the scene. And how they are ever brought into any degree of order, and how all arrive at their destination, appears a perfect wonder.

The whole column was nine miles in length. The name of the place where we are encamped tonight I do not know, but it is about nine miles from Allumbagh. Even getting over that short distance took us more than seven hours, as it was nearly six o'clock when we reached the spot where our tent was to be pitched. Captain Rudman was very kind in assisting us to get the tent up and to collect our things. We made him remain and have some dinner with us, but we were so tired that we were glad when the dinner was over, and we could once more lie down on the ground and go to sleep. Mrs. Inglis was fairly knocked up. I do not think I ever saw her look more so.

Sunday, November 29th.

We started at seven this morning, and I think, if possible, it has been a more tedious day than yesterday. The march was very long, and the train proceeded very slowly. We halted in the course of the day for about an hour, when Mrs. Inglis was able to get some arrowroot made on the roadside for poor baby, and we had fortunately taken some milk with us, and bread and butter for the other children. We passed Mhow and came to a place within three miles of the river. We did not reach our ground till ten, all fairly tired out. We must have marched nearly thirty miles today. A great deal of firing was heard at Cawnpore. No one appeared to know what it was, but it was evident that fighting going on. Another night again without being able to undress, but nevertheless we all sleep soundly.

Monday, November 30th.

We started this morning later than usual; we were, however, up early waiting for orders, but as none arrived, we thought it better to have breakfast. Colonel Inglis came and had some tea with us, but he was in such a hurry that he had not time to take anything more. We saw fires at Cawnpore, evidently stores or bungalows being burned. We heard that there had been some fighting there yesterday, when Brigadier Wilson and several of the 64th were killed. I was very sorry to hear of the death of the former, he had always been a kind friend to me, and I know how much his family will regret him. Our troops went out to meet the enemy, I believe, under the orders of General Wyndham, and we were but 1500 against 20,000. We hear various reports, but it appears certain that the

Gwalior Force is attacking Cawnpore, and that is the reason, no doubt, that they are hurrying us on. It really seems as if we never should get out of our difficulties; fighting seems to follow in our train, or rather, I should say, to precede us wherever we go.

After we had finished breakfast. Captain Edgehill came and told us we ought to be ready to start at ten o'clock. We had only one mile and a half to go; but that short distance took us an hour. We pitched our small tent as soon as we could, and the air being delicious, we sat out and read for some time; and then Colonel Inglis and Colonel Shortt came up. When they went away we read the evening service, but how little it appeared like a quiet holy Sunday, all around us speaking of war and its attendant horrors.

At four p.m. we dined; Colonel Inglis and Captain Wilson shared our dinner, and Captain Birch, who arrived just as we had finished our soup, was very glad to sit on a box outside and partake of what we had; something to eat in these times, and especially a glass of beer, being most acceptable, and not always procurable. We were told that about seven p.m. we should be ready to start, so the small tent was soon struck, and we were once more *en route* for Cawnpore. When we got upon the road, we found the mass of *hackeries*, camels, and vehicles worse than ever,—four lines deep on the road.

However, most fortunately, General Grant had ordered part of the road to be cleared for the carriages, so we got on very well with the exception of a few long stoppages and some heavy parts through the sand. When we arrived at last at the bridge, some very sharp musketry was heard close to us. I must say I felt alarmed, thinking that the party in front was being attacked, but it turned out to be our own people firing at what they thought were some of the enemy; but I believe it was a false alarm.

At last we arrived at Cawnpore, and nothing could look more wretched and miserable than this dreadful place as we came in by the light of the moon. The burnt bungalows, the broken gates, the remains of gun carriages, trees lying on the ground with their leaves and branches completely stripped off, and more than all, the thoughts which arose in our minds of the fearful scenes so lately enacted here depressed and saddened us altogether. It was now twelve o'clock at night, and we were brought to the Dragoon Barracks. Our small tent was up as soon as ourselves, and pitched in a few minutes. We had some hot tea, and once again the ground in our tent formed our only bed, and we did not dream of undressing.

Monday, November 30th.

We were so uncertain as to what would be our orders for today, that we waited till ten o'clock; and nothing being heard, we each took it by turns to bathe and dress in the tent, and it was past one before we were all ready for breakfast. We were then told that we were to be moved at once to the Artillery Barracks, but we quietly ate our breakfast, thinking that probably another order would shortly be issued, and so it turned out to be; for we are now told to hold ourselves in readiness for a start at daylight tomorrow. Captain Norman came just before we sat down to dinner, and talked a little of the affairs of the country. He seems to think that it will be rather a long business putting everything to rights again.

There is one place still in a state of siege in Central India, called Saugor, and *that* of course a force must go to relieve. It is a small garrison, I think Captain Norman said 220 men and 170 women and children; but they are said to be able to hold out for some time. Captain Wilson amused us the other day by telling us that when our force came away from the Residency, they left 30,000 *rupees* (three thousand pounds) in *pice*. It appears almost an incredible thing that such a large sum could have been collected in that way. Of course the great weight prevented its being moved. No doubt the natives had a good scramble for it.

Chapter 14

December 1st - December 14th

Tuesday, December 1st.

At seven o'clock this morning everyone in camp was on the move, and various groups were taking their *chotah hazree* outside their tents; camels were being loaded, and all the carriages were ready by half-past seven o'clock. It was very cold indeed when we started. Our move was to the Artillery Barracks, which is a great improvement on our position of the morning. It took us about half an hour to get here, and we found a very nice piece of encamping ground. We pitched the large tent at once, and made ourselves very comfortable. Poor Brigadier Wilson's old servant, Saville, came to see me today, to ask me to write to Mrs. Wilson, which I intend to do, painful as the task will be. The poor man appeared so dreadfully grieved, that I was quite sorry to see him. The last moments of the Brigadier appear to have been tranquil. He spent in prayer the half hour that he lived after he was taken into his tent.

It is fortunate that we left the Dragoon Barracks when we did, for during the day an officer, a man, and a boy, were wounded, and a camel, pony, and an elephant, were killed, by "shrapnel" from the insurgents. No one knows anything about our movements, but all seem to say that we cannot leave Cawnpore till things are quieter.

Wednesday, December 2nd.

Last night we all undressed and had a very good night, going really to bed. We were told, early in the morning, that we should march in the course of the day, and repeatedly had the fact impressed upon us that we must be ready to start at half-an-hour's notice. Captain Edgehill came and begged us to send, at twelve o'clock, for eight days' rations, which we did; but another order was then issued, that four o'clock was to be the hour. We were kept in this suspense all day, and towards evening were told that we should not go till night, and perhaps not till daybreak.

At half-past four o'clock, Carry and I walked with Mr. and Mrs. Harris to see the place where all the poor people who were murdered here maintained so fierce a struggle with the fiends outside. I could not have believed, had I not seen it, that their abode had been so wretched. They were shut up here for twenty-one days.

The intrenchment is scarcely even a good-sized ditch, and yet, at times, it was safer for the poor ladies to take their chairs and sit there than to remain in the miserable building which scarcely afforded a shelter from the sun, The roof had been entirely destroyed by round shot, and the only thing which showed there had once been a verandah were a few solitary beams of wood projecting from the main building.

It was sad to see pieces of old letters, parts of old returns of the dear old 32nd, and here and there a sheet of torn music, strewn about the ground. Mrs. Harris picked up part of an old *Bible*. As to a door or a window, not a vestige of such a thing remains; and the wretched attempt at a gate, in order to form a barricade, which the garrison had erected, showed to what extremities the poor sufferers must have been reduced. We saw the only well from which they could get water, and it was under such a heavy fire, that they had to run out when it was dark and draw the water as they could.

The enemy were in houses *close* to them, and in great numbers, and yet never had the courage to come over the miserable intrenchment. In some places there were scraps of writing on the wall, describing their sufferings. In one place Caroline found the following words, "Dear Jesus, send us help today, and deliver us not into the hands of our enemies!" Poor things, how excruciating must have been their agony. No doubt to many, the holy faith of Jesus,—the confidence they felt in our Heavenly Father, was a support which made them peaceful and happy even in their greatest extremity.

When one sees the place where these poor creatures were shut up, the wonder is that anyone ever lived to get out of it. Very many indeed died, and the only place in which they had to bury them was a well, into which the bodies were thrown at night!! But still, I believe, nearly 400 got out alive, and were reserved for a much more cruel fate. The place where they were afterwards murdered, by order of the brutal *Nana*, is now in possession of the enemy, so of course we did not attempt to see it.

Colonel Inglis dined with us. Captain Rudman came in the evening. He looks very ill, and I do not think he will be able to stand this kind of life long. The management of the troops here in the action the other day seems to have been very bad, and severe comments are made on the officer in command. We little expected to find Cawnpore in such a state. The insurgents are all round it, and are in possession of the city. I dare say the commander-in-chief hardly knows what to do with us. Most anxious he is, no doubt, to get us away; but after escaping the dangers of the Lucknow siege, I am sure he would not like to expose us to more danger than is necessary.

We sent off our English letters today, and I wrote to poor Mrs. Wilson, at Deesa, telling her of the death of her husband. As we thought we should not have more than half an hour's notice to start, we did not undress, but lay down as we were. I cannot say I slept very well, and the want of a proper night's rest knocks me up more than anything else. I feel very tired and good for nothing today. Heard that a man of the 88th was taken prisoner yesterday.

Thursday, December 3rd.

We have been expecting, since the early morning, to get our orders to move every moment. It is now past four o'clock and we have heard nothing about it; so we are still in a state of uncertainty which is most unpleasant. We went again this afternoon to the old intrenchments with Mrs. Inglis, who had not been with us the day before. As we were returning we met Colonel Inglis, and he said he did not think it likely that we should go this evening; but, however, as soon as we got back to our tent we found that Captain Edgehill had been to say the order had come for us to march at ten o'clock tonight, so we ordered our dinner at once, and sent up to tell Colonel Inglis we were now really going; prepared as we had been all day for our start.

There always remain a few things which can only be done just at the last. About half-past nine o'clock Colonel Inglis came to our tent, with Captain Birch, who came to say goodbye. Everything appeared very sad and gloomy starting at that hour of the night, and to poor Mrs. Inglis the parting from her husband at such a time and in such a manner was very distressing. I felt very much for her. He walked down with us to the place where our *gharry* started from, and there we all parted. It was miserable work; and I had such a severe cold and felt so ill, that I was in a bad condition to commence so fatiguing a journey. Our escort consists of the 34th Regiment, some cavalry, and four guns.

Friday, December 4th.

Our journey last night was tedious. Though we started at ten o'clock, we did not reach our encamping ground till eleven this morning. We marched twenty-seven miles, and were all dreadfully tired. I do not know that in my whole life I ever felt more so, for we had been able to get very little sleep during the night. The children's *gharry* most unfortunately broke down, the wheel coming off; so we were obliged to move the children and all the boxes into our carriage, which delayed us, and made us fall a good deal to the rear. Mrs. Inglis wrote a few lines to Colonel Inglis, and gave her note to one of the officers we met on the road marching up to Cawnpore with different detachments of regiments, of which there appeared to be a good many.

Our tent is pitched in a nice grove of trees; Mrs. Gall and her party are our nearest neighbours.

A very sad accident happened last night. A writer's wife, whose husband was shot during the siege, is travelling with her brother. They were in a buggy; he got out and left his rifle against the door of the carriage, which moved on, and the poor woman, thinking the gun would fall to the ground, put her hand on the muzzle of it to prevent its doing so. It went off and shot her hand, shattering it so much that as soon as we arrived on the encamping ground she was obliged to have her thumb amputated, and it seems doubtful whether she will not lose her hand. She was close to us, and it was painful to think of her sufferings, she seemed to be so patient. She could only travel on a *charpoy*, and there was much difficulty in procuring *Coolies*; but Mrs. Inglis, with her usual kindness, gave her two of hers, and she was able to get four herself. We dined at five, and afterwards I was so tired that I lay down and fell asleep for about an hour, just before they struck the tent.

Saturday, December 5th.

We got off last night about ten, and arrived on our ground this morning at seven, having marched only twelve miles, so we came along very slowly indeed; and I believe we halted for two hours during the night, but we all slept, and none of our party knew it. We are encamped in a nice place today, and are near a pretty piece of water. Mrs. Giddings breakfasted with us; she is quite alone, and Mrs. Inglis has asked her to come and breakfast and dine with us always, as she has no servants of her own. We are eight miles from Futtypore, and shall pass it tonight.

Sunday, December 6th.

The march was weary, long, and tedious (sixteen miles), with constant delays, and we were so tired and cramped up in the *palkie gharry*, that I do not know how we shall ever get through another night in it. We reached our encamping ground about seven a. m., and the morning was cold and chilly. Neither the camels nor the servants belonging to the kitchen department had made their appearance when we arrived; the former, however, soon came up, and our tent was pitched under a pretty grove of trees.

We waited some time for the *khansamah* and *kitmaghars*, and finding they did not arrive, we got out all the breakfast things, and laid the table; fortunately, we had the remains of a cold fowl with us, and one of the other servants made the *chupatties*. Just as we had seated ourselves at breakfast the *khansamah* arrived. They had all fallen asleep, at some place where they lay down to rest, and did not awake till a very late hour, causing a long delay, which for us was rather inconvenient. After breakfast it was very late (two o'clock, I believe), and we read the Evening Service. I lay down in the tent for about an hour, but got up more tired, I think. Carry and I walked through the camp, and saw Mrs. and Miss Halford. We are to start again at nine tonight.

Monday, December 7th.

Another night more fatiguing than ever; we arrived at the railroad at six a.m., and were told that we should have to get into the train at once. To describe the scene of confusion with all the *hackeries*, camels, and conveyances of every kind, would be impossible. No one seemed to know what they were to do with their luggage. Some people said it could not go with us, others that it could. We got out of our own conveyance and took possession of one of the railway carriages, putting in all our small parcels and boxes with us.

It was soon made known that the luggage *could* go with us, so we had the camels unloaded, and their loads transferred to the luggage-vans, also some things out of the *hackery*; but we found it much better to let the latter and the goats follow us. The *gharrywarr* said they would be up on Wednesday morning. There were great delays in the starting of the train, and we did not finally get off till ten o'clock, which was annoying, as the time spent in sitting in the railroad-carriage might have been employed in getting a comfortable breakfast; instead of which, we got nothing to eat till our arrival at Allahabad, which we reached between two and three o'clock.

The distance we came by rail was, I believe, about forty miles. Nothing could exceed the warm and enthusiastic welcome with which we were received at Allahabad. All the soldiers cheered as we arrived, and every kind of conveyance, *doolies*, buggies, and carriages, were in readiness to take us to the tents which, by the Governor-General's order, were pitched for us. Mrs. Inglis, the three children, and innumerable small but heavy boxes, were put into a *dooly*; but the bearers had not gone many yards, before they declared their inability to go farther, the weight being too great.

A gentleman, who fortunately happened to be passing in a carriage at the time, made Mrs. Inglis get in, and drove her up to the tent. Mrs. Giddings came in a *dooly*, and, lastly. Carry and I had to be provided, for I was suffering greatly from a swollen ankle, and was altogether so tired and knocked up that I could scarcely move a step. I was therefore looking out most anxiously for some assistance, when Dr. Scott came and told us that there was a gentleman here with a dog-cart, who would drive us up. We lost no time in getting in, and picked up Mrs. Thomson on the road, who was walking, and looking dreadfully tired. Nothing can be more perfect than all the arrangements made here by the authorities for the ladies. The tents, which are very large ones, are pitched in a pretty spot, and the whole encamping ground is shut in with *kanauts*, so that we are perfectly private.

I felt so very unwell that I really scarcely knew what was going on around me. We did not get any dinner till nearly seven o'clock; and though I had scarcely tasted anything since the previous day, I felt very little inclined to eat, and was only too glad to undress and go to my bed as soon as it was ready. Nothing could exceed the attention and kindness of those who had provided for our comfort here. Lights and soap were taken round to every tent, with sago for the children, as well as milk.

Tuesday, December 8th.

It was indeed a great relief to undress again, it being the first time for five nights: all that time we had never taken off our clothes, except to change them. I was so completely tired, that when I went to bed I got into such a high state of fever I could not sleep, and got no rest till towards the early morning, and I was soon so unwell that we were obliged to send for Dr. Scott. He seemed to think it was only fatigue, and said that I required strengthening; and he would send me some quinine. I remained in bed the whole day, almost unconscious of what was going on; but heard enough to know that they were all busy with bon and *coprawallahs* the greater part of the day.

Monday, December 14th.

The last five days I have been so ill I could not continue my journal. I felt better yesterday; but today do not feel so well. The weather is very chilly; perhaps that is one of the reasons. But I trust it may please God to bless the means used for my recovery, and spare me to see you all again.

Appendix

The Polehampton Memorial in St. Chad's Church.

In the chancel of St Chad's Church, a memorial has been erected to the late Rev. H. S. Polehampton. The inscription, from the pen of the Rev. B. H. Kennedy, D.D., is as follows:—

> Sacred to the memory of the Reverend Henry Stedman Polehampton, M.A., late Fellow of Pembroke College, Oxford, and nearly seven years curate of this parish. Appointed a Chaplain of the Hon. East India Company, and stationed at Lucknow. He was one of the small garrison who valiantly defended the British Residency against a vast besieging force of native insurgents; and amidst his sacred functions was wounded by a bullet through his body, and died twelve days later of cholera, July 20th, 1857, aged 33 years. Endowed with sound abilities, a kind heart, and liberal mind; uniting energy with simplicity, and tempering zeal with moderation, he received testimonies of grateful esteem from those to whom he ministered both in England and in India; and as he had comforted many sufferers, so in his own hour of suffering he derived full comfort from the great Scriptural promise of salvation through faith in Christ Jesus.
>
> His wife Emily, youngest daughter of Charles Blake Allnatt, Esq., having shared his perils and watched his death-bed, was, with the other surviving Europeans, providentially rescued by British troops under British commanders, whose matchless feats of devoted courage will live in history and in the hearts of their countrymen.
>
> This tablet was erected by private subscription, in remembrance of a beloved friend and pastor.

The memorial is entirely of Carrara marble, of chaste and elegant design. Over the cornice is an unfolded book, upon the leaves of which are inscribed the words, *Enter thou into the joy of thy Lord.* Behind this is the cross, and branches of the Eastern palm. The tablet is placed in the chancel, near to that of his grandfather, the late Rev. Thomas Stedman.

The following narrative of the defence of Lucknow by Brigadier Inglis supplies those interesting military details which cannot be looked for in a lady's journal:—

BRIGADIER INGLIS'S NARRATIVE OF THE DEFENCE OF LUCKNOW.

From Brigadier Inglis, commanding Garrison of Lucknow to the Secretary to Government, Military Department, Calcutta.

Dated Lucknow, Sept. 26.

Sir,—In consequence of the very deeply-to-be-lamented death of Brigadier-General Sir H. M. Lawrence, K.C.B., late in command of the Oude Field Force, the duty of narrating the military events which have occurred at Lucknow since the 29th of June last has devolved upon myself.

On the evening of that day reports reached Sir Henry Lawrence that the rebel army, in no very inconsiderable force, would march from Chinhut (a small village about eight miles distant on the road to Fyzabad) on Lucknow on the following morning; and the late Brigadier-General therefore determined to make a strong reconnoissance in that direction, with the view, if possible, of meeting the force at a disadvantage, either at its entrance into the suburbs of the city, or at the bridge across the Gokral, which is a small stream intersecting the Fyzabad road, about half-way between Lucknow and Chinhut.

The force destined for this service, and which was composed as follows, moved out at six a. m. on the morning of the 30th of June: —Artillery: four guns of No.— Horse Light Field Battery, four *ditto* of No. 2 Oude Field Battery, two *ditto* of No. 3 *ditto ditto*, and an 8-inch howitzer. Cavalry: Troop of Volunteer Cavalry; 120 troopers of detachments belonging to 1st, 2nd, and 3rd Regiments of Oude Irregular Cavalry. Infantry: 300, Her Majesty's 32nd; 150, 13th Native Infantry; 60, 48th Native Infantry; 20, 71st Native Infantry (Sikhs).

The troops, misled by the reports of wayfarers—who stated that there were few or no men between Lucknow and Chinhut—proceeded somewhat further than had been originally intended, and suddenly fell in with the enemy, who had up to that time eluded the vigilance of the advanced guard by concealing themselves behind a long line of trees in overwhelming numbers. The European force and howitzer, with the Native Infantry, held the foe in check for some time, and had six guns of the Oude artillery been faithful and the Sikh Cavalry shown a better front, the day would have been won in spite of an immense disparity in numbers.

But the Oude artillerymen and drivers were traitors. They overturned the guns into the ditches, cut the traces of their horses, and abandoned them, regardless of the remonstrances and exertions of their own officers, and of those of Sir Henry Lawrence's staff, headed by the Brigadier-General in person, who himself drew his sword upon these rebels. Every effort to induce them to stand having proved ineffectual, the force, exposed to a vastly superior fire of artillery, and completely outflanked on both sides by an overpowering body of infantry and cavalry, which actually got into our was compelled to retire with the loss of three pieces of artillery, which fell into the hands of the enemy, in consequence of the rank treachery of the Oude gunners, and with a very grievous list of killed and wounded. The heat was dreadful, the gun ammunition was expended, and the almost total want of cavalry to protect our rear made our retreat most disastrous.

All the officers behaved well, and the exertions of the small body of Volunteer Cavalry—only forty in number—under Captain Radclyffe, 7th Light Cavalry, were most praiseworthy. Sir Henry Lawrence subsequently conveyed his thanks to myself, who had, at his request, accompanied him upon this occasion (Colonel Case being in command of Her Majesty's 32nd). He also expressed his approbation of the way in which his staff—Captain Wilson, Officiating Deputy Assistant Adjutant-General; Lieutenant James, Sub-Assistant Commissary-General; Captain Edgehiil, Officiating Military Secretary; and Mr. Cooper, Civil Service—the last of whom had acted as Sir Henry Lawrence's *Aide-de-Camp* from the commencement of the disturbances—had conducted themselves throughout this arduous day.

Sir Henry further particularly mentioned that he would bring the gallant conduct of Captain Radclyffe and of Lieutenant

Bonham, of the artillery (who worked the howitzer successfully until incapacitated by a wound), to the prominent notice of the Government of India. The manner in which Lieutenant Birch, 71st N. I, cleared a village with a party of Sikh skirmishers, also elicited the admiration of the Brigadier-General. The conduct of Lieutenant Hardinge, who, with his handful of horse, covered the retreat of the rear-guard, was extolled by Sir Henry, who expressed his intention of mentioning the services of this gallant officer to his Lordship in Council. Lieutenant-Colonel Case, who commanded Her Majesty's 32nd Regiment, was mortally wounded whilst gallantly leading his men. The service had not a more deserving officer. The command devolved on Captain Stevens, who also received a death-wound shortly afterwards. The command then fell to Captain Mansfield, who has since died of cholera. A list of the casualties on this occasion accompanies the despatch.

It remains to report the siege operations.

It will be in the recollection of his Lordship in Council that it was the original intention of Sir Henry Lawrence to occupy not only the Residency, but also the fort called the Muchee Bhawun, an old dilapidated edifice which had been hastily repaired for the occasion, though the defences were even at the last moment very far from complete, and were moreover commanded by many houses in the city. The situation of the Machee Bhawan with regard to the Residency has already been described to the Government of India.

The untoward event of the 30th June so far diminished the whole available force, that we had not a sufficient number of men remaining to occupy both positions. The Brigadier-General, therefore, on the evening of the 1st July, signalled to the garrison o the Muchee Bhawun to evacuate and blow up that fortress in the course of the night. The orders were ably carried out, and at twelve p.m. the force marched into the Residency, with their guns and treasure, out the loss of a man; and shortly afterwards the explosion of 240 barrels of gunpowder, and 6,000,000 ball-cartridges, which were lying in the magazine, announced to Sir Henry Lawrence and his officers, who were anxiously waiting the report, the complete destruction of that post and all that it contained.

If it had not been for this wise and strategic measure, no member of the Lucknow garrison, in all probability, would have survived to tell the tale; for, as has already been stated, the Muchee Bhawun was commanded from other parts of the town, and was moreover indifferently provided with heavy artillery ammunition, while the difficulty, suffering, and loss which the Residency garrison, even with the reinforcement thus obtained from the Muchee Bhawun, has undergone in holding the position, is sufficient to show that, if the original intention of holding both posts had been adhered to, both would inevitably have fallen.

It is now my very painful duty to relate the calamity which befell us at the commencement of the siege. On the 1st July an 8-inch shell burst in the room in the Residency in which Sir H. Lawrence was sitting.

The missile burst between him and Mr. Cooper, close to both, but without injury to either. The whole of his staff implored Sir Henry to take up other quarters, as the Residency had then become the special target for the round shot and shell of the enemy. This, however, he jestingly declined to do, observing that another shell would certainly never be pitched into that small room. But Providence had ordained otherwise, for on the very next day he was mortally wounded by a fragment of another shell which burst in the same room, exactly on the same spot. Captain Wilson, Deputy-Assistant Adjutant-General, received a contusion at the same time.

The late lamented Sir H. Lawrence, knowing that his last hour was rapidly approaching, directed me to assume command of the troops, and appointed Major Banks to succeed him in the office of chief commissioner. He lingered in great agony till the morning of the 4th July, when he expired, and the Government was thereby deprived, if I may venture to say so, of the services of a distinguished statesman and a most gallant soldier. Few men have ever possessed to the same extent the power which he enjoyed of winning the hearts of all those with whom he came in contact, and thus ensuring the warmest and most zealous devotion for himself and for the Government which he served.

The successful defence of the position has been, under Providence, solely attributable to the foresight which he evinced in the timely commencement of the necessary operations, and the great skill and untiring personal activity which he exhibited in carrying them into effect. All ranks possessed such confidence in his judgment and his fertility of resource, that the news of his fall was received throughout the garrison with feelings of consternation, only second to the grief which was inspired in the hearts of all by the loss of a public benefactor and t warm personal friend.

Feeling as keenly and as gratefully as I do the obligations that the whole of us are under to this great and good man, I trust the Government in India will pardon me for having at tempted, however imperfectly, to portray them. In him every good and deserving soldier has lost a friend and a chief capable of discriminating, and ever on the alert to reward merit, no matter how humble the sphere in which it was exhibited.

The garrison had scarcely recovered the shock which it had sustained in the loss of its revered and beloved general, when it had to mourn the death of that able and respected officer. Major Banks, the officiating chief commissioner, who received a bullet through his head while examining a critical outpost on the 21st July, and died without a groan.

The description of our position and the state of our defences when the siege began are so fully set forth in the accompanying memorandum, furnished by the garrison engineer, that I shall content myself with bringing to the notice of his Lordship in Council the fact that when the blockade was commenced only two of our batteries were completed, part of the defences were yet in an unfinished condition, and the buildings in the immediate vicinity, which gave cover to the enemy, were only very partially cleared away.

Indeed, our heaviest losses have been caused by the fire from the enemy's sharpshooters stationed in the adjoining mosques and houses of the native nobility, the necessity of destroying which had been repeatedly drawn to the attention of Sir Henry by the staff of engineers; but his invariable reply was, 'Spare the holy places, and private property too, as far as possible,' and we have consequently suffered severely from our very tenderness to the religious prejudices and respect to the rights of our rebellious citizens and soldiery.

As soon as the enemy had thoroughly completed the investment of the Residency, they occupied these houses, some of which were within easy pistol-shot of our barricades, in immense force, and rapidly made loopholes on those sides which bore on our post, from which they kept up a terrific and incessant fire day and night, which caused many daily casualties, as there could not have been less than 8,000 men firing at one time into our position.

Moreover, there was no place in the whole of the works that could be considered safe, for several of the sick and wounded who were lying in the banqueting-hall, which had been turned into a hospital, were killed in the very centre of the building, and the widow of Lieutenant Dorin and other women and children were shot dead in a room into which it had not been previously deemed possible that a bullet could penetrate. Neither were the enemy idle in erecting batteries.

They soon had from twenty to twenty-five guns in position, some of them of very large calibre. These were planted all round our post at small distances, some being actually within fifty yards of our defences, but in places where our own heavy guns could not reply to them; while the perseverance and ingenuity of the enemy in erecting barricades in front and around their guns, in a very short time rendered all attempts to silence them by musketry entirely unavailing. Neither could they be effectually silenced by shells, by reason of their extreme proximity to our position, and because, moreover, the enemy had recourse to digging very narrow trenches about eight feet in dept in rear of each gun, in which the men lay while on shells were flying, and which so effectually conceal them, even while working the gun, that our baffled sharpshooters could only see their hands while in the act of loading.

The enemy contented themselves with keeping up this incessant fire of cannon and musketry until the 29th of July, on which day, at ten a.m., they assembled in very great force all around our position, and exploded a heavy mine inside our outer line of defence at the Water-gate. The mine, however, which was close to the Redan, and apparently sprung with the intention of destroying that battery, did no harm; but as soon as the smoke had cleared away, the enemy boldly advanced under cover of a tremendous fire of cannon and musketry, with the object of storming the Redan.

But they were received with such a heavy fire, that after a short struggle they fell back with much loss. A strong column advanced at the same time to attack Innes's post, and came on to within ten yards of the palisades, affording to Lieutenant Loughnan, 13th Native Infantry, who commanded the position, and his brave garrison, composed of gentlemen of the Uncovenanted Service, a few of Her Majesty's 32nd Foot and of the 13th Native Infantry, an opportunity of distinguishing themselves, which they were not slow to avail themselves of, and the enemy were driven back with great slaughter.

The insurgents made minor attacks at almost every outpost, but were invariably defeated, and at two p.m. they ceased their attempts to storm the place, although their musketry fire and cannonading continued to harass us unceasingly as usual. Matters proceeded in this manner until the 10th of August, when the enemy made another assault, having previously sprung a mine close to the brigade mess, which entirely destroyed our defences for the space of twenty feet, and blew in a great portion of the outside wall of the house occupied by Mr. Schilling's garrison.

On the dust clearing away, a breach appeared through which a regiment could have advanced in perfect order, and a few of the enemy came on with the utmost determination, but were met with such a withering flank fire of musketry from the officers and men holding the top of the brigade mess, that they beat a speedy retreat, leaving the more adventurous of their numbers lying on the crest of the breach. While this operation was going on, another large body advanced on the Cawnpore Battery, and succeeded in locating themselves for a few minutes in the ditch. They were, however, dislodged by hand grenades.

At Captain Anderson's post they also came boldly forward with scaling ladders, which they planted against the wall; but here, as elsewhere, they were met with the most indomitable resolution, and, the leaders being slain, the rest fled, leaving the ladders, and retreated to their batteries and loopholed defences, from whence they kept up, for the rest of the day, an unusually heavy cannonade and musketry fire.

On the 18th of August the enemy sprung another mine in front of the *Sikh* lines, with very fatal effect. Captain Orr (Unattached), Lieutenants Mecham and Soppitt, who commanded the small body of drummers composing the garrison, were blown into the air, but providentially returned to earth with no further injury than a severe shaking. The garrison, however, were not so fortunate. No less than eleven men were buried alive under the ruins, from whence it was impossible to extricate them, owing to the tremendous fire kept up by the enemy from houses situated not ten yards in front of the breach.

The explosion was followed by a general assault of a less determined nature than the two former efforts, and the enemy were consequently repulsed without much difficulty. But they succeeded, under cover of the breach, in establishing themselves in one of the houses in our position, from which they were driven in the evening by the bayonets of Her Majesty's 32nd and 82nd Foot. On the 5th of September the enemy made their last serious assault. Having exploded a large mine, a few feet short of the bastion of the 18-pounder gun, in Major Apthorp's post, they advanced with large scaling ladders, which they planted against the wall, and mounted, thereby gaining for an instant the embrasure of a gun.

They were, however, speedily driven back with loss, by hand grenades and musketry. A few minutes subsequently they sprung another mine close to the brigade mess, and advanced boldly; but soon the corpses strewed in the garden in front of the post bore testimony to the fatal accuracy of the rifle and musketry fire of the gallant members of that garrison, and the enemy fled ignominiously, leaving their leader—a fine-looking old native officer—among the slain. At other posts they made similar attacks, but with less resolution, and everywhere with the same want of success. Their loss upon this day must have been very heavy, as they came on with much determination, and at night they were seen bearing large numbers of their killed and wounded over the bridges in the direction of cantonments.

The above is a faint attempt at a description of the four great struggles which have occurred during this protracted season of exertion, exposure, and suffering. His Lordship in Council will perceive that the enemy invariably commenced his attacks by the explosion of a mine—a species of offensive warfare for the exercise of which our position was unfortunately peculiarly situated, and had it not been for the most untiring vigilance on our part in watching and blowing up their mines before they were completed, the assaults would probably have been much more numerous, and might, perhaps, have ended in the capture of the place.

But by countermining in all directions we succeeded in detecting: and destroying no less than four of the enemy's subterraneous advances towards important positions, two of which operations were eminently successful, as on one occasion no less than eighty of them were blown into the air, and twenty suffered a similar fate on the second explosion. The labour, however, which devolved upon us in making these countermines, in the absence of a body of skilled miners, was very heavy.

The Right Honourable the Governor-General in Council will feel that it would be impossible to crowd within the limits of a despatch even the principal events, much more the individual acts of gallantry which have marked this protracted struggle. But I can conscientiously declare my conviction, that few troops have ever undergone greater hardships, exposed as they have been to a never-ceasing musketry fire and cannonade.

They have also experienced the alternate vicissitudes of extreme wet and of intense heat, and that too with very insufficient shelter from either, and in many places without any shelter at all. In addition to having to repel real attacks, they have been exposed night and day to the hardly less harassing false alarms which the enemy have been constantly raising. The insurgents have frequently fired very heavily, sounded the advance and shouted for several hours together, though not a man could be seen, with the view, of course, of harassing our small and exhausted force, in which object they succeeded, for no part has been strong enough to allow of a portion only of the garrison being prepared in the event of a false attack being turned into a real one.

All therefore, had to stand to their arms and to remain in their posts until the demonstration had ceased; and such attacks were of almost nightly occurrence. The whole of the officers and men have been on duty night and day during the eighty-seven days which the siege had lasted, up to the arrival of Sir J. Outram, G.C.B. In addition to this incessant military duty, the force has been employed in repairing defences, in moving guns, in burying dead animals, in conveying ammunition and commissariat stores from one place to another, and in other fatigue duties too numerous and too trivial to enumerate here.

I feel, however, that any words of mine will fail to convey an adequate idea of what our fatigue and labours have been; labours in which all ranks and all classes—civilians, officers, and soldiers—have borne an equally noble part. All have together descended into the mine, all have together handled the shovel for the interment of the putrid bullock, and all, accoutred with musket and bayonet, have relieved each other on sentry, without regard to the distinction of rank civil or military.

Notwithstanding all these hardships, the garrison has made no less than five sorties, in which they spiked two of the enemy's heaviest guns and blew up several of the houses from which they had kept up the most harassing fire. Owing to the extreme paucity of our numbers, each man was taught to feel that on his own individual efforts alone depended, in no small measure, the safety of the entire position.

This consciousness incited every officer, soldier, and man to defend the post assigned to him with such desperate tenacity, and to defend the lives which Providence had entrusted to his care with such dauntless determination, that the enemy, despite their constant attacks, their heavy mines, their overwhelming numbers, and their incessant fire, could never succeed in gaining one single inch of ground within the bounds of this straggling position, which was so feebly fortified that had they once obtained a footing in any of the outposts the whole place must inevitably have fallen.

If further proof be wanting of the desperate nature of the struggle which we have, under God' blessing, so long and so successfully waged, I would point to the roofless and ruined houses, to the crumbled walls, to the exploded mines, to the open breaches, to the shattered and disabled guns and defences, and lastly, to the long and melancholy list of the brave and devoted officers and men who have fallen. These silent witnesses bear sad and solemn testimony to the way in which this feeble position has been defended.

During the early part of these vicissitudes, we were left without any information whatever regarding the posture of affairs outside. An occasional spy did indeed come in with the object of inducing our *sepoys* and servants to desert; but the intelligence derived from such sources was of course entirely untrustworthy. We sent our messengers daily calling for aid and asking for information, none of whom ever returned until the twenty-sixth day of the siege, when a pensioner named Ungud, came back with a letter from General Havelock's camp, informing us that they were advancing with a force sufficient to bear down all opposition, and would be with us in five or six days.

A messenger was immediately despatched requesting that, on the evening of their arrival on the outskirts of the city, two rockets might be sent up, in order that we might take the necessary measures for assisting them while forcing their way in. The sixth day, however, expired, and they came not; but for many evenings after officers and men watched for the ascension of the expected rockets, with hopes such as make the heart sick. We knew not then, nor did we learn until the 29th of August—or thirty-five day later—that the relieving force, after having fought most nobly to effect our deliverance, had been obliged to fall back for reinforcements; and this was the last communication we received until two days before the arrival of Sir James Outram on the 20th of September.

Besides heavy visitations of cholera and smallpox we have also had to contend against a sickness which has almost universally pervaded the garrison. Commencing with a very painful eruption, it has merged into a low fever, combined with diarrhoea; and although few or no men have actually died from it effects, it leaves behind a weakness and lassitude which, in the absence of all material substances, save coarse beef and still coarser flour, none have been able entirely to get over. The mortality among the women and children, and especially among the latter from these diseases, and from other causes, has been perhaps the most painful characteristic of the siege The want of native servants has also been a source of much privation.

Owing to the suddenness with which we were besieged, many of these people, who might, perhaps, have otherwise proved faithful to their employers, but who were outside the defences at the time, were altogether excluded. Very many more deserted, and several families were consequently left without the services of a single domestic. Several ladies have had to tend their children, and even to wash their own clothes, as well as to cook their scanty meals, entirely unaided.

Combined with the absence of servants, the want of proper accommodation has probably been the cause of much of the disease with which we have been afflicted. I cannot refrain from

> bringing to the prominent notice of his Lordship in Council the patient endurance and the Christian resignation which have been evinced by the women of this garrison. They have animated us by their example. Many, alas! have been made widows, and their children fatherless, in this cruel struggle. But all such seem resigned to the will of Providence, and many, among whom may be mentioned the honoured names of Birch, of Polehampton, of Barber, and of Gall, have, after the example of Miss Nightingale, constituted themselves the tender and solicitous nurses of the wounded and dying soldiers In the hospital.

The Brigadier then enters into specific details of the services rendered by the most distinguished officers, &c., whether living or dead. He also bears testimony to the unsurpassed courage and loyalty of the native troops; expresses the deep and grateful sense entertained by the garrison of the services rendered by Sir James Outram and General Havelock and their troops in effecting the relief of Lucknow at so heavy a sacrifice of life, and concludes with these words:—

> We are also repaid for much suffering and privation by the sympathy which our brave deliverers say our perilous and unfortunate position has excited for us in the hearts of our countrymen throughout the length and breadth of Her Majesty's dominions.

LEONAUR

ALSO FROM LEONAUR

AVAILABLE IN SOFTCOVER OR HARDCOVER WITH DUST JACKET

OFFICERS & GENTLEMEN *by Peter Hawker & William Graham*—Two Accounts of British Officers During the Peninsula War: Officer of Light Dragoons by Peter Hawker & Campaign in Portugal and Spain by William Graham .

THE WALCHEREN EXPEDITION *by Anonymous*—The Experiences of a British Officer of the 81st Regt. During the Campaign in the Low Countries of 1809.

LADIES OF WATERLOO *by Charlotte A. Eaton, Magdalene de Lancey & Juana Smith*—The Experiences of Three Women During the Campaign of 1815: Waterloo Days by Charlotte A. Eaton, A Week at Waterloo by Magdalene de Lancey & Juana's Story by Juana Smith.

JOURNAL OF AN OFFICER IN THE KING'S GERMAN LEGION *by John Frederick Hering*—Recollections of Campaigning During the Napoleonic Wars.

JOURNAL OF AN ARMY SURGEON IN THE PENINSULAR WAR *by Charles Boutflower*—The Recollections of a British Army Medical Man on Campaign During the Napoleonic Wars.

ON CAMPAIGN WITH MOORE AND WELLINGTON *by Anthony Hamilton*—The Experiences of a Soldier of the 43rd Regiment During the Peninsular War.

THE ROAD TO AUSTERLITZ *by R. G. Burton*—Napoleon's Campaign of 1805.

SOLDIERS OF NAPOLEON *by A. J. Doisy De Villargennes & Arthur Chuquet*—The Experiences of the Men of the French First Empire: Under the Eagles by A. J. Doisy De Villargennes & Voices of 1812 by Arthur Chuquet .

INVASION OF FRANCE, 1814 *by F. W. O. Maycock*—The Final Battles of the Napoleonic First Empire.

LEIPZIG—A CONFLICT OF TITANS *by Frederic Shoberl*—A Personal Experience of the 'Battle of the Nations' During the Napoleonic Wars, October 14th-19th, 1813.

SLASHERS *by Charles Cadell*—The Campaigns of the 28th Regiment of Foot During the Napoleonic Wars by a Serving Officer.

BATTLE IMPERIAL *by Charles William Vane*—The Campaigns in Germany & France for the Defeat of Napoleon 1813-1814.

SWIFT & BOLD *by Gibbes Rigaud*—The 60th Rifles During the Peninsula War.

Lightning Source UK Ltd.
Milton Keynes UK
UKHW041254250820
368797UK00002BA/550

9 781846 779534